Knock on Woodstock

For

Michael Lang,
My angel and provider of a ticket to freedom,

and

Richie Havens,
Whose poetic expression of freedom and soul
nourishment became my own mantra.

Knock on Woodstock

*The Uproarious, Uncensored Story of the Woodstock
Festival, the Gay Man Who Made it Happen, and
How He Earned His Ticket to Freedom*

by
Elliot Tiber

1994

FESTIVAL BOOKS / NEW YORK

Disclaimer:
The author makes references to a variety of persons living, dead, or in suspended animation. All references are satirical and sometimes comedic, however, no actual true or accurate information is implied. The reader is advised that fact and fiction, according to the absurd, twisted, world of the author, are often unclear and any offence or implied derogatory statements about any persons, living, dead, or in suspended animation, is purely coincidental unless otherwise stated. Foul language is not used in the telling of this story.

For reproduction rights, contact the publisher:
Festival Books
c/o Festival Conservancy, Inc.
163 Amsterdam Avenue, Suite 321
New York, NY 10023

This book is available at a special discount
when ordered in bulk quantities.

Published in conjunction with
Joel Friedlander, *Publisher*
Post Office Box 3330
San Rafael, CA 94912

First Edition

ISBN 0-9641806-0-x Hardover
ISBN 0-9641806-1-8 Softcover
Library of Congress Catalog Card No: 94-72214

10 9 8 7 6 5 4 3 2 1
Manufactured in the United States

Dedication

The author dedicates this book to the following persons who have made invaluable contributions to the quality of his absurd, twisted, comic life:

Andre Ernotte (my companion for 20 years and life-support system); Alyce Finell (Angel, Muse, hope/faith/charity); Dr. Michael DeMeo, for the Paxil, Zoloft and encouragement; Act Up; Larry Kramer; Katherine Hepburn; Gay Community Center; Dr. Lewis Falb of The New School; David and Goldie Blanksteen, and Charles and Jane; Rachelle and Sam Golden, and Bryan and Stephen; Renee Teichberg Brisker and Yuri Brisker and Alyce Pickholtz; Ann and Aaron Teichberg; Dr. Louis Falb, The New School; Lonette McKee; Shayna-Punim-Tiber; Fran Lee (my surrogate Mama); Audrey Wood; Bertha Klausner; Sammy Davis, Jr.; Gregory Peck; Orson Welles; Neil Diamond; Barbra Streisand; Shirley Kaplan (a.k.a. 'No Snakes-Shirley'); Linda Lepomme and Piet; Gerd Wiedestedt; Suzanne Sarquier; Dr. Fran Budabin Lassiter; Vivian Davis; Jan Miner; Jane Collins Snowday; Annie Cordy; Fanny and Gilbert Ernotte (my Belgian parents); Bernard Giraudeau; Anny Duperey; Jacques Bourton; Nicolas Resimont; RTB TV, Belgium; Ministries of Culture Belgium, Walloon-Flemish; Annette Insdorf, Columbia University; Allain Guilleaume; Pierre Druot; Suzy Rossberg; Mort Shuman; Miche Brel; France Brel; Janis Joplin; Joe Cocker; The Marx Brothers; Jonathan Winters; W.C. Fields; Mel Brooks; Josh Mostel; Gena Rowlands; Queer Nation; Dr. Mathilde Krim; Lilly Tomlin; Liz Taylor; K.D. Lang; Out; Madonna; Gay Pride; and the rest of the Mishpacha, and chocolate bars everywhere. And special thanks to Mitch Douglas, my genius agent at ICM; and Alma, for everything.

The Woodstock Festival staff, including Michael Lang, Executive Producer; Lee Mackler Blumer, Security and Administration; Stanley Goldstein, Headhunter and Coordinator and Mensch; Joel Rosenman, Adminstrative Troubleshooter and Advertising; Jon Roberts, Financier; Penny Stallings, Administrative Assistant; Bill Hanley, Sound; and Max Yasgur, my neighbor, milkman and summer friend.

And to Jack Teichberg, since 1969 still at Woodstock, 'resting,' and Sonia Teichberg, (n.c.).

Acknowledgements

A heartfelt thanks to those who have been closer than close friends, Lee and Irv Regent, dear souls whose nurturing, loving and support are treasured forever. They gave me a home when I had none.

This book was made possible through the very special comedic insight of Fred Rothchild, a visionary who appeared out of cloud nine on a sunny day in my life. And lovingly shrinkproofed and supported by Dr. Milt Robin, my nemesis. The meshugaas team to come on board the roller coaster that was my eternal good mazel was filmmaker Phil Katzman and Carole St. Onge, Fran Fisher, and Marcia Wolfson, Patty, Gianni, Tom, Andrew, Laura, Neal, Greg, Michel, Patti, Hefi, Danny, Pedro, Paul, Karen, Hiroshi, Johannes, Wolf, and the entire family of "Ticket To Freedom: Woodstock."

And a special *merci* to Steven Kaufman, Steve Corvi, and Edith and Al Goodman, and the staff at the HHAR for taking care of S.T., and to the mishpacka of Manhattan Plaza for their ten-year subsidy of my writing. And to Rick Frishman and Dena Merriam and Planned Television Arts.

And last and most, my sincerest gratitude to my editor, Joel Friedlander, for his enthusiastic support, vigilant dedicated focus, and a la fax/mode intimacies!

Contents

Author's Note

As of October 1993, Mike Lang, Joel Roberts, John Rosenman, announced plans for Woodstock II, this time in Saugerties, 20 miles from Woodstock.

Bethel announced their own Woodstock 1994, on the farm, for a family-value, Muzak kind of music festival. Families—not gays, lesbians, or other diverse types. Presumably, whites, legitimate citizens, married, legal children, and no beards or cursing or refugees of any 12-step programs.

And, a group of ex-Woodstock Festival fanatics announced their own memorial festival somewhere near Bethel. No money, no profits, no greed. Just music and memories.

Since we had to go to press before August 15, 1994, the results of the three festival announcements will be known to the reader.

Whichever festival celebration you chose to go to, Don't look for me and my Orson Welles hat and cape and purple cigarettes. I wasn't invited. Go know.

Foreword

Ticket to Freedom

We never really seem to know why it takes joy, pain, courage and humor to make up what we call Life in general, when in fact, all of these things seem to play through our normal day as the emotional fare towards the success of sleep. But, somewhere deep in each one of us lies a well (a small one), which harbors our dreams, and in this deep place we keep the tools from which we design our personal freedom to just be a Human Being.

Sometimes, left field (or should I say most of the time), steps in and we are whisked off into a world only we could see, on our own personal quest for liberation from what anyone else says, does or designs, that does not lend itself to the good of it all.

This book is a long-untold story of what left field is all about and how ultimately wise it is.

Richie Havens

Preface

Footnote to History

In the third week of August, 1969, an estimated one million people, then designated as "hippies," descended upon a quiet, small, economically and spiritually dead redneck town—White Lake, New York, part of the greater town of Bethel. People came from all parts of the United States and all parts of the world. They came in all sizes, shapes and ages, though the press would have had you believe they were all under the age of 23 and had long hair, did drugs, and had sex with anything that had a pulse. Yet, considering the vast array of types and lifestyles noted, there was no mention at all of any gay men or lesbian women being there. We were totally invisible. Nothing new in 1969. But now, in 1994, enough is too much. We were there, we were queer, we were musicians, artists, tech crew, professionals, laborers, humanitarians, doctors, nurses, farmers, students, politicians, lawyers, teachers, mothers, fathers, brothers, sisters, cousins, lovers. In short, we were—according to Kinsey percentages—ten percent of whoever and whatever else was there.

This was a varied group of people, but one with a common desire: to hear music, the music of a new generation. Music performed by groups and individuals, some famous then, most famous now. The event was the Woodstock Music and Art Fair, which took place on three muddy and rain-soaked days that would go down in history as the cultural turning point for a generation: August 15, 16 and 17, 1969.

Theories abound as to why, where and how all these people came to Woodstock for this festival, which its organizers originally thought would attract maybe a few thousand like-minded souls. Sociologists point to the coming of age of one of the largest generations of all time. Economists cite the confluence of the end of the post-World War II boom economy, the decline of the industrial age, and the dawn of the information revolution. Historians analyze the effects of a confusing series of wars and a string of assassinations. Mystics declare the dawning of a new age as predicted by Nostradamus, Jeanne Dixon, Jesus Christ and Shirley Maclaine. However, the key element of the festival and its true origins and why all these people would be drawn to as hopeless and dead a place as White Lake, New York was none of the above. Glossed over by history is the real reason they all came.

The real reason—never before revealed in print, on television, or even in seances—was that for fourteen years, I was a nice Jewish boy from Brooklyn with a dream. The dream was that one day, maybe a few hundred people would come to White Lake to listen to my music festival in the swamp behind our ugly tourist trap and, of course, rent rooms, thereby enabling me to pay the bills and show some income on the books and ergo, sell the fucking ugly motel and end its disgusting death-grip on me, ergo, rescue me from indentured servitude to my dysfunctional, over-the-edge parents and their disastrous speed trip to join the messiah in hell!

From 1958 to 1968, I granted myself a permit, and ran my own music and art festival on the swampy lawn of the El Monaco-White Lake Swinging Singles and Invisible Gay Resort Motel, as it was unknown except to a too-precious few. A festival which I assured myself and my parents would one day bring in a hot-to-buy-a-motel buyer. I didn't believe me then. My mom and pop thought me mad, but, hey, I was their son. Who would expect them two dopes to categorize their son as a crazed bent twisted absurd clown on a tightrope made out of air?

And just who was I that I turned out to be the sperm-giver to this later named 'Woodstock Nation?' I wasn't born a nation-sperm manufacturer. I started outside of the proverbial 'bottom of the barrel.' In addition to my aforementioned status as festival and motel begetter, the list of quasi-activities that I have engaged in during my ridiculous life includes being a screenwriter, playwright, sculptor, painter, display maven, color marketing consultant, piggy bank smile painter, Sunbeam electric shaver demonstrator at shopping malls, Fred Astaire

Ballroom Dance Instructor in Times Square, house sadist at various sex clubs, retail marketing man, and the esteemed professor of Absurd, Twisted Comedy at the New School for Social Research in New York. "Absurd, Twisted Comedy," a literary genre that may include only me.

Nee Eliyahu Teichberg, when I reached majority age, I instantly changed this to Elliot Tiber, after that defunct *New York Times* theater and culture column, "Along the Tiber." Terrified of Mom and Pop's certain traditional reaction, I lied and told them Tiber was a shortening of 'Teich' and 'berg.' This change of identity cost eighteen dollars. It was a pathetic attempt to sidestep the Teichberg Curse—a malevolence that caused the endless economic straights of my family. Perhaps this curse has something to do with my endless hyperbole? Nah, this curse had to do with choosing the wrong parents at the wrong time in the wrong century. And once that dreadful choice was made, cruel and inhuman punishment, albeit with absurd comic relief, was the reward installed permanently.

But of special importance in my list of achievements were the fourteen years, from 1955 to 1969, when I ran, operated, and desperately promoted that obscene motel in the joyless noise called White Lake, New York, in the famous-for-fifteen-minutes town of Bethel. That town is no longer famous and, as per the residents' express wishes, not on any maps known to civilized people. The ancient controversies I talk about a bit further on were reincarnated in 1993 and 1994 as the Twenty-fifth Anniversary Festival plans were being argued. Not such old news, since the *New York Times* found it 'fit to print' the current controversies. Twenty-five years later, as if in a time warp, the locals don't want the dirty hippies in their backyard. Only, those former hippies are now the new generation of parents with bank accounts enough to rent rooms. What to do? Hang in there, we'll get to that, too. Neither I, nor my dysfunctional parents, nor the birds knew this very motel was to become the headquarters for the Woodstock Music and Art Fair, and the hotbed of Christ-killers, hippies, druggies, sexual perverts, and music. For three days the birds virtually disappeared from Sullivan County.

I am some kind of absurd footnote to history. I did not survive my heinous Bar Mitzvah in pre-riot Bensonhurst, (next door to Larry

King on Bay Parkway), Jewish guilt for everything including breathing, (Oy, if only they had 12 steps in 1948), obsessively overeating
terrible disgusting vile overcooked kosher food, but I did survive
Woodstock. Not only did I survive, but Woodstock gave me my ticket
to freedom, as you will see.

My inaccurately labeled *obscene* commentary has kept me from
card-carrying membership in popular society. My homosexuality and
compulsive S & M sexuality have kept me from being a card-carrying
member everywhere else except in certain places. And considering the
state of the state, my preference for solitude, privacy, my Yorkie, VCR
and days and nights of films, has turned out to be the better choice.
The proof is I have no grey hair, weigh less than I did at 19, and enjoy
perfect everything.

Never a sad day, never depressed, never lonesome or wanting, I,
fortunately, am addicted to the bizarre. Given the choice between
acceptable social events, family gatherings, and community 'do's, I
have always embraced spending a New Year's Eve either with bars of
Hershey's Chocolate or, in pre-AIDS years, wallowing in the pits of
the Mine Shaft. A couple of thousand anonymous sexual encounters
proved to be more rewarding than all those miserable frenetic New
Year's Eve parties I gave and went to during my first 28 years. The
refined pleasures gleaned from slapping faces, torturing hot Skidmore
literary major swimming team members wearing only jock straps made
of barbed wire or steel chains, can only be surpassed by having all the
above inflicted. Being a 'top' or the 'S' of the S & M populace was too
much darn work. But, I adjusted. It was a lot better than cleaning
toilets in White Lake and running Swinging Singles weekends at the
El Monaco. But, I'm getting ahead of myself.

Those sub-basement prison cells and the cowboy bunks and the
replica of Central Park paths, or the mock subway trains where you
could hit on a 'conductor' or a college jock (the big money was in
renting costumes), were much more stimulating than my duties as
President of the White Lake/Bethel Chamber of Commerce, trust me
on this.

Ergo, this story of a music festival that no one wanted in their
backyard, which finally happened because I needed to rent rooms so
I could get out of the Catskills and schlep my leather stuff to Little

West 12th Street's leathersex emporium, the Mine Shaft, may give definition and answer questions that nobody bothered to ask me about till now. Nobody asked me now either, but, since I found out, A.W., that I am not immortal, I am volunteering to set the record straight and bring Woodstock out of the closet. To coin a phrase or two: *Better late than never. If God meant for me to fly, he or she would have given me money or at least have given me a Rockefeller for a father, Ergo, I go.*

This phenomenon called Woodstock, that a quarter of a century later is still making headlines, and still causing debate and legal battle, was/is something more than a music festival. Yes? No? We did replace "Man on Moon" stories on front pages worldwide back then. Hindsight acknowledges that the Woodstock Festival is "The" event that defined the 1960s and defined a generation. The event, the music of the counter-culture of then, was jet-speeded into the spotlight of political and religious arenas. But twenty-five years ago, the media only reported about the mayhem and drugs, turmoil, mud, sex, dirt and filth. And for twenty-five years, every kind of sociological, psychological, religious, and political observer has been attempting to fit the whole snake pit into a tidy can of worms.

So, what parts of the equation are, if I may use the poetic word of popular choice today, fucked up here? This confessional may sort out parts of the puzzle, and perhaps even solve many of its unknowns. This is my story of the event that literally changed my life, and helped redefine America. I am proud to have played a supporting role. To those of you who were there, and to those of you who wish you were, Happy Twenty-fifth Anniversary. Welcome to the Woodstock nation, and welcome home.

Elliot Tiber, New York, NY 1994

1

NIMBY—
Not In My Backyard!
Or, Why No One Wanted the
Woodstock Festival in Their Town

There was one simple underlying principle that made the fact that I happened to have a music and art festival permit significant. The principle is what has since been institutionalized in the 1980s as NIMBY: Not In My Backyard.

NIMBY is a concept that cuts through class, religious, economic and racial lines. It is one of the great unifying factors of our country. Dumps (toxic or otherwise), half-way houses, rehabs, housing for people with diseases you'd otherwise pretend don't exist... these are the stuff of NIMBY. A million dirty, doped-up, oversexed, long-haired, foul-smelling hippies were prime candidates for those of the NIMBY school. One hundred thousand gay men and lesbian women also overqualified as entries into the NIMBY philosophical posture. And in 1969, in upstate New York, such a gathering was enough to encourage town after town to invoke their constitutional right to NIMBY. Ergo, they voted either to refuse The Woodstock Music and Art Fair a permit, or to rescind one they had unwittingly granted. In 1969, I thought this was very short-sighted of upstate New York. The local media were doing articles about dope, sex and the evils of rock and roll. Their emphasis was on LSD, hallucinogens, grass and the open, illicit dealing that was a given once hippies and rock fans assembled. The local Sullivan County paper, the *Times Herald Record*, a (self-proclaimed) family paper, was feasting on stories about local drug-related incidents, raids, abuse and hints of all the disasters that

1

would happen if Woodstock were really to take place. The Monticello rag—*The Republican Watchman,* a weekly whose name should give you a clue—took front-page status away from its usual headlines about the 4-H Club, and milk and egg price developments, to report about the impending doom; first to Walkill, then to Sullivan County. The only items these Pulitzer Prize-winning hopefuls didn't report, to the best of my recollection, were local landings of extra-terrestrials on their flying saucers, ready to enslave the citizenry in order to tap into their brain reserves. Looking back, they never mentioned if the E.T.s were gender-specific. Crossdressing and transsexual identity obstacles were totally ignored.

I was still in the closet publicly, upstate and in New York City, for safety reasons. While I was a tenure-track teacher at staid, self-indulgent Hunter College, the inappropriate revelation about my nether-world preferences was a clear given. That the community citizenry of the church-going variety were certain my old Jewish mother was a prolific whore did not keep me (and others) from making periodic attempts to gain our own constitutional freedoms.

The hot news of the Festival had, as its first positive side effect, an increasing confidence in the strength of unity. Suddenly, crunching numbers of five thousand, ten thousand long-haired, sexually ambivalent music makers and the ensuing hordes of groupies, hangers-on, crews, and sexual deviates such as myself, propelled a euphoric sense of community power to me. Ergo, I supported, aided and abetted the Woodstock Festival. My people were coming.

But my great visions for moving mountains with number crunching of 10,000, was way off the mark. Go know to figure on a million people coming to White Lake—all in one week yet! I thought Woodstock was going to be a nice little music fair with maybe 2,500 people and a few rock musicians. White Lake's population was, in good times, 2,500. With more of *us* than *them,* I was in heaven! In my wildest fantasies, big numbers had no possible connection to revolting White Lake. I never fathomed that Woodstock would overturn my life and the lives of more than the million who were there. And it turned around the lives of tens of millions more, worldwide, who were not there but wish they were! That I was trapped in this desolate and depressed mountain area, and the outside world would come to me,

2

was never anything that crossed my overworked brain. That this was to be a moment in history that would literally move mountains, and not just the Catskill Mountains, was not even thought about, let alone understood then.

Just as my neighbors' mantra was NIMBY, my mantra was, "Rent my rooms and get me out of the Catskills!" I was mired in a pre-Prozac purgatory, a slave to my mother, bonded to my pre-12-Step guilt, and clinging to a leather, S & M, fetish lifestyle in the closet for relief! And had I even suspected how big this opportunity would be, I would have *cashed in.* We all would have. Mike Lang, the Festival organizer, John Roberts, Joel Rosenman, and other of the key creators would have. Warner Brothers would not have been the only financial winner, as it turned out they became. The musicians who played for free, would have. If nothing else, I wouldn't have trashed the piles of crisp, clean, original posters and the unsold tickets from my office, which people are paying thousands of dollars for today as collectibles. Those posters and tickets would now be able to provide me with a retirement pension that would allow even for paying my Blue Cross bills!

When I read the quotes these days of naive visionaries who feel Woodstock should have been non-profit from day one, and any future festivals should be void of tainted money and greed, I want to force those simpletons to listen to Joan Rivers' mantra: "Oh, grow up!" over and over and over, until it sinks in! What is for free? The musicians who play the music need bread and fudge cake. The performers need to pay rent. The producers need to pay their investors a return. Isn't it gift enough to have the producers package the great sounds and voices and enable you to participate? Aren't the gifts of witnessing the talents and joining in the reverie gift enough? Think about it. Think. And hey, if you want a free festival, who stops you? Do it yourself! Don't dictate to those who've done it how they should have or could have done it to meet your criteria. These dopes are the ones who speak the loudest and get quoted most often by journalists. It's colorful. Oh, please!

I came to the rescue of the homeless Woodstock Music and Art Fair. Not out of any great knowledge, discernment, or prophetic impulse. Not out of any great love of hippies. Not out of any great love for tie-dye. Not out of any love or knowledge of drugs more

3

potent than Bayer Aspirin or Pepto Bismol. No, I came to the rescue of the Woodstock Festival because when I heard upstate New York's battle cry of NIMBY, all I could think of was how badly I wanted to be out of *their* backyard. I prayed to some possible great spirit—not God—to let them rent my rooms, buy the motel and boot me out of that odious mountain backyard. Let there be no misinterpretation, please. Never then nor now did God enter into any of my thoughts or prayers. Talking to a chocolate bar wrapper was and still is more fulfilling than talking to any God. Even the Belgians admit that Hershey chocolates are the best thing this side of heaven. You never get that gut reaction from any session with God. Oh, please. Let it rest. Let it fade away.

2

The Womb of Woodstock: White Lake and the El Monaco Resort Motel and Swingles Pit; The Deeper Meaning of Route 17B

Before you can really understand how the Woodstock Festival took place and what inspired me to offer the Festival my precious permit, you need to know more about the mysterious and macabre womb of Woodstock; White Lake and the El Monaco Motel, White Lake, New York, circa 1955: one volunteer fire department, one hostile plumber, 20 saloons, a few over-priced small stores whose owners were into the thumb-on-scale and short-change school of retailing, population of maybe fifteen hundred. Circa 1993: Likely less population, more bigots, more fools, less is more, except sometimes. White Lake is in Sullivan County, 50 miles west of the town of Woodstock, 90 miles north of New York City, and yet, still no place and, often, not on maps that were not printed in White Lake. Advertised but untrue as a quick, 90 minutes from the City by car. It was more like two-plus hours of ugliness, driving on endless concrete highways surrounded by faux dead people strapped into vehicles on wheels.

The corner of Route 17B and Route 55, where the historic El Monaco Motel reigned, was and maybe still is four miles from Max Yasgur's farm, where the Festival actually took place. This international crossroads was, and maybe still is, about 399 feet or 200 meters from White Lake, the not-so-pristine body of water, as you will later find out, where hundreds of thousands of dirty rotten hippies would bathe naked in 1969.

The town has no industry, no business that can be considered viable, no visible means of support or life. The town had a dozen oddball hotels ranging from the early 1920s to the present mishmash of despicable motels. The population of sparse locals changes its color every summer when the dreadful city people come up for fresh air, and returns to country dreadful three seconds before Labor Day every September.

There were four basic groups of locals. First was the Jewish resort owners. The meaning of the word "resort," as it relates to the dumps to be found in Bethel, bears no relationship to the usual image seen in most travel guides. Forget gleaming white buildings, pristine bodies of water, manicured greenery—evergreen or palm—servants, clean rooms, gourmet dining, or topflight entertainment; the expected norm. Potential genteel guests accustomed to indoor plumbing and other amenities, included a room key that works, are also part of resort expectations that must be left at home before this journey.

The Catskills in the 1950s, particularly the town of White Lake, used the term "resort" in a manner that could be legally challenged in any court of law as 'with intention to defile.' Victorian buildings that had long ago parted with their grandeur, most without proper fire-proofing or occupancy permits, open cesspools, outside toilets or a bath down the hall serving 20 rooms, floors so uniformly slanted that for years I thought it was an international style that had been imported from some mysterious Slavic country, over the border, in the dark, at midnight, by Hedy Lamar or Micha Auer. Why, was something I never went into. I leave that to future historians of Catskills culture. The dining rooms, usually decorated in the linoleum nightmare period, provided practicality at the expense of an inspirational artistic environment. This strong, long-lasting material was entirely suited to the nature of the paying guests—"savages," "imbeciles," "pigs," "trash," "illiterates," "boors," "slobs," "schnurrers," and additional categories not easily delineated. Loud, pushy, aggressive, selfish, minimally educated by choice. To be polite, let's just say the guests were less than genteel. Perhaps its too late to be polite?

Most of these old hotels were willed to the grandchildren of the original pioneers who slapped them together. And these inheritors of Yiddish Americana didn't know what to do with them. There were so many accidental fires over those mountains that even one more would surely bring down the FBI of insurance investigators.

Not for nothing did international hotel outfits like Hilton or Sheraton overlook White Lake. Europe, the Caribbean, Hawaii, even boring Florida, attracted crowds with credit cards. White Lake did not accept credit cards. Most business in Greater Downtown White Lake did a cash operation with I.O.U.s dominating the field. White Lake could not afford to handle plastic, since those little machines cost ten dollars. When stretch limousines and Cadillacs with wealthy parents drove in, en route to visit their offspring in the local camps, they flashed American Express or Diner's Club. I flashed them by opening my raincoat and tipping my Orson Welles hat. If I were in the office, I'd talk them to exhaustion about my Aunt Myopia, President of American Express, and our history of family *tzuris* preventing Express from giving us their little machine. If these rich types—with credit cards, that is—got my mom in the slanted, eclectic, broken-shack office with the ironing board as the registration desk, it was an entirely different business approach:

"Gentleman. Listen on me. I'm an old struggling refugee from Russia, a persecuted Jewish mamma, trying to buy warm milk for my babies. I'll hold onto this plastic card until you can get me cash from your wife, or from that woman in your car. This is a decent family motel here, and if that isn't your wife, I have to charge you an extra dollar since I'll need to use fresh linens when you leave and besides, those kind of women make a big mess in my rooms."

I couldn't be everywhere at once, and if I was otherwise engaged in doing laundry, cleaning toilets, making pancakes, parking cars, fighting off local rednecks from stealing television sets, I'd rush to the office and try to negotiate a suitable cash payment and avoid discussion of the status of the floozie woman in the car. I was successful a few times. No matter, Mom would later check on those rooms I rented, wake up the unsuspecting renters, usually after midnight, and demand other terms and conditions, or threaten to evict them or to call the police. She always won. She never wondered why we had no repeat business. Never. To this day, in her thwarted mind, she is of the opinion she ran a profitable first class resort motel. She is only riding on three wheels of her wheelchair.

The other resorts were better or worse, depending on what *shtetl*[1] the parents came from. The one common thread being that there was absolutely no demand for rooms, and no guests were getting off at Exit Number 105 from the Thruway. So, it didn't pay to renovate the old hotel buildings. It didn't pay to renovate our new old buildings either. Windows dangled from rotting frames, ivy grew up from the bog and swamps into the rooms, stairways swayed and creaked, boat docks onto the lake took on the manner of seesaws, but in the declining direction to the bottom of the sea, and former lawns and flower beds were breeding grounds for living creatures that defy categorization.

The overall ambiance, if one were to drive through in error, was gray, tired, ugly, decay, and spots of brightly-colored *Yentas*[2] in summer muumuus shlepping on-sale, bent, canned foods, yesterday's breads, past-expiration-dated foodstuffs, and copies of the *New York Post*. It was difficult to buy the *New York Times* in that neck of the woods. You had to special order it from the cosmopolitan downtown section of Monticello or Liberty. A few boat rental places provided holey craft with ancient motors that spewed black gas fumes and left oil slicks big enough to suffocate the fish. Local cooks didn't have to labor to catch fish for their guests. They'd just go to the shoreline with a pot, scoop up the dead ones, and boil the water, add ketchup and salt, and voila, gourmet kosher cooking!

For some unknown reason, there was virtually no business, no money to tear down these ancient wooden structures that were competing with the Leaning Tower of Pisa for a spot in the *Guinness Book of Records*. I called the *Guinness Book of Records,* but they never responded. Fire insurance was not available, so arson as a survival technique was out. The Catskills were known for its deluge of mysterious fires the first Tuesday in September, just after whatever few vacationers there were, left. So, many of these slanted floor firetraps slanted a bit more each year until they just fell down by themselves. Others were reincarnated as 'Motels,' especially appealing

[1] Russian/Yiddish for a ghetto village where Jews were forced to live, as musically told in *Fiddler on the Roof,* on Broadway.
[2] Yiddish for a busybody.

since motels didn't have to provide dining rooms or room service or other civilized amenities. Lots were abandoned, sometimes reopened by squatters as Bed and Breakfast places. A pitiful few were run in a haphazard, frightening manner that was good enough for certain groups of "less than genteel" slobs, tourists who never travelled and had no real resorts to compare these schleppy offerings to, and who accepted whatever slop was dumped on them.

The second group of people claiming their place in this peculiar historical retrospective were the local townsfolk who serviced these resorts. Maids, handymen, cooks (many self-proclaimed chefs just released from mental institutions), housekeepers, office workers, gardeners, and so on. Their common denominators were alcohol, unknown histories of child and adult abuse—both givers and receivers, often simultaneously—and the common resentment of the resort owners that satisfied the human need for anti-semitism.

Many of the locals in Smallwood, that Nazi-bent enclave a mile inside White Lake, did not announce their German heritage, but a penchant for pronouncing "v" as "f" and "w" as "v," coupled with a predilection for schnitzel, beer and sauerkraut, were highly suspect. Nazi flags were never publicly displayed. Poetic signs however, were, for instance: "No Dogs. No Jews." Goebbels, Eichman, Ivan The Terrible, or their immediate heirs, had summer cabins in this hidden enclave. Portraits of Hitler over fireplaces were certainly at home with the Nazi-flag bedspreads that gave that all important splash of color to brighten up an otherwise dull room.

I had three occasions to enter such log cabin retreats. While my dad was doing his White Lake Roofing Company stuff to pay motel bills, I accompanied him on three estimate visits. The shock of this Germanic, WWII-inspired folklore, the first I had ever seen in my life, never wore off. Pop knew how to deal with these sick dogs. He would quote fifty-thousand dollars for an hour's work and demand a check in advance made out to the UJA Orphans' Relief Fund. Naturally, he never got those jobs. But we did get our names on their Jew-hate list, which later on during Woodstock, must have been convenient for the bashers.

1969 was ten years too early for sensitivity awareness groups. How else to explain some of the gracious telephone calls made to me:

"You fukkin Kike Queer! You chewz is gonna get whutt yoo dizeerv! We're gonna burn your faggot-Jew motel down with your Jew whore mother on a fukkin' cross!"

This was not an intellectual crowd. This was not a humanitarian, philosophical crowd. This was a beer-and-whisky crowd; someone was supporting the 20 roadhouses. This was a motorboat-and-miniature golf crowd. This was a crowd that lived to kill living things. If it wasn't hunting season, it was fishing season. If it wasn't deer, it was pig. If it wasn't pig, it was, at the very least, target practice on dogs and cats. Their idea of a great conversation was to discuss what they killed; how big, how fast, how many.

This was not a music-and-art crowd either. Loud, top-40, hit parade songs, if the words were one syllable and not too intellectual, played at maximum decibel, were 'Le Must.' As for art, original oil paintings by the yard were available in the lobby shops of the resort hotels. Often, the artists painted as potential connoisseurs watched in awe, money in hand. Arrangements to have the picture at the checkout desk were an inducement, since most vacationers couldn't take the excessive hassle of shlepping a picture to their room en route to the pool-side games of 'Simon Says.' Prizes for various artistic and sportif contests ranged from mink stoles to a free weekend—off season, of course—and were the major drawing cards. And for the very outre, a portrait of a deer on black velvet was not hard to find.

Pool-side discussion groups of current best sellers, international chess championships, intellectual concern with the level of BBC dramatic programming, and Proust in the original French were to be found everywhere. Else. Loud shouts about baseball scores, prices on Wall Street, prices at the local supermarket, what name talent was playing at Grossinger's, Concord, or Brown's, and how to sneak in without paying; these were the subjects of choice and importance. Also, who was shtupping whom and who was available for shtupping, and who had a private room key for shtupping. Women generally announced as loudly as they could:

"Oy, my husband is working so hard in that hot city. Pity he won't be coming up until late Friday night! And my room, Number 1203, is such a large lonely room, at the end of a hall, quiet, nobody sees, nobody knows. And lonely. When my husband leaves for the city on

Monday mornings to go to work, I'm alone again until Friday. Some vacation," they would shout as they surveyed any available men that might be within ear- or eye-shot. Subtle crowd. Tasteful crowd. Refined and Defined crowd. Eeeyuch.

The third group of people was the owners of the bungalows, or, as I called them, "the bungleholes." Do not confuse the Catskills usage of the word "bungalow" with the Newport, Rhode Island usage, which generally implies a 42-room mansion with servants. These Catskill bungalows were generally linoleum-floored cabins on stilts. These were not Japanese-style stilts, which are sturdily set into the ground, an architectural design that evolved over centuries of effort. These stilts were propped up on stones: free stones, rocks, or petrified cow droppings—whatever was abundant within five feet of the site—were the foundation bases of choice. The only positive thing one might say about their construction is that each entire unit was probably biodegradable. They usually had two linoleum-saturated bedrooms, a linoleum eat-in kitchen, and the requisite screened porch, with the obligatory big yellow bug light from G.E. (before they made good things for life), and ergo, the perfect vantage from which to view the wildlife.

Wildlife, in Catskills vernacular, meant their bungalow neighbors and the swarms of flies and gnats and mosquitos that hovered about the bug light. For some unknown reason, it was an unwritten law that the bug light was always too close to the swinging screen door, thus allowing bugs to swoop inside the porch whenever the door opened. Putting the bug light away from the fragile entry was never considered. Wildlife observation from these bunglehole box seats was easy sport, since they were arranged in circles like wagon trains, the result of an atavistic urge for protection against unseen enemies. This was not pure paranoia. Jews were not allowed in other hotels in the Northeast region in exotic Connecticut, Maine, Rhode Island, Vermont, so they built their own resorts. Jennie Grossinger gets the honor as the first pioneer in the Catskills. She built a way of life.

The selling point of these bungalows was that you could cook for yourself. In Yiddish it is called "kachalein," "cook it yourself." This met the needs of the Jewish working masses who couldn't afford the luxury of full service hotels and classy restaurants. Non-kosher ones to be sure. The Jews, out of necessity, invented this do-it-yourself style vacation, and influenced generations of standup comics and second and third generations of folklore to be remembered fondly. By some. By me, Eeeyuch! Accordingly, there was a kosher butcher stationed near every major bungalow colony, and a rabbi on or near the premises.

In the center of most of these bungalow clusters was a larger bungalow without bedrooms, just one central room, with slanted floors. The Jewish colonists called this the "Casino." It was the "cultural center" of the colony hosting "Bingo Night," "Canasta Night," "Yenta Night," and "Saturday Night Entertainment." The show, open only to official bungalow/hotel renters, usually involved an accordion, a stand-up comic wearing at least one toupee, and members of the owner's offspring who would do magic tricks, or worse, recite an original poem. And finally, there was the tummler—a master of ceremonies of sorts. The tummler had two jobs, one at the show itself, where he usually told one or two slightly off-color jokes between acts. His second job was as the show's promoter, which meant he annoyed everyone all day by recruiting attendance to this show wherever he could find a breathing human by the pool, at lunch, under a tree. You could be hiding behind a rock reading Proust, or hiding under the crawlspace of your bungalow; the tummler would find you. He—it was always a male—would tease you with visions of the door prize. The mink stole, or a portrait of the hotel, or an extra dozen deserts, were sure-fire bait for most vacationers. Those occasional oddballs that preferred to read Proust, maybe in French yet, soon enough counted their losses and returned to the city, since the "no refund under any circumstances" policy was the standard. The entertainment crossed many borders and included off-color jokes, standup and sitdown comics, tango and rhumba dance teams, warblers and zingers.

The fourth group of people was everybody's business, literally. They were the tourists, parents of kids at one of the many camps in the region, and pure vacationers who came not out of "visiting day" guilt, but people who were escaping the hot city. Others, none of whom I ever was able to speak to at length, actually wanted to be there and came on purpose. They announced that they wouldn't ever be caught dead in the Catskills, (an anti-semitic remark), but for the fresh air, chemical-free water, and pollutant-free air. And they found all this available, but only in certain secret locations, far from the bunglehole casino and out of reach of those who were not informed or deserving.

These card-carrying members of nature-first groups were looked upon as nuts, and were tolerated, if they had cash to pay for their rooms. It was entirely suspect that anyone would come to White Lake and not take advantage of the vacation amenities the bunglehole owners provided at no charge. At the end of a 24-hour day fighting with these ugly tourists, collapsing on an Adirondack deck chair, on the cement lawn by the renting office, I would hear vacationers overdose on the fresh night air and the lushness of this paradise. I would get nauseous, but had to say nothing then. Now, I'm saying it.

And then there were the swinging singles, an extinct breed popular during the 1950s and '60s. Mostly single Jewish women, all claiming to be under 28, in search of a husband with a medical degree or, at least, with some kind of profession, anything. Short of these require-ments, teeth and hair would do. Most of the swinging single Jewish males were in search of a rich, very rich, woman to marry so they could never work again in their lives. Short of marital bliss, a clean classy whore who didn't charge, and would vanish after the weekend, before checkout so one couldn't get stuck with paying their bills. These available females had to be tall, big-busted, blonde, good teeth, good breath, great in bed, sexy enough to impress the other guys, and trained (previously by someone else), to give massage, head, back rubs, mix drinks, pay the bar tabs, make no demands, accept the phony city telephone number as correct and, in general, not to be glue. The ideal bimbette in this group would be one who would disappear should a better looking 'broad' appear on the horizon. Not to make any demands was topmost in the list of priorities.

These males were all hot. Hot bods, hot buns, potent, available, great smiles, great personalities, clean socks and, hopefully, clean underwear. Knowing what catches they were made it easy for the available women to snuggle up to the most ideally suited one. It never worked out. To be sure, thousands of swinging singles got married, had kids, and show up regularly at the participating hotel 20 years later to be honored as 'family,' and a free weekend—off season, naturally.

This was not a democratic clientele. This was a straight crowd. No problems existed with anyone crossing any sexually ambiguous lines. Gays or lesbians simply did not exist in the Catskills. We existed, but maintained extremely closeted profiles. Sure, here and there, locals would find it curious that some big woman built a cabin in the woods by herself. There were some of these women, all without husbands or children, who had 'girlfriends come up for weekends' and okay stuff like that, but none of them were dykes. There were the occasional misfit, unmarried men who kept to themselves and bothered nobody. It was peculiar how these men avoided local beer joints, picnics, Firemen's Day parades and hotels with children's activities. But the locals felt it had to do with bad marriage blood in the past. If not a tragic divorce, for sure there was some terrible car accident or early death from cancer. A homosexual in the mountains? Unthought of. We were there and purposely, for safety reasons, invisible. More later.

Meanwhile, getting back to the straight available females: they had no self-esteem, were overdressed, wore too much makeup, too much parfum, spoke too loudly, and displayed desperation all over their persona. After initial attempts at meeting up with Mr. Right met with disastrous results—meaning "No!"—they went for the jugular. Dropping any male and forcing him to have sex was the activity of choice. Sex, or if that didn't satisfy, the midnight buffet, all you can eat, free, included in the package price for the weekend. Their gourmet tastes included panic hunger for extra-gooey pizza, huge burgers with everything on them, jelly donuts, chocolate malts, french fries with bacon, and anything on bagels, and large oversized giant portions of anything. And pool-side barbecues.

The only good barbecues were the 'free' all-you-can-eat ones included in the room rate. These extra social get togethers, usually thrown by management on Sunday at eleven, served to hurry up checkout time. By giving some generic hot dogs and burgers to the frustrated, hungry mob under the guise of a last minute singles get-together or farewell party, they could get them to check out of their rooms in time for the cleaning staff to set up for the next batch of vacationers, foaming at the mouth by noon.

14

Yes, this was the sitcom in my motel in the bucolic town that would, 14 years later, host the Woodstock Festival. Yes, Woodstock would find its womb in a town populated by those for whom grass was something you mowed, a pot was a vessel for chicken soup, hot and cool were meteorological terms, wired meant having electricity in your bungalow, laid back was what you did on a hammock (an item never included in the rent, you had to bring your own), hip was just another body part with a joint to complain about, and joint was a crappy restaurant.

▲

White Lake was a desperate town. There was pathetic little traffic on Route 17B except for the locals going to and from the raceway in Monticello, the county seat and a village of fifteen thousand. Actually, that moderne Route 17B that the Woodstockers arrived on wasn't always the shining example of modern engineering it was in 1969. Just a few years before, it was a one-and-a-half lane tar road. Someone up there in Albany paid someone who paid someone else to make 17B a superhighway. The powers that be purchased land left and right for the five-mile stretch to Monticello, paying good prices to the distressed landowners.

I was so desperate to make a bit of money to pay bills that I rushed to build my Underground Cinema, slanted shack and bar-disco-office to the very edge of my property. Looking at the road maps, it was clear that the highwaymen would have to buy off that chunk of my property to have the road go straight on its route. My pop and I schemed and planned and sat back waiting for the road men to come in with the state's public domain condemnation papers, making us a fair offer for taking a 25-foot chunk of our lawn and destroying our movie, office, disco, and bar. We weren't dancing for joy since the most we could get would be enough to make repairs on the other buildings, and pay off one season's mortgage.

The Teichberg Curse was there—they made no offers. They simply let the highway go its course and, to this day, sticking out onto the road, is our former bar and disco, now a pizza joint. It was clear to me afterwards that those in charge decided not to give those kikes and their faggot son any benefits from the road-building program.

One of our neighbors boasted that she got forty-thousand dollars for less than two feet of lawn. Another said he'd gotten enough to move the hell out for just ten feet of ground. And these were properties that had no commercial or any other value to begin with. Oh, neither of these landowners was Jewish, or gay, thank you.

The annual mini-invasions of kushinyerkas[1] who came upstate to drop their kids off at summer camp, show up for visiting day, and come up to bring the kids and dirty laundry back, were limited to two weekends; not enough to change the economic outlook. These rich parents meant business, albeit pathetic, for the motel. They also meant some distraction from the collection of local barflies and lost tourists.

About nine miles past Yasgur's farm there are fishing spots on the Delaware River. The ugly killers of swimming things, when tired of sleeping in bags under the fresh-air skies, would sometime wander into my parking lot. How wonderful for me. Killers needing rooms, beds, baths and keys. The conversations didn't run deep, but at least they ran. Mostly, those with Mercedes explained how they were paying off the installments, those in Fords envied those with Cadillacs. I'd hear how unfair life was and how a Mercedes and a Cadillac and ungrateful children had not brought them happiness.

So, here I was. Overeducated, and forced to spend my weekend nights talking dead water things, flashy car stories, and, once my abstract paintings were put on sale, boasts about their children's artistic talent surfaced. If I was feeling shrewd, I listened intently and agreed with them heartily and they would, in gratitude, buy one of my own oil paintings for a few hundred dollars. That I had studied with the masters of Abstract expressionism—Rothko and Rheinhard and Motherwell—made no impression. A forty-five thousand dollar painting for two hundred dollars was a good buy or it wasn't. I had put forty-five thousand dollar price tags on the paintings myself, crossed out that figure, and wrote: "Sale, reduced to $200 cash." And who would pay attention to a sweaty, exhausted, absurd-talking motel

---

[1] Russian/Yiddish for women who pinch tomatoes in the supermarket, and then ask for a price reduction because the goods are damaged.

tummler who claimed to have studied with the greats who were in the Museum of Modern Art? I'm sure they felt they were making a donation to some twisted diseased mind, and it was in the mitzvah or good samaritan category that made some buy my paintings. When you check into a roadside motel in the Catskills, you don't look to buy abstract expressionism from the same guy who is cleaning the toilets and making the Greta Garbo pancakes. Or do you?

These same people would also wonder why they had to pay extra for towels when they had booked our Presidential Wing. The very educated would also point out the confusion in our name—the El is Spanish, the Monaco is French, they would say with all the elite attitude they could muster. Others would bemoan their fate of being stuck in the Catskills in general ("It's only for the kids"), the El Monaco in particular, when they hailed from Park Avenue and 72nd Street. I took that as my cue to ask, "Would you like to buy a bustling beautiful resort?" I would point to the permanent "For Sale" sign on the front desk. Remember, this was all during pre-Prozac days. As they spoke, my depression became more and more severe. I would fantasize that one of these rich gentlemen would fall in love with me, and take me away to Paris, and let me live in sedate seclusion forever. And if he were turned onto leather and whips, so much the better. That didn't happen.

Just before dawn, discussions with some of these amazingly dull tourists was a definite group therapy I conducted without the proper psychiatric license. Their kibitzing with the toilet cleaner, bed maker, pancake maker, and protégé of Marlene Dietrich, Alec Guiness and Orson Welles, apparently was more rewarding than shtupping the 'wife' in Number 247, the shanty by the pool. Those in the Presidential Wing, elevated by the 26.3 slanted steps to the terrace level overlooking the pool filtration system, felt some higher notion of philosophical insight, and devoted enormous energy to establishing their self-worth. Some of the more fascinating intellectual discourses covered international issues such as:

"How come they call that there double decker motel building, which looks just like the motels in Florida with their pink and blue doors, the Presidential Wing on one side, and the sign on the back calls it The Isadora Duncan Institute for Kushinyerkas?" Or, "They say that the air up here in the mountains is so pure that someone is losing a fortune not bottling it! Do the locals live to be a hundred?" Or, "Got any hot tips for tomorrow's race at Monticello Raceway?" And, "Betcha get plenty of hot stuff here, like, you get to drink all you want from the bar, free, you got a passkey and can access all the hot numbers that check in?" Drool, drool, drool. Oh, please.

Geographically, White Lake is a town that includes White Lake. The Chamber of Commerce's ruler measures this lac blanc[1] as five miles long. Sometimes the chamber said it was eight miles wide. Suffice it to say that whoever owned lake-front property controlled access to this public lake—except in August 1969 for three days when the hippies in dire need of bathing water, invaded—naked! And it was understood that it was fine to kill Bambi during hunting season and bash faggots and keep out Jews, but don't put your naked penis or other stuff into the lake!

Except for the Festival's lawless days, if you wanted to use the lake, you had a pay a fee to a property owner and listen to a three hour sales pitch. Every inch of lake was always for sale, for a reduced cash price. Generic deeds were available by the pound in my topless leather bar after midnight.

Back on land, if you wanted services of any kind—plumbing, food delivered, electricity working, sewers cleaned, snow plowed, or local drunks vacated from your front porch—you'd have to be a member of the Misfits and Mean Club, a.k.a. locals. Electricity in the wilderness is not a luxury. We only had one light that seemed to work, sort of. It was our "No Vacancy" sign. We never ever needed it until Woodstock.

On one stormy night, the sign went out. Here, our beacon on an otherwise dark deserted road not travelled, was not there. Mother, desperate as usual for business, lay down in the middle of Route 17B in front of the first of our three driveways, stopping the meager traffic, hoping to divert some lost truck or car. After all, it was raining hail, dark, foggy, miserable, and the only light for miles since the Upper Delaware fish-killing place nine miles back, was the orange traffic light and her flashlight-lit hand-held sign:

[1]French for 'white lake.'

18

Stop! I could be your mother!

Mother shrieked as Pop rushed to phone the electrician.

The electrician showed up at 7:00 a.m., drunk of course. I wasn't worried about Mom, since no truck nor bus nor car in the dead of night or rain or snow would dare run her over. On some of these occasions, though, I did fantasize what the world would be like without mothers. Jewish mothers. Mom never let that happen to her again. She paid a malcontent county electric repairman ten dollars and unlimited cholunt[1] in the bar to hook up the permanent "Vacancy" sign to the state electric pole. End of problem.

▲

Lest you think I was sitting on some shelf in White Lake waiting for Woodstock, I should point out that in the decade preceding Woodstock, I had about 17 concurrent careers, all of which displeased me in bits and pieces. Except those I hated with a violent passion. My erratic temperament didn't provide me with the necessary ass-kissing ability one needs to work for other people. However, just the fact of getting hired for some new and better-paying and higher-titled job with Blue Cross benefits included was the zap my insecure ego desperately required. I didn't have a track record in stick ball, nor knowledge of baseball names and scores.

To give you an idea of the level of my self-esteem before self-esteem was even dreamed of: I was jealous of this handsome boy in my class at the Yeshivah of Flatbush named Marty Burns. He had dark hair, was not fat (already a major accomplishment), smoked Camel unfiltered cigarettes behind the fence with Freya Danzig—a tall beauty I was in love with who didn't see me—and Marty cracked his knuckles. Cracking knuckles was a sure sign of masculinity and sexual bravado.

I tried to hang out with Marty Burns. I fantasized that he would tie me up and force me to crack knuckles and smoke cigarettes. All I succeeded in was cracking knuckles and smoking. Years later, talking to another refugee from the Flatbush boy-nunnery, I was told Marty fooled around with him and fucked Leo Klein, another toughie who

---

[1]Russian overcooked stew.

19

smoked cigarettes and had an obsession for putting his hands in my back pockets and tying me up and hiding me in cardboard boxes in an unused classroom. Big stuff, but it was stuff, and I didn't want you to think I had nothing going for me but to wait for Woodstock.

So, back to my career moves. Not by accident, I had topless leather boys in a borscht-belt-cum-Nazi bagel bar. With each rise in status and addition of responsibilities, there was an equal rise in clinical depression. I didn't know about clinical depression in those days. I must have had something, since the CEO of Federated Department Stores (Bloomies, Bullock's, Macy's, etc.), consulted with me about what to do with Los Angeles, San Francisco, and Houston. Me? My heavy visual merchandising track record, if you did not count the hardware store from hell on 20th Avenue in Bensonhurst—and those crepe paper windows with red thumb tacks I designed and installed,

Hugh Downs, the Interior Designer Fritz Lohman, and me at the
National Design Center Show in New York, circa 1967

and which mother removed to resell the tacks—then you had to rely on my instinct for taste and biz. Oy, and they paid me for that, too. And I gleaned a sharp portfolio of pictures to back up my rush into clinical depression.

So, having schlepped across the country and around the world selecting standards of good taste for the classy wealthy to install in their homes, I was then ready to clean toilets and make up beds and brush away pubic hairs in slanted-floor motel rooms in White Lake. I didn't know, of course, that all this was a way of preparation for the Festival that was to begin a new nation.

These non-career successes as a department store design and color consultant and color marketing expert were aided in a major way by cruising Greenwich Village gay bars and, later, leather sex clubs. My jerk BFA degree in Fine Arts from Hunter College was worth less than the sheepskin it was printed on. My frantic, panic-driven hungry desperate need to support myself and grab some pieces of the brass ring and that apple pie Betty Grable was fighting for in all those dumb movies, made me do the work of ten people—sans benefit of coke. I didn't even drink, so I had to conjure up the courage and chutzpa[1] from thin air. The air I chose to depend on was that breathed in by the crowd surrounding those leather slings in the village fuckbars, S & M leather sex clubs, and private loft parties on Fourteenth Street in the meat packing district. These hot men in full leather, or part leather part chain outfits, or in ripped T-shirts and ripped jeans, as I was beating them into submission or they were slapping me in my gut and/or butt (depending on the mood and season), provided me with in-depth previews as to the latest in color and design fashion trends. So my nightly romps were tax-deductible, though I didn't earn enough to deduct. Mixing biz with pleasure surely must have originated in the pits of a leather fuckbar.

Nothing new about making love or, if your prefer, fooling around or, if you prefer, having hard sex, and noticing the unusual clothes, hairstyles colors accessories that your partner(s) have chosen to don for the night. I never did feel quite comfortable in mentioning these nighttime influences, even though the straight world not only men-

[1]Yiddish for 'ultimate nerve.'

21

tioned their influences, but promoted them in gossip columns, fashion rags, and on television talk shows. Witness today that nobody blinks when Donald Trump dumps Ivana, who instantly goes into fashion- and jewelry-consultant mode—talents and tastes she acquired in bed with the Donald. When I tricked with the now-infamous photog- rapher of S & M and stark nudity, Robert Mapelthorpe, I didn't feel comfortable enough with myself to mention his influence on me and the world at large. I did whisper that we made love under a huge floor-to-ceiling Nazi flag that hung as a room divider in his Soho loft. It unnerved me to be tied up to a leather waterbed with hoods and gags and electric wires keeping tight control of my movements. It unnerved me to ask Robert what that flag was doing there and what it meant to him. I knew what it meant to me. Robert was into a whole uniform S & M trip, and symbols of violence and brute force were a turn-on. It wasn't the symbol of choice for me, but then I wasn't asked for my decorating advice.

When I met him, Robert was with Patti Smith, the poet and performance artist. He was also with hundreds of guys in leather and in birthday suits. He stared at me, a.k.a. cruising, for an hour. I was focused on his powerful eyes and his head-to-toe leather piece of work. Skin tight leather jeans, leather chaps, appropriate chains and hand- cuffs in just the right amounts in the left places, a leather hood slung over his left shoulder, and a lean, mean, menacing aura. The stuff love and passion are made of. In case the reader isn't aware of it, yes, there are love and passion outside the world of Burger Kings, The Gap, and whatever Calvin Klein says. Actually, most of, if not all of Calvin Klein, Versacce, Gap, and the other major trend-setting houses have their most successful looks and lines based on leather fuckbar dictates. Times have changed, and in the mid-1990s, the younger generation is so attuned to Madonna and leather and skin piercing and androgenous ambiguity, that it is no longer necessary to keep these things hidden. My only sorrow is that all this stuff wasn't out in the 1960s, or back in the 1950s, so my generation could have enjoyed more freedoms than we did.

So there we were, in the bar area of the decayed Mine Shaft fuck club, choking in the smoke and hard pressed for space, what with at least two thousand men around us, cruising each other. I have to assume he saw what I dressed up as, since I saw what he would have me see. Ergo, Robert saw a tall, stocky, mustached, dark-haired sadistic type, in leather jeans, jacket, and police sunglasses, standing mean (how I wish I could say lean machine but can't honestly), against the cigarette machine. Lighting up one after another, and taking tokes on joints supplied by a long stream of hungry leather queens sliding by me, waiting for me to slap one of their faces with my heavy workman's leather gloves. And Mapelthorpe's stare kept me in one place, ignoring the mad pleas of others to take them downstairs into the pits and devour them.

Mapelthorpe saw through my sadistic facade, ignored my hand-cuffs strategically placed on the left side—meaning I was top and the sadist, but to those knowledgeable, the sure sign of the masochist and bottom—and he slid over to me, took off my sunglasses, slapped my face hard, with feeling and meaning, and put his cuffs on me. Hey, it was instant falling in love with love. And Marlene Dietrich was right next to the juke box singing just that as he dragged me down the slanted wooden flight of stairs into one of the hundreds of hungry, waiting taxi cabs.

I was throwing my caution to hell, since I'd never permit some hot leather-sexed stranger with handcuffs and a knife and gun hanging in full view, to whisk me off to some loft in Soho. I didn't know who Robert Mapelthorpe was. Before and after we did all that perverted sado-maso stuff that Jesse Helms later belittled on C-SPAN, Robert showed me some of his enormous collection of exotic photographs. It was so overwhelmingly beautiful and mind-altering to my limited point of view, that coming down from whatever we were snorting or ingesting took a few days. Robert shared some of his unique way of seeing with me, a decided improvement over what I had, up until then, considered avant garde. Not to belittle what I had gleaned from my studies and travels to that point, but I was so startled to encounter this monumental artist underneath that bigger-than-life Nazi flag, that my remembrances of those hours are not too straight.

When all was done, I invited him to ride upstate with me to glorious White Lake to share in a swinging singles weekend at the El Monaco. He had other plans. He also said he didn't know where White Lake was, which was a crushing blow. Infuriated, and into switching roles on demand, I found it necessary to give him some crushing blows, and we had a farewell song and dance atop some hot coals he devised. Oy, such *nachas*.[1] I miss you and am sorry you had to go so young. But a brief Mapelthorpe is better than no Mapelthorpe.

So, my career en route to Woodstock, as you might gather, was abetted by that 99 percent of the designers and trend-setters who were gay and previewed their latest ideas in the sex bars. And when I showed up at the CMG, Color Marketing Group, with the top experts at Kleenex, Sandoz, GE, and other mega-corporations, whose honchos were married family types, I had the edge. While these mega-corporate types did in-depth research studies, then tabulated results and had expert analysts determine who and what and why, I already knew who and what and why, and was able to predict what was going to be out there in the street. I knew the latest trends and styles as they were just dawning. Ergo, this fuckbar information, an oblique side benefit from my closeted, sexually ambivalent, crazed lifestyle, enabled me to earn some sort of income to pay my bills and finance the motel.

Ah, so you see the connection between my ambivalent sexual mayhem and the birth of Woodstock? If we only had ACT UP, Larry Kramer, K.D. Lang, Madonna, and some of the self-esteem 12-step programs have helped us earn, what a different story Woodstock might have had. If I had had the courage and inspiration I gleaned from bearing witness to the more than four thousand gays and lesbians passing through the treasured doors of the Gay Center in New York City then, as I do now, I think it not crazy to assume Woodstock would have had several million taking the territory and using Max's farm to take a stand. Invisibility might have had a jump start by 20 years. Ah, but that is just wishful thinking, and hindsight is worth less than nothing.

The trendy, cutting-edge models, mavens, and societal leaders dressed in ripped jeans, body jewelry through noses, eyelids, tits and penis foreskins probably have no notion that the source of their wardrobes and lifestyles were born in the back rooms at the Mine Shaft 15 years ago. I briefly mention these summations to give the reader

---

[1] Yiddish for pleasures.

some hint of the mindset I was in while simultaneously being President of that Chamber of Commerce, and promoting Woodstock.

▲

I was probably one of the first artistic, recycling nuts of the late 1960s. The ugly slanted-floor casino that housed 40 years of card games and standup comics was recycled by me into an art gallery. When that failed (White Lake didn't need an abstract expressionist gallery), I recycled it into a swinging singles dance palace. When that failed (nobody showed up to dance to my warped albums), I recycled it into the Underground Cinema and opened with "Scorpio Rising," an early S & M gay porno feature that achieved some notoriety in the cult world of nether-land. Then Woodstock came, and I recycled it into an emergency drug-crashing safe house. I got out, and now, it is transformed into a pizza joint.

Each of those recycling transfigurations required permits. And I secured those permits. If not for me and all those recycling permits, I wouldn't have had "the" permit to give to Woodstock. That all-important permit I used in 1969 for Woodstock was the same permit I used for my Underground Cinema, White Lake Music and Arts Festivals 1960 through 1969, El Monaco Topless Waiter Festival 1968, Empire State Festival of the Arts, and scores of prior 'do's that never materialized except in my head and on a few signs.

The connection between this architectural bastard, mislabeled 'casino,' to the birth of the Woodstock Nation, can be obliquely understood by my heavy-duty preoccupation with the legit art world. Oh, not to discount my psycho-neurotic need to participate in the success syndrome, or else I'd have been content to join group exhibits at the local high school's annual bake sales and fund-raisers. Nah, being exposed to the greats—Rothko, Motherwell, Rheinhard, Baziotes, Seligman and Jimmy Ernst—fucked over my Bensonhurst brains for good. Had I believed the shit the rabbis were dishing out in that Flatbush, kid spirit-killing emporium, I never would have been inclined to invite dirty druggies to pristine White Lake.

And my connection to the fine arts? Aha! That is what the rednecks and townies and faggot-haters of the town board in Bethel didn't give consideration to. Oh, they knew that somehow in the big city (as they called New York City), I was connected with the arts, but that was fag stuff. Not to pay attention to. They read in the local rags about my paintings selling in Fifth Avenue salons, and the names of my teachers, but what value did any of that have in relation to bowling, beer drinking, killing Bambi's relatives, and the good life in the country? None. They didn't know the kind of head they were dealing with, and underestimated a Jewish invention that they rue to this day, some 25 years later. Mazel. I had my share of mazel on a few fronts. And mazel came in heavy doses when Mike Lang moved Woodstock to my front lawn.

I think back to my initial entry into the arts plastique, painting, and their connection to my signs, (a preview of Warhol's commercials?). I knew from Abstract Expressionism? No, nothing. I was an artist, that I knew, a student at Hunter College, where I had to go for my freshman year, since I didn't have the grades to get into Brooklyn College. (Those days you had to be educated to qualify for an education; no open enrollment studies in *kvetching*[1] then.)

And the rumors were that the fathers of a major new art movement—that was going to be recognized even in Paris—were all teaching at Brooklyn College. Enough of a lure for me with my two chins, and passion for giving legitimacy to my raggedy, brown smoke-stained bohemian suede jacket and Village artist garret. I studied with Rothko with an uncontrolled fervor I had no idea I was capable of. When Rothko couldn't afford his Lucky Strike unfiltered cigarettes and sandwiches, I offered and he shared mine. When Reinhardt couldn't cope, we spent long silent hours in his Union Square studio. We lived and felt his pain, together and apart, and shared time and other stuff.

With no support network to count on, and being an invisible alien to my family and most everyone around me, this unique reception by these kindred souls and artists became compensation for me, at that time. It was part comfort for the abuse and bashing hurled at me from all directions. If I had any brains for big-time promotion and foresight, I could have collected enough sketches and signed drawings from them to have retired a millionaire. Rothko did give me several signed

[1]Yiddish for complaining.

pen-and-ink drawings he worked on with me, but, as you will read later, my dopey mother thought they were junk and tossed them into a fire.

Doing my own White Lake Gallery fed my dumb dream of some mysterious messiah coming to save me. There, with my abstract expressionist paintings on view, with the prestigious W & J Sloane's, Lord & Taylor Gallery, and B. Altman Gallery price tags dangling in prominent view, I fully expected a car to drive into the motel compound and present me with a personal savior. This savior was to walk into the casino-cum-art gallery, or casino-cum-music hall or casino-cum-underground cinema, and fall in love with my abstract expressionist paintings. Short of that, he would fall in love with me. And he would give me a gold American Express Card and a batch of signed checks, then swoop me into his Lincoln Continental and awaken me from the entire White Lake nightmare. The dream continued that this messiah had a dark beard, black eyes, and wore tough leather chaps and handcuffs, praise Allah or somebody. As it turned out, this messiah had long curly blonde hair, no shoes, shopping bags of money, and entered the motel compound in a helicopter. And that messiah was Mike Lang, the producer of Woodstock. By the time Woodstock got to me, I was a young man with a wet dream, and that dream was about to come true, but a million-fold. And the whole world came to share in it.

So Mike and John and Joel and Stan and Lee didn't know why I was out of breath when they first exited that helicopter on my lawn. My Monday through Friday mornings in the spring and summers were nine-to-five jobs and evening free-lance mural painting and decorating in the city for a paycheck to pay for the fucking motel. Come Friday mornings, everyone I knew flew out to Fire Island to join in the round-the-clock partying. Me, I'd undergo a profound transformation for a party of different sorts.

I'd leave behind my life of art, cruising, and death-defying jobs, get into my black Buick convertible, and drive 90 miles up to the Catskills. My head turned with all the frivolous, fun-filled stories my gay brothers described about free life on that paradise of an island. Included were the many improv plays, shows, Judy Garland and Ethel Merman picnics, and hot Sunday T Dances. And sex, sex, sex. In the dunes, behind and above the dunes. Endless parties and everyone swinging and living. And I was driving in the opposite direction. If I had had any brains I would have seen clearly how stupid a decision that was. I didn't have fully developed brains. Not like the brains that 50-something has provided me with. Earned, I may say. I played endless mind games in order to survive the raw ugliness of the New York State Thruway each of those Friday afternoons. I imagined each car on that cement deathline was rushing to get to White Lake to my music and arts pavilion. If I couldn't go to the Boatel in the Pines or orgies in Cherry Grove, I'd create something akin to all that in my compound. Hah, dope of dopes!

I trifled with my highly suspect brains wondering if Mamma got a maid to clean the rooms. If she did, miraculously, I'd have some precious time off from motel toilet training. If Mamma had managed to find two people, breathing and able to function at the most minimal level required by law to be counted among the living, I'd be relieved of mowing lawns, shlepping bed boards into the swamp-view bungalows, and chasing away the tiny spiders that seem to favor fifth-rate motel rooms. At least for one day.

I arrived in White Lake breathless to commence those weekends of bliss and joy. Munching on the locally-made-by-loving-Nazi-hands bagels, I became my mother's motel toilet bowl-cleaning slave, room renter, lawn mower, cook, pool boy, cesspool cleaner, guest relations manager, hotel security, fat son, and general schlepper.

▲

I was born in a Yona Shimmel Knish[1] box, from Coney Island behind Nathans Famous, in Bensonhurst in 1935. My understanding of past lives and reincarnation to pay for grave sins committed was limited back when I was one year old. How could I know it was all a big mistake? I was without the power to put a stop to the quickly-growing farce that life was propelling me into. Yet, my sharp instincts valiantly tried anyhow. At two, I went naked out on the roof of our estate villa at 2067 73rd Street in Bensonhurst and screeched piercing sounds that made it evident I was ready, willing, and able to jump.

[1]A Lower East Side knish store, an icon.

Neighbors called the Fire Department. Some hot, black-haired, handsome Irish fire fighter, in his cherry picker, scooped me into his arms, still screaming, and assured me that I was safe. Oy did I learn a lesson in mendacity a moment later! He released my death grip on his strong comforting arms, and handed me to my dysfunctional hysterical mother.

"Wait till I tell Poppa how rotten you are! He'll beat you up, and you won't get your Pepsi Cola or Yona Shimmel's knishes for a whole year! And naked yet, in front of all the neighbors. And the goyim can all see your *pupik!*"[1]

And she would quickly hide my pupik with some shmatta. This bit of biz no doubt reinforced my self-esteem about masculine parts,

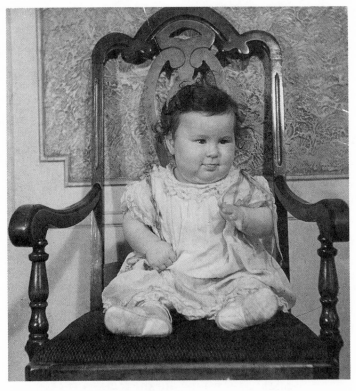

In Bensonhurst, 1935

[1]Yiddish for penis.

but go know. At two, it was impossible to analyze it. Now, at 50-something, ask me if I care?

When my oldest sister, Goldie, saw me begin the venture into motel fantasy life, she warned me, clearly:

"Don't do it Elli. Don't throw away your life on them and their stupid motel. You're young and don't know what you are doing. You will throw away your good young years on some crappy motel in crappy White Lake? Stay in the city. You're lucky they sold that rotten Bensonhurst hardware store and moved, far away. Don't follow them in their meshugaas! Save yourself now. That stupid motel will never work out."

In hindsight, she was absolutely right. But hindsight wasn't ever available until later. Ergo, I thought it was doing the right thing. Big mistake in judgement here. I was blind from so much masturbating that I couldn't see the handwriting on the faux white brick walls installed by the Garden State Brickface company who guaranteed those faux bricks would never crack. They lied. One dark rainy night, a local Nazi drove his tractor lawn mower into the side of the Heaven's Gate Wing, (the name of choice that particular night since, as I will explain later, I used my artistic talents to hand paint lots of signs; in those pre-magic marker days, no easy feat).

This Nazi's rough, red hair and face blemishes apparently created some loose wires in his head. He had stopped by earlier that day to offer his tractor lawn mower services. Since I couldn't afford to take even one more dollar from my city paycheck that particular day, I thanked him and said that the FBI wouldn't permit mowing down the high government, secret experimental nuclear vegetation topping my grounds.

"You fukkin Kike Faggot! You fukkin widd my braynze? I'll gitt you cokkksukker jewboy and your whorin mother!" he said, when a simple "I'll leave my business card in case you and the FBI change your minds," would have done nicely, thank you.

My apparent over-education and trained aesthetic sense ruled out any possible peaceful relationship with the social elite of White Lake. And as soon as it was evident to the community that I was not going to marry one of their daughters, wouldn't participate in killing helpless animals, and had no beer-bar dart-throwing track record, my entire social standing was determined. When they appraised my quasi-permanent, big black Orson Welles fedora hat and capes, there grew the distinct possibility that I wouldn't be warmly welcome at the annual Fireman's Parade and beer blast. And these leaders of the cultural and social sets read my signs promoting music and art festivals, and unanimously placed me on top of their Jew Faggot hit list.

▲

In order to have a life away from hillbillies, Jewish mommas, castrated poppas, and swarms of straight-only populations, I needed money. Big money. Money enough to buy into the real Monaco or, if not, at least beach-front property in the lost city of Atlantis. Music festivals in White Lake, clearly, were not the most direct route to freedom. Streisand's mantra of "People Who Need People" evidently didn't refer to relying on White Lake's selection of nifty neighbors.

White Lake was not a great place to be if one was talking money. I was not particularly savvy at turning local cow dung into tax-free bonds. My fever for wealth and freedom blinded me from common sense. With Pop and Mom continuing their choke-hold on my brains and penis, I joined in this spree of buying odiously overpriced land across from downtown White Lake. Then I even helped build the ugly motel. That done, we waited for cars filled with tourists to come rent our Floridian-style rooms. The folks leafed through Cadillac brochures and lists of Miami Beach vacation spas. I leafed through Fire Island flyers about Sunday hoo-has. I read about the boys in the dunes in Tunisia, about Marrakesh and Amsterdam.

When no tourists came to rent those 10 rooms, instead of throwing in the towel, giving the place to the bank and running away, we bought the neighbor's falling-down bunglehole colony, built our two-story Presidential Wing, and waited for more tourists. When that didn't work, I started changing the name of the motel each week. So instead of nobody renting motel rooms from the White Lake Motel, they didn't rent from the El Borracho Club. Then I took some more city paychecks, and we built an extravagant twenty-by-forty foot in-ground pool. I proudly added to our signage:

El Monaco - White Lake Motel - Resort & Cabana Club
Day, Week, Season, Pool, and FOR SALE CHEAP.

This subtle subterfuge brought in a few cars who liked the key word on the sign: CHEAP! The mortgage was higher and higher, and I got more and more free-lance work in the city to pay off the ever-mounting costs of expanding this get-rich-quick scheme motel.

And so we expanded once again, and moved the casino from the back swamp to the front swamp, and renamed all the buildings and opened the pancake house and added the topless bar, and still, they didn't come.

I copied the success of Fire Island, and chased away the few bargain-hunting Yentas that became our steady clientele. We were now, according to our signage, a swinging singles resort. Given the terrific management team in place, plus the brilliant strategies of lawn cricket, ping pong was free ping but you had to pay ten cents for the pong, (this failed right away), and a mad Russian mamma and a lovesick Austrian father, any fool could have seen that these efforts were not the power routes to independence and success.

In hindsight, perhaps I should have had a brain scan to see if part of me was riding an elevator without any buttons. There were no Geraldo talk shows on which to confess child abuse, priest abuse, or other dysfunctional problems that attract film deals for six figures. Go know. The kids today, they have it made. With one gunshot, one father or mother raping one in pre-puberty, or just one nursery school teacher touching private parts, big six-figure TV movie-of-the-week deals can be had. Obviously, ironing pubic hairs on the motel sheets for 14 years, entertaining world-class Yentas around motel offices, doing pool-side orgy matchmaking, do not qualify for movie deals! So, plotzing there, having begun with nine rooms that didn't rent in 1958 and 74 rooms by 1969 that didn't rent, I finally got a sign from hell:

"If only I could get 100 people to come to the motel, each paying $1,000, I'd have one hundred thousand dollars! If I only could find a way to interest ten thousand people to come to the motel, each paying $1,000, or twenty thousand each paying $500, or thirty thousand each paying $250, or one million each paying 50 cents—even in 1969 dollars—that would be enough to get out, send my deranged parents to some Betty Ford kind of clinic." (This was all pre-Betty Ford however).

So you see, my head was busy turning in 360-degree directions for solutions and salvation. As the upcoming song said, "By time we got to Woodstock..." Only the song wasn't written as yet. Go know.

The Teichberg Curse—a genetic predisposition toward "economic decay/disaster"—played havoc with my life. As the salmon are compelled to swim upstream, so the Teichbergs sought out poor business opportunities. Sought out grew into ferreted out. That grew into unfocused digging of one's own grave. However, back in Bensonhurst, the Teichbergs bought property on Twentieth Avenue where Spike Lee now films and Al Sharpton holds black protest marches. That real estate plummeted in value by the minute once the Teichbergs moved in. I blame Spike Lee. If he had been born sooner and did his movies in front of our store, we could have been in the movie, even if only in the background. A desperate, fat-faced, three-chinned, Pepsi Cola-drinking, candy-woofing white Jew boy with faggot tendencies hanging out the window as Malcom X or some band of malcontents marched, might have been featured on *60 Minutes* or the focus of an in-depth study on anti-semitism or, at the very least, a photo in *Life* of Bensonhurst child abuse? Instead of working seven days and nights in Teichberg's Hardware and Housewares store from hell, I could have hollered out the windows into the cameras and Hollywood moguls would throw seven-figure movie and TV contracts in my face. Where were the soothsayers when I could have used them? If Spike Lee had been there, cameras turning, I would have spit out colorful venomous insults to the Jews and the Italians. In the 1940s, there were no Puerto Ricans or Haitians there to insult and hate. We had such a limited menu. Bensonhurst in those days didn't have any such colorful mosaic to draw upon.

Cher didn't show up. Vincent Gardenia lived nearby, but I didn't know him or that fact. Woody Allen, Streisand, Elliot Gould, and Larry King all lived within spitting distance of my Teichberg villa on 73rd Street. I didn't know. If I did know, they wouldn't have cared anyway. They had their own Teichberg Curses to deal with. So, on my own, I learned one thing:

"When in doubt, eat something. When depressed, eat something. When sad and lonely, eat something. Eat. Eat. Go, know."

But with hindsight, I can surmise that if not for the Teichberg Curse, there never would have been a Woodstock Festival to start the world on a salvation course! Aha! Those cherry cheese knishes are still working overtime in the stomach of life. Some poetic binging? So, to clarify the point here, it is evident that when the Teichbergs "discovered" White Lake, as desolate as the town already was, it took on new downward momentum.

When the Woodstock people got their first gander at El Monaco, aside from the sweaty, overfed nervous Elliot Tiber, what did they see? It wasn't a motel, it was my mother's collection of dirty rooms, unwashed but re-ironed linens, keys that were misnumbered, door knobs that turned the wrong way, and big yellow bug bulbs wrongfully placed directly over each room's door, providing an international arrivals airstrip for bugs the size of buffalo.

If nothing else, our rates and policies were so flexible they were double- and triple-jointed. They reeked of negotiability. You could rent by the day, the week, or the hour. A mystery I've never solved involved those who would rent a deluxe room with a smell of the whispering pines, pay cash in advance, and never show up, never write for a refund. For just a bit more cash than the un-posted rates, you could have the deed and a lifelong sigh of thanks from the son. Since there were no offers I knew about, I did provide a registration card signed by Humprhey Bogart, who was rumored to have stayed in the Belle Fluer Wing overlooking the cesspool.

There were good reasons why our keys had no numbers. A disgruntled locksmith employee stopped by one cold rainy night with a truck full of locks and keys. He couldn't afford the room rent, so he bartered a deal that couldn't be beat. A hundred locks and keys, but none with numbers. Pop made a key rack without numbers. Mom put all the keys in a pasta pot, shuffled them around, and dumped them onto the key rack. This system saved big bucks on the conventional lock/key system used by the Hilton and Marriott chains. Hilton never called me and I never called them, however. In order for our system to work, it was imperative that one never actually lock the door, or else it couldn't be opened except with a master key. Pop held onto that master key for life. Not one night went by in 14 years that some fool guest didn't lock the door. For a reasonable tip, Mom would schlep out at four in the morning and use the master key to unlock the foolishly-locked locks. Of course, it would be unseemly for the proprietor to charge a 'fee' to unlock a door: Mom wore her maid's uniform under her bathrobe so asking for tips was not an embarrassment.

The El Monaco followed the letter of the occupancy laws in force in White Lake. Room rates were posted and posted and posted. In order to avoid legal and criminal prosecution, I had the signage departments of Macy's and B. Altman's Fifth Avenue make up price lists to fit every occasion. No matter the circumstance or time of day, year, or century, I had room rate signage that would back up our preposterous system. A few dozen rate cards were hanging from rubber bands above the cash drawer. A ceiling fan circulated them. As a potential guest discussed the cost of a room, the fan circulated. Mother, Pop, or I would simply point to any variety of rates, and in certain circumstances, an agreed-upon figure was arrived at. How did I do this dance of dollars for 14 years? Desperation can be a strong motivator.

Rooms by the hour took on a completely different system. It took my mother a while to understood just what these hourly rentals were. A limo would drive up. A local big shot—even the Catskills have big shots—would emerge with a blonde, rent a room and be gone in an hour. At some point, my mother "got it." Being an orthodox Jew, she ran to the local rabbi who assured her that God would overlook the hourly rentals in view of her economic needs, especially if a small donation to the Temple building fund was forthcoming.

Apparently, after her spiritual consultation, mother, who won't drive, flick a light switch, take a phone call, or write a post card on the Sabbath, welcomed every limo, every philandering husband, and every blonde bimbo to enjoy the sexual abandon that a discreet hotel proprietor could provide. And, of course, she gleefully charged them what traffic would allow, literally, a fair rate for a room and a prayer.

This clever system did not net a profit in 14 years. Not once. Was it simply our genetic predisposition to distress? Before getting down to the coincidence of Woodstock, White Lake and the Teichberg curse, I better explain how I got to White Lake in the first place. No, an alien spaceship did not drop me accidentally from a UFO en route to Chitzen Itza.

▲

Oh, it wasn't always such a high lifestyle for us little Teichbergs. We were not always privileged to have our mountain retreat. When we were kids, at the end of summer, other kids would come back from "the country," a.k.a. "the Catskills." We heard how they swam, they fished, they climbed, they played. And what did we Teichberg kids get? I got to go to Yeshiva of Flatbush. From 7:00 a.m. to 4:30 p.m., six days a week. At 4:30, things really picked up for me. I headed straight to the hardware store and helped Dad work on roofs until dark. Then I did time at the hardware store. At eleven I'd crawl home, wolf down some dinner and do my homework. Vacation time was different. The Yeshiva was on break, so I got to spend the *whole* day on roofs, and the evenings at the hardware store.

I began to whine about the country. I just wanted to be normal and be like everyone else and go to the country. I didn't even know

The first day of the motel, on Route 17B, 1958

36

what the country was. It was just some mythical place that didn't have a hardware store, and I wanted to be there.

Then one day Mother came home and announced we were going to the country. It was summer. My older sisters were by then married. So it was just my baby sister, Renee, me and Mom and Dad. I thought out loud: "Anything has to be better than that lousy hardware store and those hot tar roofs." Wrong.

The country turned out to be Pauline's Rooming House in White Lake. It was your basic White Lake frame house with slanted floors and rooster wallpaper. There were twenty makeshift rooms, one bathroom down the hall. Not exactly architecturally-built rooms. Shower curtains and sheets hanging from old wire hangers, more often than not, defined the 'room' one rented, and for which one earnestly thanked Pauline. There were no motels in White Lake in 1955, when we first came up. Not that Mom would spend good money on a motel anyway. The fourth floor attic was cheaper than the third floor shower curtain. Ergo, our room was in the attic. It had little dormer windows and a low ceiling. On the floor were two mattresses—one for Mom and Dad and the other for Renee and me.

We looked out the dormers and concluded that we'd landed in heaven. There were trees. There was a lake. There was grass. There were stars in the sky. There were bugs that chirped like birds through the night. We were intoxicated. Mother went into one of her Slavic voodoo dances when she realized that, not only was she paying cash to a stranger for a little crappy room with two mattresses but, by not being the landlady, she was losing the cash payments of the 19 other families. Now, this is a business, she thought. If we buy a house out here, get rid of the hardware store, we could make a fortune and live like this full time! Renee and I were excited. We thought we were going to be rich any moment, live on a lake forever. And best of all, we were going to get rid of that hardware store and our indentured servitude. It never occurred to us that, in comparison with the hardware store, the motel business would be like descending a couple of rings in hell.

It just so happened there was an old dilapidated Victorian house very much like Pauline's house, just 75 feet down Route 17B. It had a porch, an attic, a well and a cesspool. And it was for sale. Mamma took this incredible coincidence as a sign that it was "Beshert," which is Yiddish for "Destiny." Had she walked around the block, she would have discovered that virtually the whole town was for sale, with a lot more for a lot less.

But she didn't walk around the block and, in her enthusiasm to respond to her destiny, began a bidding war with herself and managed to purchase the run-down house which she would convert to a motel. What she spent could have bought someone else's troubles in the form of an ancient abandoned hotel with 200 rooms, dining hall, a theater seating five hundred, a pool, and a few dozen acres. Instead, the Teichberg Curse, in a feeding frenzy, sucked her into this strip of swamp, not even on the lake, but across the road. Even an abandoned, chicken-shit-filled farm would have been a wiser choice. On the county list of dead-end locations with absolutely no future spot on any tourist horizon, White Lake was number one.

That was the auspicious beginning of the El Monaco Legend and step one toward my great moment in history as the host of Woodstock.

3

A Town Miscast By Fellini's Plumber's Second Cousin on His Stepbrother's Side

A town is, of course, more than a collection of buildings. A town is its people. And, to really understand the impact of the Woodstock Festival, it's important to have a sense of the character of the town's characters.

White Lake in the 1950s and '60s was a town that could have been cast by Fellini on a day when he was not in touch with his artistic, humanistic, or political sensibilities.

Because the town was so small—1,100 or 1,500 people, depending on who was paid to count since some counters didn't include certain ethnic groups or people of color—everyone was politically influential, with the exception, of course, of the Teichbergs. The Teichbergs didn't fit in. We were on hit lists, but not economically viable lists. No matter, I had my own lists, to wit: Marie was of paramount importance in this political scheme.

Marie—no relation to Marie Antoinette—was the phone company. Since White Lake didn't generate enough business to warrant phone numbers larger than three digits, Ma Bell rented Marie's living room and entrusted her with a switchboard and the great intellectual and ethical task of connecting our phone calls. Marie's knock-kneed, clapboard house across the road from our motel would later became the Sullivan County National Bank office that would service the Woodstock Festival accounts in 1969. If Marie wasn't home, or if she was demented, not in the mood, drunk or angry at you, you didn't get calls, because everything had to go through her switchboard. And if you did get calls, she often listened in. Any personal information was then spread to all points. Marie wasn't very professional in her eavesdropping skills. She'd repeat every word, with a three-second delay, to her husband, Rusty, while you were in progress. Salacious conversations, of which I provided quite a few, garnered the additional bonus of muffled snickering and snorting.

Marie never made it into the Woodstock lore because five years before the festival, the phone company created a proper phone system with automatic switching machines. One day, shortly after the takeover, Marie disappeared. Nobody asked why or when or what. The Sullivan County Bank took over her house, remodeled it into a *National Bank* (according to the sign), and in 1969 it would play its own Woodstock role.

Vasmer, the grocer, had to always comment:

"Not many cars in your parking lot, I noticed. You know, we don't need no motels here. Got enough people here."

Joe or Bud, a drunk roadhouse owner who lived above his bar, ruled his household of *Deliverance*[1] sons with a brown bottle—in the nastiest places, I always suspected. He snickered whenever I stopped by to hit on his parmigan hero sandwiches (which were terrific, even though his slave-wife was forced to do cooking out back 24 hours a day, with no time off for birthing). Eating Mom's dreadful kosher cooking made any other ethnic cuisine, no matter how crude, delicious. To me.

"I passed by at closing time last night and saw you had some mighty strange, big fat women coming out your bar. Do you charge extra for big gals doing that dirty stuff in your motel rooms? The boys and me were wondering if you can ever get the bed sheets really clean after those kind of women used them? Me? I'd never rent rooms to no dirty lesbos!"

This cretin had formulated his in-depth philosophical position and passed the information along to me loud enough for other locals to digest.

"Two lame and blind nuns. Those women last night were both injured in Korea. They are nuns and were wounded taking care of our

[1]The name of a motion picture, denoting mountain low-lives.

40

boys. Blinded by mortar shells and, poor bitches, drink to forget what they went through. But hey, if you think they shouldn't be welcome in White Lake, let's talk at the next Chamber of Commerce meeting," I replied loud enough to make a dent in the drunk crowd, leaning on the bar, listening to every word.

I felt that fighting back with a jab at their misguided patriotism would accomplish more than feeding their sexist, racist jabs. That was then. Today, I'd handle it differently. I'd get a GLAAD (Gay Lesbian Action Against Defamation) group to zap them out of this world!

Though I didn't know any of the locals in Walkill that Woodstock Ventures had to dance with, their uncolorful, brain-dead residents were surely similar to those surrounding me in White Lake. For example, the corner gas station proprietor 50 feet from the El Monaco driveway. Proximity and neighborliness demanded we buy all our gas from him, even though his prices were higher than everywhere else. But when tourists drove into his station asking specifically for the El Monaco, he would tell them he had never heard of it. What kind of lost tourists, 50 feet away, couldn't see my plethora of road signs with dozens of motel names, including El Monaco? This is part of the Teichberg Curse. Paul was anti-semitic, homophobic, and made big efforts at concealing his heavy German accent. His smile was a nervous one. His wife was a cooking spoon with a gas-nozzle nose. He used to sit watching old black and white war movies rooting for the other side.

Even though 99 percent of our neighbors were of the same trivia-trash ilk as Pauli, there were a few rare other neighbors, sweet and treasured misfits. Riva Pefufft, a decent educated woman, out of place and out of water, was disconnected from the greater White Lake character. One of the kinder, gentler souls, she was not accepted into the beer guzzlers wive's shut-up-and-cook-and-clean auxiliary. Her husband was a mystery, and not a word about him was every mentioned. A great dreamer, elegant, genteel, literate, she was thin, tall, with regal bearing and classic fine features. If Woolworth had had an authentic classical statuary department consisting of library study carrels, she would be the forlorn manager of it, in her usual floral synthetic-fiber dress. Mrs. Pefufft was a poor man's Viveca Lindfors, with a voice like Wallace Beery. She was connected, if not devoted to, her pretensions by the fact that she inherited her prime White Lake property, the Cadillac Hotel.

Directly across the road from us and on the lake, the Cadillac was an ancient ruin. A wood-frame hotel with several buildings and bungalows surrounding the obligatoire kosher dining hall. In addition, the Swiss chalet-style entertainment pavilion leaned a good 74 degrees in several directions at the same time. Not vertically, unfortunately. By the time the Teichberg Curse arrived, Riva had no choice but to pull the plug on the Cadillac. I hated to see that old warhorse of the 1920s and '30s demolished, but understood.

I had one chance before it fell down to have a kosher dinner there. Riva was in her glory. She danced from table to table as if she were at Comme Chez Soir in Bruxelles. She didn't notice that the collection of Yentas and bargain hunters were only interested in the blue-plate special. Whatever the meal, if it included soup, salad, and desert, with all the free seltzer you could drink, it was the meal of choice. Her feet didn't notice the slant.

No question, the buildings stayed up on the strength of her willpower alone. The Fire Department, heartless as usual, gave her the official death notice. Even White Lake had its occupancy permit laws. They gave her the demolition demand after they had enjoyed a huge family-style meal, on the house of course. These gentile fire fighters didn't like Jews. They didn't like young women whom they perceived to be lesbians. In fact, Riva's daughter was a poet, a highly sensitive Oberlin College student who was shy and out of place and didn't bed down with the fire fighters' sons. I was on intimate terms with her until she disappeared. I never knew if she was a lesbian or not. It never occurred to me to pry.

Riva was the town's bedeviled true visionary. She believed White Lake had a future and would one day host millions. She was right and wrong. It did host millions, but it didn't have a future. Her plan was to build a 155-story hotel complex on the lake with an additional 50-story condo atop a revolving casino, with an unlimited view of Pennsylvania, just nine miles away. Riva had plans drawn up at great expense, filling an entire shopping cart. She schlepped those plans down to the highway every Saturday morning when there was some tourist traffic, hung up a sign that read, clearly and professionally:

42

"Pffuft's International Hotel, Condo, and Revolving 155-story rooftop restaurant. Now taking cash deposits. Use of Olympic Pool and Health Club and Gambling Casino for members only. $1,500 deposit neccesary."

Seeing her sit out there, well dressed in sheer floral polyester scarves, neatly braided grey hair secured with a distinguished ribbon some Hungarian princess once gave to her great grandmother (she always said), tickled me, yet left me with the sadness one reserves for a loved one gone unhinged. It was difficult to remain a human being with compassion and concern in a hell such as White Lake. Business was the only focus, and its casualties drew no pity.

Riva offered shares in this fantastic enterprise to my dad. She suggested the El Monaco as a down payment, with his "little roofing company that never was" thrown in for good will. For this he would own three percent of the 8th through the 14th floors, the other floors having already been optioned. Although her options fell through, she somehow added a new swimming pool and three early American-type houses onto her lake front. Membership offers in her sparkling pool to passersby didn't materialize.

"Why don't you rent seasonal memberships?"

"I do not wish to cater to strangers. Only owners of the condos or guests in my International Hotel are eligible."

"But all you have is the pool. Until you have the 155 floors built, why not get a bit of income from daily pool rentals?"

"But that would take away from the prestige of a limited membership. No, I do not wish to cater to strangers. Of course, Elliot, you are most welcome to swim in my pool, but only as my guest."

Riva gave me a 'guest pass,' smiled her usual warm genteel smile, and manned her condo table on the roadside. She read her current book until finished, then, without a break, reached into her shopping bag and pulled out another, instantly immersing herself in it. With strained reluctance, Riva eventually let the road signs fade away, moved into one of the model Americana houses herself (she needed a place to live), and read Marguerite Duras as she waited for Don Quixote or the messiah. I felt kinship with her because of her obvious lack of connection to reality.

4

Surviving, or
Hang in There Until Woodstock!

A Harvard Business School Case Study.
Creative Marketing Strategy: An Overview

If only I had known Woodstock was around the corner, I'd never have to have taken so many desperate measures in order to survive. However, since not even one psychic soothsayer in Chelsea (where I moved to be closer to the leather bars), predicted this cataclysmic change, I was left to my own devices. I used my color marketing expertise to repaint the doors. My strategy was to impart a look of tropical joy to the grim, desolate rundown White Lake pale that was to be seen everywhere in the town. My pop was busy fixing those parts of El Monaco that were falling down, one step ahead of potential tourists. The less the tourists spent on the rooms, the more quality and service they demanded. Demanding and getting were not allied. I cleverly painted each door a different Florida pastel. I painted impressive room numbers and names on doors, walls, arrows I stuck in the ground, and on my endless array of highway signs. One day, a registered interior designer from Manhattan, a visiting parent in search of an overnight room, Letitia Baltimore or Barclay nee Vishinsky, sat in her taupe BMW staring in amazement at me and my dozen paint brushes, and offered her valuable advice free.

"I am a member of AID and NSID. It is my professional opinion that if you painted everything a subtle shade of grey or beige, removed all those vulgar signs, and hung an American Eagle over the entrance, you'd attract a discreet clientele."

Mom showed her a deluxe suite in the Paul Revere Wing, an instant name I painted on the side of the building nearest her car—as

44

she spoke—in honor of her Americana suggestion. She exited the room aghast.

"I've travelled across the entire country and stayed at some of the best and some of the worst roadside motels. I have never seen such a disgraceful, unsanitary, unappealing mess as this... (looking up at the dripping sign), Paul Revere Wing! Yeeuch, it is vile and you people ought to be prosecuted."

If I could have foreseen that Woodstock was but moments away, I would have had a different answer to give this fine colleague. But, as it was, I had to invent excuses, to wit:

"MGM will be filming here next week, and we are putting the finishing touches on this set. Rita Hayworth and Gregory Peck are shooting *The Motel From Hell* here. I can let you have Gregory Peck's room for fifteen dollars, but only for six days. Greg will be needing his room by Thursday."

Mother didn't understand one word I said. She did understand that the woman suddenly found the Paul Revere Wing had *a certain charm*. Mother's vision was focused on the *certain charm* of the cash in her hand.

One of the architectural features my pop and I installed was disastrous on all counts, except for the practicality it offered when Woodstock finally arrived. We engineered five driveway entrances to the compound. We were on two highways, so that accounted for two. The barn and farmhouse in the compound had another; that's three. The rains one summer created a crater-like mud path that ultimately dried up to form a jungle-type roadway. That was four. And we actually blacktopped an exit drive at the far side of the compound so that cars, and later horses, wouldn't sink into the swamp when trying to maneuver. That was five. I think there were two more hidden in the untrimmed brush, but with so many directional "Entrance" and "Exit" signs to paint, there wasn't much time for an overall planning scheme. When Woodstock came, they made good use of all those driveways with their barrage of trailers, portable toilets and 18-wheel trucks.

It wasn't obvious to me then that my artistic bent, coupled with my affinity for promotions, was betraying me and leading me ever deeper into debt and chemical depression. Making signs provided me with some kind of weird, twisted hope for a passport to any world that didn't include ethnic and familial provisions. So, I made site-specific signs for each driveway in order to satisfy the assorted buildings in the compound; El Boraccho Motel, White Lake Motel, Elliot's Hideaway, White Lake Summer Theatre, El Monaco Underground Cinema, Empire State Art Gallery, White Lake Topless Waiters Disco, Graffiti Toilet For Women Only, and my favorite: "Wha?"

Mamma and sister Renee in 1958, our first year at the motel

When a potential customer drove up, we would each take our posts at the different driveways. Whoever was approached first quoted our top price. If that didn't sell, we referred them to the next driveway, where they got a lower price, and to the last driveway, where they got our rock bottom special. Strangely, many people didn't catch on that we were all the same place. Then again, we never had any repeat business. Lady Bird Johnson's Highway Beautification Act didn't affect White Lake. The news of President Johnson's election didn't come to White Lake until long after President Ford arrived. Millie at the Post Office did not take to the Johnsons and refused to hang his official photo alongside her favorite: Ike with Hitler. How she managed a photograph of Ike and Hitler fishing on White Lake was never explained.

Human Resource Management: A Paradigm of Efficiency

Then there was efficiency of human resource management. In addition to manning a driveway, my pop fixed roofs, did all the repairs, and tripled as the chef. His cooking skills were not a nice thing to see. At breakfast, those few guests we had on weekends needed their morning coffee, and pulled apart Thomas' English Muffins, slightly toasted, but not too, and not under either. His huge, strong worker's hands and mental exhaustion didn't prepare Pop for catering to such raffine requirements. Pop hacked open the muffins with a hatchet, threw them on a grill he had made out of a discarded lawn mower and piece of wire fencing, which he had hooked up to his home-made generator. When burning smoke filled the linoleum coffee shop, he slam-dunked the paper plate with black muffin and a blob of elegant Hotel George V pat of butter (stale margarine in el cheapo labels the hotel supplier discounted), onto the wobbly table.

Oh, this coffee shop was a gerry-built one to replace the only other coffee place in a mile, that in Newman's Drugstore, which we couldn't send anyone to for a variety of reasons you'll find sprinkled throughout this narrative. Our sophisticated travellers expected to be able to have breakfast within walking distance of their rooms. Not unreasonable, so we fashioned the end motel room, closest to the highway, into a coffee shop. I insisted Pop wear an IHOP apron and little floral cap on his head, but his tarred overalls were the only vestiges of manhood he had left, so he wore them forever. His rough laborer's hands were covered with years of tar, paint and hard work. Not a delicate pretty sight, nor compatible with demanding tourists, Pop's repertoire of polite niceties was severely limited. Along with his hot temper, short patience, and irritability—sexual abstinence does this to certain people—our travel guests often quickly decided they were not as hungry for breakfast as they first thought. After some of them saw Newman's Drugstore's crowd of cretins, they reconsidered Pop and his tar-topped cold rolls.

When Woodstock Ventures ultimately took over this coffee shop as temporary office and feed bag, they never commented about what fate had provided them. It must have been such a relief, being out of Walkill and into a welcome environment, that they overlooked the out-of-control Jewish Mamma kitchen.

Mother kept serving up her chicken-fat laden pot luck dishes, overcooked and burned flanken casseroles, and rendered chicken necks to unsuspecting crowds. This acceptance reinforced her deranged view of her talents as hostess of the highways. I reported her to the local health department, but they were just as ineffective as the other service agencies in this outpost of hell. The Monticello hospital was fed up with endless requests for stomach pumping, and sent warning signs to be posted. However, every available spot for signs was already being used by moi, and theirs never made it. However, their signs did have a nice smooth backside, which I freely used for my own messages. Sales of Ex Lax and Bromo Seltzer at the registration desk were always brisk. Mom never connected her cooking with bromo sales.

What moderne motel doesn't have telephone service? Don't ask. We had signs that said, "Telephone service is being updated for your comfort and convenience." Pop was our motel telephone operator. Papa lacked basic phone-skill instincts. No matter how hard I tried to train him in a few professional phrases such as, "El Monaco, how may I help you?" he would still pick up the phone and say,

"Haloo? Vat's dis? Vy you calling? Vachoo vant? If you got children, don't come here. We don't rent to children. They ruin mattresses, make noise, pee in the pool, make noise, and if you got kids, we got no vacancy!"

"But our children can sleep in a bed with us."

"No vacancy."

"Our five kids are used to sleeping on the floor."

"No vacancy."

"We reserved a room for us and our children eight months ago."

"No vacancy."

"I'll report you to the White Lake Chamber of Commerce!"

"Mine son is the president of the White Lake Chamber of Commerce. Still, no vacancy."

Fiscal Policy: Firm But Flexible

Mom and Pop ran a tight ship, in certain respects. Since I was in the city weekdays, they had free rein to set motel policy behind my back. And a stringent fiscal policy was its spine, its core, its fundamental underpinning. Mom's central business law was: NO REFUNDS. When customers asked for refunds, Mother's answer:

"I didn't walk here from Minsk in Russia in 20-foot snow drifts, with cold potatoes in my pockets and pimples from the Cossacks just so I should give you a refund on your room! A curse on your head and on your children's children!"

Closely related to "NO REFUNDS" was "NO CREDIT CARDS, AND NO CHECKS."

"We don't take checks because people stop checks! You look like those tourists who were here last year who stole linens from Room Number 321? If you can't afford to pay for a first-class motel, you shouldn't travel, maybe?"

Some brainy customers made the logical inference that there might be valid reasons to stop a check, and either took their business elsewhere, or were intimidated into paying cash. Credit cards were an expensive luxury El Monaco couldn't afford. Visa insisted on at least one hundred dollars a month in billings to open an account with a motel. One hundred dollars? Oy. I had to do four consultant hours with potential decorating clients on West End Avenue, or two jobs on Park Avenue for one hundred dollars. Visa didn't call for rooms and I didn't call them for the hundred dollars.

Zen And The Art Of Motel Management

80 days to Woodstock and counting...

As you will see later on, when Woodstock finally took over my motel, there wasn't time to be embarrassed about laundry matters. However, up to that hectic moment and change in life, there wasn't enough income from my city designer employment to pay for a washer-dryer. I had to improvise a dance over 400 sheets and 800 pillow cases and hundreds of towels needed on those weekends when we were full. Yes, there were three weekends a summer when campers' visiting parents and desperate lost travellers accidentally tumbled into El Monaco.

Looking back, I suppose seeing the mix of meshugga signs and slovenly appearance, travellers assumed it was an odd-job-lot motel, and that bargain prices were to be had. But, even the worst of the bargain hunters demanded crisp, fresh clean linens and towels. For the first five years, I tossed the dirty laundry into a ditch in the basement, hosed hot water and lots of chemicals over the piles to kill germs, swooshed it all around with two-by-fours from the Nazi lumber yard across the road, then shlepped it to the edge of the swamp out back, hanging it out to dry on the whispering pines. (We advertised whispering pines because the stock photos of pines were cheaper than taking actual photos of whatever those trees out back really were.) This I had to do before dawn. From past encounters with upset paying guests, I knew that seeing the linens drying on swamp tree branches with zillions of moving little black things rising up from the bog, was unsettling. Perhaps unsettling is a bit mild.

"Are you fucking crazy here or what? Don't you hillbillies know about sanitation? Who knows what kind of diseases we can get from your dirty unsanitized linens?

"You don't know who you are dealing with here! My brother-in-law is the President of (insert any famous company, country, organization). I can buy and sell you!"

Sell? The second-most beautiful word next to 'buy,' and magic to me:

"You can indeed 'buy' me out. Why don't we draw up legal papers. You can own this world-class hotel in an hour, sooner if you prefer. I hadn't thought of ever selling, but you look to be (insert your choice here: nice people, bright people, deserving people, brilliant business people)! For cash, we can give you the keys to the kingdom in less than 15 minutes. I don't have to pack nothing. And you can deduct your personal room rate from the price. Is there some price that would fit into your scheme of things better than some other price?

"Okay, you talk a hard deal here. Are we talking two figures? Three figures? Six? Shall I have my people contact your people or are we talking cash under the table here? Hello? No vacancy!"

The sixth year, it dawned on me that I would die an early death if I continued this linen stuff. I was doing a West End Avenue apartment. Fourteen rooms for Lilly Levoe, grieving widow of four fur coat factories and mother of a spoiled, whining daughter. Lilly insisted I design and install a forest in her 60 foot entrance hall to make her live mynah birds feel at home and loved. Thinking of the cost of a commercial-weight washer-dryer, I added on the appropriate amount to the bill for foliage flown in from Kenya. Lilly and her birds were ecstatic warbling around in her indoor, plastic planted forest, and I was relieved of washing pubic hairs from the linens and questionable stains from towels.

A valuable lesson in motel management was gleaned from all this. Training guests not to need more than one set of towels or sheets during their stay was an absolute requirement.

75 days to Woodstock and counting...

By the time I got to Woodstock, eight years later, I had refurbished Lilly's forest eight times in order to replace the broken down washer-dryers. Each season, these industrial-strength machines gave in. I didn't know it but, during the week, while I was teaching art at City University, New York Tech, and designing American Eagle toilet seat covers in Pasaaic New Jersey, (punishment too much for any sinner), Mamma was taking in vash from the other motels. With each sheet and towel she dispensed mother's advice. Business was booming until the health department tested the bacteria count of her loads.

"Either you use detergent and hot water or we close you down! Mrs. Teichberg, you need a laundry permit to operate a commercial operation in your basement."

Permit meant paying off some clown in the town clerk's office, and we knew better. She stopped her taking in laundry operation until a better plan could be worked out. When I found out, I grabbed a kosher knife and tried to stick it in her heart. Only two things prevented that joy. I couldn't find her heart, and the barfly White Lake cop, Blackie McFarknol, pushed his belly between my plunging hand and her chest. She pressed charges, Blackie had another very dry Rob Roy, and refused to put me in jail.

70 days and counting...

I knew I couldn't keep up the pace of walking with potential guests across Route 55, illegally onto a neighbor's beach front, and out-talking, out-pacing, out-distancing folks into thinking they were all the time on El Monaco property. Swimming in the Catskills meant a sparkling clean, blue-bottom pool within spitting distance of one's room. Who could afford a swimming pool? My feet just gave up. Pop's health wouldn't permit his running the 1000 foot dash to the lake.

Mom's feet were getting spookier by the day. Her skinny legs looked like chicken sticks, and even a mamma with a misplaced heart deserved better. So there was no choice but to build a pool.

"A pool? You have to find ways to get the fuck out of there! Each season you keep burying yourself deeper and deeper in debt in that losing situation! You will never be able to earn a dime, and you won't have any money when you're 65, and you'll end up with newspapers

- 70 Units—brand new motel rooms, suites, efficiency apartments, vacation cottages and guest house
- Beutifully situated on 15 acres of natural woodland, landscaped lawns and hiking trails
- New steel swimming pool with crystal clear filtered water, poolside patio, pool open 24 hours
- New TV lounge, Casino-game room
- Handball, basketball, volleyball, ping pong, lawn tennis, badminton, nature trails on the premises
- Barbecue pit for cook-out enthusiasts
- Only 5 minutes to Monticello Raceway

WHITE LAKE • SULLIVAN COUNTY • NEW YORK
EXIT 104 QUICKWAY TO ROUTE 17B AT ROUTE 55

For a Holiday in a Fun and Sun setting

THE **El Monaco**
RESORT
MOTEL and COTTAGES

LESS THAN 2 HOURS FROM N. Y., N. J. AND PENNA. METROPOLITAN AREAS
5 MINUTES FROM MONTICELLO RACEWAY

- Centrally located to many children's camps
- Planned teenage activities by village Chamber of Commerce
- Summer high school sessions in nearby Monticello
- Supervised day camp for the kiddies available at modest charge
- Baby sitter service
- The perfect spot for your hunting and fishing headquarters

Vacation Paradise
WHITE LAKE

THE MOST BEAUTIFUL LAKE IN SULLIVAN COUNTY
OPEN ALL YEAR

The El Monaco Resort Motel

around your feet in a public shelter. Sell that dreadful place! Don't buy a pool. If you can't sell, donate it to some charity, take the tax deduction, the folks can go to a nut house, and you move to California and get a life!"

So sayeth my shrink of the moment, Dr. Lament Huning. She was right, of course. I just didn't fully comprehend the depth of the bottomless pit I was digging for myself. I sent out thousands of 'artist paints murals to spec' postcards to a list of interior designers. I translated my painting ability into doing classical-styled Italianate or Greco-inspired fountains, gardens, statuary, topiary, and so on, onto dining room walls, old pianos in need of restoration, and Salvation Army war chests needing new life. My marbleizing or forget-me-nots in mauve and heliotrope, priced by the square inch, paid barely enough for a fucking minimum-size commercial pool.

The smallest pool possible for a world class resort was twenty feet by forty feet, a.k.a. a large bathtub outdoors. This cost, in the mid-1960s, $10,000. In 1994, the same pool is $100,000. For me and my level of income, $10,000 was already stratospheric. Obviously sick and disturbed, I was determined to invest just this one more time, and turn around the El Monaco and make a fortune on my swinging singles plan. Or, with a pool, there is a chance to sell out. I shouldn't have paid any attention to myself. Go know.

I painted neo-Greco-Roman gardens at 475 Park Avenue for the Baroness Von Ponz, owner of Opel cars. Her fake-titled decorator, Pini San Marco something, refused to pay me. He claimed I did not have any authentic experience in neo anything, and that my work was such schlock he had to repaint the entire foyer white and engage another muralist. He locked me out of the foyer, had my paints in a box on the street, and stopped payment on his faux checks.

I did have a live witness to verify the quality of my art work: It was Edna Luetz, the then Nazi chair of Hunter's Art Department where I taught. Edna had credentials, but was totally insane. I had taken pictures and had her come up to witness this great Sistine Chapel-lookalike mural on the baroness's foyer walls and ceilings. A judge ruled in my favor. The photos of the murals showed nothing but a vague classic garden under a hazy mauve glow. I had to depend on my own expert testimony, to wit:

"Your honor. This faux Duke Pini whatever, comes here, gives me faux checks, takes the Nazi car lady's money to use for his fascist Italian comrades in San Miniato, and I'm left with my old Jewish refugee mamma—who walked to New York from Minsk in 1909 or 1913 from Cossacks raping and defiling helpless Jewish families after midnight during a 30-foot snowstorm—shlepping 5,000 feet to show some anti-semite's lake front to demanding tourists, who would live to retire in the holy land if only I could collect this money and pay for the pool."

Go know that Judge Uri Kariewskkinik was a Russian emigré himself from Minsk.

"My mamma, may she rest in peace, probably was on that same cattle boat your mamma was on. My mamma washed floors from Minsk to Minnesota, in order to pay for my legal education. Duke, pay your bill or you are dead ravioli here!"

These are things that Woodstock Ventures didn't know when they took over the El Monaco. They just saw this sparkling turquoise-blue pool, and took for granted that every motel has a pool. Oy.

The fact was, we installed the postage-stamp-size outdoor tub and it attracted no new business at all. The few kushinyerkas that did rent rooms complained the pool was too small, and there was too much chlorine in the water, and they didn't have enough pool towels, and there should have been more chaise lounges, and outdoor showers, and cabanas, and umbrellas, and a pool-side bar, and a handsome lifeguard who gave room 'service' and personal massages to horny housewives whose husbands were shtupping waitresses at the raceway or in other motels. All this gave Mom the notion for a new business. And so, like the masochist I was, I painted yet more new signs, like,

Pool towels rented, see Sonia the pool maid. Chaise lounges rented, see Sonia the pool maid. Pool drinks, umbrellas, suntan lotion, showers, and massages available for rent. See Sonia the pool maid. Cash only. Tipping encouraged.

Economies of Scale: When Quantity Counts

68 days or 73 days and counting...

Even broken-down roadside motels such as proliferate in the South's Gulf Coast and in Appalachia, have telephones. Not El Monaco. That was a luxury my meager teacher's salary couldn't afford. Even a second-rate psychic could have predicted that Woodstock would need in-room phones.

Mamma to the rescue. A disgruntled ex-employee of Ma Bell's drove in one night with a truckload of previously-owned Bell phones and a used switchboard from some Hilton Hotel in Korea. His name was Herbie and we knew he was legit because he had fixed our original phone a few times. He said that for $500 we could own these phones, and never have to pay a fee to Bell again. Mother offered him $70 if he'd include the necessary switchboard. Herbie drank away his $70 in bar whiskey. We put a phone in every room. Papa wired the switchboard so that all the little bulbs lit up. The catch with this phone system was that it was hooked up to nothing but itself. In other words, it didn't work. But it did look good and it provided me with the opportunity to make new signs:

**Pardon our silence, new phones are being installed.
We thank you for your patience. The Management.**

These signs remained, pristine and undaunted until 1969, when the Woodstock Festival management moved in and had to bring in real phones and a functional switchboard.

As the phone system brought us, unwittingly as it were, into modern-day motel marketing, we now needed color televisions, window screens and shower tiles that did not plop off the wall as soon as some hot water hit them. One rainy night, a disgruntled tile man drove in with bargain imported Italian tiles for motel bathrooms for only five dollars per room. The Teichberg Curse was lifting. Some watchful angel from motel hell sent trucks with disgruntled color TVs that had no innards, motel bed vibrators with coin slots fit for Tunisian kopeks, and mattresses filled with peanut shells from Georgia. Accompanying those shells were large Georgian roaches nibbling away at the gourmet leftovers of the peanuts. Naturally, I had to make more new signs.

**For your luxury and comfort, the El Monaco will be installing
luxury televisions, luxury imported mattresses, vibrators and
shower tiles. We thank you for your patience.
Your room rate reflects these improvements.
A reminder: No Refunds for any reason, valid or not.
The mis-management is not responsible.**

Breakthroughs In Nomenclature and Marketing

69 or 83 days and counting...

Mamma insisted on strategic and flexible terminology. A room
was anything you could put a number on, including the back porch
of the main house. Well, it wasn't really a porch, it was a slanted floor,
outside, with a shower curtain supporting some ancient marine
mosquito netting gleaned from a Sullivan's Department Store left-
over-from-the-war sale. Mom filled a carton with 'all you can carry'
for five cents. The netting was included.

Other preferred time-share/space-share cubic footage was defined
by curtains, with appropriate signage. One of my favorite ones said
"The Doll House, not affiliated with Ibsen's anything." Behind the
curtain was a spring and no floor space. A mattress would have used
the vertical air space, so was not included. Luggage had to be excluded
since underneath the box spring was a sealed cesspool cover, to which
the law required emergency access. There was nothing solid enough
to hang a clothes hook on, so any clothing was stored under the
pubic-haired sheet.

During peak season this room was popular due to its affiliation to
Ibsen and its very, very cheap price of under ten dollars per night per
four people. Advance booking was done two summers in advance,
sight unseen, no refunds. There was still one more feature to this
bargain accommodation in the center of downtown White Lake. One
couldn't occupy it until 4:00 a.m. The shower directly above it leaked
onto the bed. Barflies and disco-dancing swingles finished showering
only after the bar closed. And other guests used the community shower
above beginning at 6:00 a.m., the checkout time for this luxury annex.
Had I known then that during the summer of 1969, six members of
the top brass from Woodstock and Warner Brothers, and Paramount
and MGM, would be sleeping like sardines in this room, I would have

photographed it for Andy Warhol to make famous later. Pop tried to fix the leak, but that wasn't possible without removing the foundation walls of the theatre barn next door. How the two were related is still unclear, since my dad took that information to the grave with him. Pop was stubborn. He didn't think this was a legit room, and wanted no part of its life.

Flexible terminology also applied to supplies. Mamma discovered from the soap supplier that if you were willing to buy soaps with other hotels' names on them, they were 90 percent below cost. This made our motel very 'internationale.' We had soaps with wrappers from around the world. Those guests who were ashamed to say where they were actually staying could steal soaps that said; Grand Hotel Europa, Grande Hotel Madrid, Grande Hotel Roma, or The Orient Express bus tours! The problem was that these soaps were so old they could not whip up any lather. Not even a bubble. Occasionally, savvy guests would complain and I would explain it was the hard mountain water that caused lack of lather. Well, it *could* have been. My only other excuse was that a formal complaint was being made to the Grand Europa headquarters in Majorca, and that took time. There were no faxes in the 1960s. During the Festival, every last bit of Grande-any-thing soap was used up, lather or not.

Component Pricing and the Bottom Line

As you will see a bit later on, when Woodstock Ventures asked what the room rates were for the entire motel, I was at a loss for exact words.

"Flexible pricing" was essential for the success of the El Monaco. Flexible pricing meant several different prices for every room, and additional charges for such luxuries as: ice and the plastic cup it would be delivered in, delivery and tip not included; windows that opened; curtains for the window; shower curtains; extra soap; an extra towel; parking space in front of one's own room; guest parking; tourist tax, (self-declared since the county didn't have one); school tax, (your kids go to school—you think ours don't need to?); lawn mowing tips; luggage insurance; key deposits; towel deposits; aggravation tax; sur-charges for checking in early or late; surcharges for checking out early or late; rental of wake-up alarm; repair surcharge for damaged television; surcharge for key with number; you get the rest.

Some stubborn guests asked to see a printed rate card. For these outrageous people, I had to step in and dance them around:

"If you want to stay here, you'll have to abandon any previous notions of the hospitality industry's standards. They do not apply here. We were the model for the Bates Motel in Hitchcock's *Psycho*, and we can show you the very shower curtain Janet Leigh grabbed as Tony Perkins stabbed her to death. We are overpriced, understaffed, falling apart, ugly, uncomfortable and, if you had any choice, you'd be any place else. The fact you are still here willing to take this abuse and pay for it tells me that there are absolutely no rooms to be had in the entire county, ergo, please either take the room, or remove your car from the parking lot as there is an hourly rate to park cars here. Next!"

I was being honest with the people. Most laughed and thought the routine so innovative and brimming with local upstate color that they said they were satisfied with whatever we had. Others seemed provoked to the edge of criminally insane behavior; those we charged a bit more for the aggravation. Doctors paid top rates. Working-class people got lower rates, but didn't get some of the extras, such as towels or a plastic cup. If my father was around for the price fixing, he would of course add, "Are there any children in this party? That's $200 extra."

After a few years of experience, keys were put in this "extra" category, too. Mom learned a strange fact of the hospitality business: People are prone to keep their keys. She charged five dollars (about $50 in 1994) extra for a key. When customers complained, she explained this was a house rule because "customers nowadays don't know how to behave." This key policy did not last very long. Too many customers considered "the key" a necessity, if not a requirement, and the Cold Potato/Minsk speech just didn't cut the mustard here. Discussing this with Mother was futile, so I took action. I punched out all the locks and hung signs which read,

Installing state-of-the-art high-tech computerized key systems for your convenience and security. This technology will not be ready until the day after checkout, so don't expect and you won't be disappointed.

Mother explained to irate customers that the holes in their doors increased air circulation and were actually a benefit. After all, another system, such as air conditioning, would have doubled the room rate.

Environmentalism and The Bottom Line

92 or 61 days and counting...

Mom was putting the environment up front. She figured that if there were no fresh stains, sheets could be shaken free of any loose organic debris, ironed and sent back to the remade rooms. This revised operating procedure was based on the need to conserve electricity since electricity cost money.

It was a like a game of musical sheets we would play. I'd put freshly laundered sheets on the beds, replace the odious towels with fresh ones, and slip in extra towels. Mamma would run in after me, strip the beds and replace them with her recycled and ironed sets. En route out, she would replace the clean towels with those that were not used more than once the previous day. To make sure the towel fairy didn't show up to replace her choices, she nailed these towels to the wall. It was beyond Sisyphus; I was afraid we'd be spreading syphilis. But there was nothing I could do to stop her. She said she had no intention of spending her old age, broke, alone, in the streets, her feet wrapped in newspapers.

Strategic Marketing Errors: Tips From The Trenches

En route to the Festival, in all fairness, I should tell you about a few of the brilliant marketing schemes that I couldn't pull off. Is White Lake not the place for an international airport? A few years before Woodstock arrived by air—via helicopter—Sullivan County opened the White Lake International Airport. I did not solicit the airport. It arrived. I was so desperate, in my wishful angst, that the absurdity of the airport never came to mind. I was so far gone that I believed the airport could help the El Monaco struggle for any kind of status that would involve an income, or at least bail money.

The opening of the airport sent me into a sign-painting spree. All over the airport, El Monaco signs sprung up like daisies, declaring brightly:

Only Two Miles To the World Class Resort, the El Monaco.
One mile to El Monaco, home of international music festivals.
You just passed El Monaco,
the world-class everything to everybody.
Welcome to El Monaco Motel & Singles Resort. Straight, Gay,
Lesbian, TVs, Cross Dressers, Sexually Ambiguous, Child
Molesters, Anti-Christers, all Welcome.
NO CREDIT CARDS. NO REFUNDS.

After the first three weeks, since not one customer came from the international jet set that were no doubt landing after midnight at the shiny new terminal, I had to resort to plan B.

Paying a steep fee to the airport, I installed a bright red courtesy phone that connected directly to the motel office. This was not an off-the-truck special phone. It had insides and even worked. Unfortunately, it never rang. I painted a sign on the side window of my Buick:

El Monaco International Motel
Airport Shuttle Service

I was getting suspicious as I circled the shiny marble floors of the sparkling new terminal. There were several ticket sales windows that looked like real airport counters. There were signs that indicated baggage claims, taxis, busses, and a variety of other airport-type services available. I looked up at the electronic tote board to see the expected list of incoming flights and schedules. Zilch! Nada! My perky red El Monaco Air Shuttle cap atop my then thick, black-haired head askew by now, I rushed to the Terminal Manager. The Manager said: "What list? No flights in. No flights out."

Pan Am, TWA, British Airways, and 45 other carriers did market studies and decided there was no demand for air travel to or from White Lake. My little perky red shuttle hat was a total bust. Disappointed, but not yet alert enough to see the handwriting on the wall, I confessed the awful truth to Mom and Pop.

Maybe it's the Teichberg Curse again? Who was I talking to? These were the Teichbergs! My name was Tiber, no relationship. Among the three of us, there wasn't enough smarts to just dump the whole mess, cut our losses, plead insanity and check into some government shelter for basket weaving.

134 or 89 days and counting...

I'm not certain if Woodstock Ventures understood the full impact that a modern-day harness track within spitting distance of their Festival would have. It never came up. And considering that the Raceway eventually also joined the long list of businesses that sued Woodstock for alleged lost income, maybe we were being shortsighted. Maybe we had tunnel vision? Hello?

At the time, the second Monticello Raceway was also known as the second coming. Just five miles down the road from my signs. We caught the racetrack fever. No question we'd be rich with racing fans, drinking Rob Roys and renting rooms by the hour. Winners would come and go, leaving money trails behind them. We'd be making money hand over fist. Then some big shot would stride over to the registration desk and buy us out for cash on the spot.

The few first race track-related biz inquiries that took me by surprise were from Monticello hookers who wanted to 'rent stools' in my bar. Go know what that meant. I didn't then; I do now. I was thrilled somebody wanted to come to my bar, for any reason. The hot motel-bed biz, so lucrative in every other motel in the county, was now going to come to my rescue. I had wet visions of thousands of hookers, sitting on El Monaco stools, long lines of cars from the raceway to White Lake, taking numbers, waiting for their hour of heaven on Mamma's pubic hair covered sheets. I dreamed about big money that would buy me freedom. I was too dopey to know I could have had freedom anytime I wanted it. Something else was holding me back. I didn't know.

This dream propelled me to convince the Raceway promotional guy to give us a trot of our own. Grossinger's, Concord (without the 'e'), Brown's, even Goldberg's Mountain Top Valley View Hilltop Bungalow Colony had trots named after them. I got the first trot to be named after a White Lake resort in history! Surely, this would have gotten the money people to sit up and notice, and come pay me back for all those years of dumping my city salary checks into this bottom-less ugly pit? Wanna bet on it? Don't.

The deal was the El Monaco would award a silver cup to the winner and it would be mentioned on local radio and listed in the papers and programs. And the big time was dangled in front of my dopey eyes: Even the racing column of the *Daily News* would list us. Pop immediately suggested changing the prize from an expensive silver cup to a free weekend at the El Monaco, exclusive of drinks, ice, tips and towels. Mom insisted the grand prix be a free portion of her homemade stew, cholunt.

It all turned out not to matter much. Nobody won the El Monaco Trot. The day of the Trot came. Not one TV station called for interviews. If I had wanted to present the silver cup, I would have had to buy an entrance ticket for $1.50. We didn't take in $1.50 in two days, so it seemed imprudent to throw it away on a race that was doomed from the start. I painted a horse's head and nailed it atop the El Monaco sign, with a banner that said:

Welcome El Monaco Trot at the Raceway.
Trot Special Rates. Half Price Horsey Drinks.
Free Cholunt & Pepto Bismol.

Nobody came to watch our Trot. The free listings didn't draw horseflies either. A local Nazi pre-skinhead skinhead knocked down the plywood horse head. The local radio station gave me a phone interview.

"No, I don't know anything about horse racing. Trotting? No, never seen a race, except when I drive by the track, I can see the horses shlepping those wagons behind them. Such a bore. I'd rather be in the dunes in Tunisia. What silver cup?"

Still, there were plenty of brothers and sisters at that track. A huge bus that followed the races rented parking space and showers at El Monaco. They entertained drivers, owners, groomers and horse lovers underneath our Underground Cinema building. Hello?

209 or 84 days and counting...

A mysterious raven-haired beauty drove into the parking lot just as I was closing up the bar. Paulette Bontemps careened her white convertible across three parking spaces. My folks were fortunately dead asleep. We had maybe three rooms rented. It was early June, so White Lake was in its usual burial-grounds quietness. There were a couple of after-hours waiters from Brown's Hotel hanging out. Paulette slid into the bar, choosing to squeeze onto a stool that one of the waiters was sitting on. Slender and curvaceous and obviously a turn-on to straight men, Paulette giggled and teased her way into these guys' hearts.

"Hey, honey. I need a cabin for a few months, maybe forever. I never plan ahead. Something private away from the road. A couple of bedrooms, and trees? I got this thing for trees. Hey, I lost all my money. You guys got enough money to rent me a cabin here?"

She slid her hands into their pockets and under their butts. Something about her prompted one guy to plop a fifty on the bar. The other made noises about a check. Paulette wove herself in serpentine-like fashion around them, then passed the fifty to me, and urged the other one to write out a check for another fifty dollars.

"One hundred dollars will get you two weeks in our Milton Berle Comedy Cottage. Five hundred will get you the whole summer and you can even stay for the winter, though there is no heat in those bungleholes, and no water after the first freeze. Hello?"

Paulette was instantly escorted by her two new friends, and installed herself. In the morning, there were a half dozen cars parked in the bogs around her cottage. Pop looked for her registration card, and didn't see those half dozen cars listed. Later on I had an intimate conversation with her, to wit:

"If you are entertaining gentlemen callers, please have them park their cars outside along the road. It gets hairy when you have more cars by your bunglehole than the whole motel has. I have two Jewish parents here."

We became fast friends. She was the wild, absurd, twisted, nutcase I was, and we found time to laugh a whole lot. In my situation, it was miraculous to find a kindred soul. And she was able to focus on 24 hours of party time. I never did know one ounce more about her than she decided to put out. Her sense of humor was the other side of hysterical, and she had a way of dealing with the ridiculous that appealed to me. I confessed my entire stupid life story, and before 48 hours had passed, she was including me in her parties. She saved me from an early death.

When she brought in crowds of guys to the bar, she would announce out loud to admirers:

"Hey, if you want to make it with Bontemps, you gotta wanna make it with my brother, Elliot here."

And she teased and taunted an array of hot guys that she likely plucked from some other planet. Some got angry at her mind games, at which she excelled. She provoked them into using all or part of her assortment of S & M toys. Coincidentally, Paulette was into heavy submission and domination role-playing. Perhaps some guiding angel from Atlantis or Mars directed her to me.

When she wasn't playing sexual musical chairs, she played her oboe or her flute. She composed and sat atop a tree branch at the edge of the forest, pad and paper, humming and writing and jotting. As far as I can remember now, her music could be compared with Philip Glass's repetitive patterns and styles. Now and then, during those brief breaks when I could sit with her and rap, she dropped clues as to concerts in Amsterdam, Vienna, and Copenhagen. Whether she played solo or with an orchestra was not known; successful or not, I never knew. It was clear that she didn't like nosey people, and I was a witch myself when it came to privacy. We did work together for a few precious hours though. Her music moved me to get back to some serious painting. She'd play, and I'd work on a couple of canvases. Painting, however, is not a part-time thing, and so nothing substantial came from this collaboration. But she sure did make our whispering pines sing a bit.

With virtually no business, the only income for a month was from Paulette's entourage, and ever-growing popularity. Then, the end of this Eden was near. She got a mysterious phone call from Amsterdam. Her brother had smuggled a couple of million dollars' worth of diamonds into JFK and she was going to pick him up. She said she'd be back, and with lots of money to party forever. I never heard from her again. Weeks after she left, I put her things into a shack for storage. I found a never-used wedding gown, sealed in a box with a clear plastic top for viewing. There were no other clues as to who she really was or where to reach her. She did get some phone calls later on during

Woodstock, but nobody ever left a message or a clue as to where she might be.

But for the duration of her stay, I was not so lonely and miserable. The quality of hash and grass she seemed to have unlimited supply of was very high. And, so were we all.

I was not cut out to be host of the highways. While waiting for Woodstock, and desperate for some business, I discovered my own misguided marketing effort, the "Thank You Note" series. In the weeks before the season began, in an Emily Postian inspiration, I sent thank you notes to the previous season's guests, acknowledging their patronage and inviting them to come again soon. Couldn't hurt, right? Just costs a postcard and a stamp. *It was possibly my worst move.* How was I to suppose that most of those happy married couples that did check in were, in fact, not married to each other? They signed in as Mr. and Mrs., so that was it, no? Angry wives and husbands called and threatened to sue for libel and slander. I dealt with those complaints by referring all calls to our main offices at the Paris Hilton. Some were quite surprised to find out that we were only a division of Hilton International. Hilton International was also surprised, and a call from them made me change tactics. I redirected legal inquiries to Marriott International, then to Holiday Inn and later to Sheraton Hotels. It wasn't easy to play musical hotels, but it was a dirty job that someone had to do.

42 or 54 days and counting...

Woodstock would have a very long list of severe enemies before, during, and after it did its stuff in Bethel. Lapenis was one such opponent of drugs, rock and roll, and humanity.

1969 was the year of the outdoor loudspeaker penis wars in White Lake. The esteemed Lapenis Bungalow Colony across the road was not only much bigger than the El Monaco—it had 1,000 bungalows, an outdoor amphitheater presenting live Broadway-type shows, a penis-shaped pool, and a huge contingent of snakes, vermin, and other Yentas dressed up in spray-lacquered hair—and clearly, much more lively. Leon Lapenis, its oversized owner, had a fetish for hollering into the public address system. His gravel voice bounced off the lake and echoed for miles in every direction. People complained and cursed and threatened. Invasion of privacy. Intrusive ugly and loud disturbing of the peace. Complaints fell on deaf ears, an expression born in the town clerk's office in White Lake. Nothing helped. He was the biggest taxpayer in White Lake, and had his three oversized sons as hit men, and his loud-mouth wife as the shrew of shrews, and they were in charge. A three-digit-kilo man, clearly laterally related to *hippopotamus famili*. His mode of transportation was limited to his three-story high tractor ever since he was arrested for drunk driving and permanently lost his driver's license.

Leon made up for this dent in his masculinity by using industrial-strength loudspeakers. He made sure everyone on White Lake knew just how big a man he was by the sheer decibel level of his speakers. His speakers were not only big, but strategically placed, so that the sound would land directly in the El Monaco compound. He never forgave us for attempting to do summer music and art and cinema festivals for a clear-cut reason:

"You putz! You come here with your fucking faggot theater joiks from the city and mess up the minds of my tenants? My tenants come to me and pay double the prices bekuzz dey gett da best in Broadway shows! Weee don't neet no fukkin competition in White Lake. I own White Lake. We never had plays and music festivals and art shows and we never will! I'll bury you and your fukkin creepo friends!"

I should have followed his honest advice, but my sense of being violated and my rights being usurped colored my stupid decision to continue. I only got revenge when Woodstock arrived, and there was no way to get in or out of his compound.

I complained to the police, but they were the same police whom he paid off to overlook his shady real estate deals and assorted health and safety violations. His clientele were loud and liked loud noise, so they did fine. But I was quickly losing my battle with reality. So, I took matters into my own hands and set up a set of Navy speakers from some World War II battleship. Now, these were speakers loud enough to still shatter windows in occupied Japan via time warp.

I summoned up my last reserves of energy—whatever was left after having cleaned seventy-two toilets—and strategically planned my attack for 2:00 a.m. on Saturday morning, when I aimed my speakers at the Lapenis Colony and blasted them with Elvis' "Blue Suede Shoes." That's when I began my celebrity paging, too:

"Barbara Streisand, phone call in the Presidential Wing. Paul Newman, pick up line two on the courtesy phone by the pool. Marilyn Monroe, (it didn't matter if they were dead or alive), your limousine is waiting."

Ever more desperate for relief and revenge, I inserted "live coverage" from the El Monaco Trot, complete with horse hooves and dinging bells. It would have been devastating for any normal person. Not Messr dame Lapenis. Town folk and residents of the other resorts drove by in droves to ogle the El Monaco's phantom celebrity guests. It didn't add to the coffers any, but it did lower my blood pressure and provide me with relief, albeit, a temporary and frustrating one.

The irony was that very soon I would be paging live mega-stars such as Janis Joplin, Joe Cocker, Joan Baez, Richie Havens, and the honchos from Warner Brothers. And shortly, I would be broadcasting not just to Lapenis' but coast-to-coast, and then some.

5

Me, The President, and My Jewish Festival Permit

Desperate for ways to drum up business for the increasingly not-ever-for-profitable El Monaco, I became civically minded: I became active in the inactive White Lake Chamber of (*horrors*) Commerce. Happy to be anything that didn't include Mother's minion, I volunteered to be the White Lake Chamber of Commerce Marketing Director and Cultural Affairs Counsellor.

The active property-owner members included Mr. Bernbaum of Bernbaum's Lakeview Colony. Twenty-one bungleholes with no pool, but with a view of a six-foot patch of the lake. Access to the lake was not possible since his ex-wife owned that six-foot patch and went to her deathbed instructing her attorneys to never, ever sell or lease that patch to him.

Thelma and Sol Mondlin owned a Victorian rooming house that they filled with starving poets whom they nourished emotionally as well as nutritionally. They couldn't afford to do this. Sol drove a taxi to support this well-meaning folly. These two gentle souls provided emotional support for a wide range of artistic lost souls who ended up in White Lake for no good reason. I was one of the lucky ones who was part of their friendship circle.

Silly Ross, 225 pounds of tough demanding brutal pragmatic energy. She owned 1.2 cottages which she rented only to widows or divorced women who were lonely for female companionship. Her mouth was enormous, her deep pockets sewn closed. In the city, she was foreperson of a shmata[1] factory on Seventh Avenue. Nobody

---

[1]Yiddish for a rag.

68

messed with Silly. She voted no for everything that concerned men or maleness. Okay, why not?

Betsy Farmished had a 1920's hotel with 150 rooms, of which 149 were sealed for safety reasons. She occupied the kitchen and entry hall which the fire department propped up for her. She had hopes of a renaissance in Kauneonga that would restore the glory to her heyday. Sophie Tucker and Eddie Cantor stayed at her hotel. Garbo reserved rooms once, but never showed. Betsy was not on any visible medications. She spoke continuously whether or not anyone was in proximity.

We had a few mysterious tourist-biz people who provided services for vacationers. Sam Firstnik sold nightcrawlers to fishermen. Al Bookman sold fruit and vegetables from his hearse. Not everyone enjoyed buying produce from the back of a hearse, but since Al's prices were lower than the market, and he told funny stories, he earned a living of sorts. Al only needed to make enough to pay for his wife's and daughter's summer rest.

Trudy's Lakeview Lakehouse—not to be confused with Rudy's Lakehouse, not to be confused with Judy's Lakehouse B & B—was tidy if a bit ancient. These Rooms On The Lake provided exactly that; a room leaning over the lake. If the house wasn't vertical, hey, you get what you pay for.

They all duly elected me President of the Chamber of Commerce within five and a half seconds. Little did I or the townspeople know what wild hysterical ramifications this honor would mean in 1969.

One of the first major progressive improvements I made as La President was to have Pop quickly erect yet another shack on the highway next to the motel entrance. Four-point-two feet south of my Underground Cinema, and 22.3 feet north of my Yenta's Pancake House, and 45 feet from nowhere. I went into sign-making mode and made a sign that said:

White Lake Chamber of Commerce
FREE INFORMATION

The booth held an assortment of brochures and handmade flyers from the dozen Kochalain resort dumps on the lake. The owner-members of the C.O.C. sat in the weeds near the booth. Each one, foaming at the mouth, hoped that the next car filled with travellers and cash would be directed to their resort. Also, they did not trust that the booth would be equally fair to each member who had donated $3.69 towards the structure. However, after seven hours of hungry stares at any passing car, it was clear this effort was a total bust. Being the fleet-footed, quick-thinking young effervescent President of the C.O.C., I painted yet a new sign:

Roads Washed Away Ahead.
No U-Turns. Detour.
Last Motel before the end of the road.

No use analyzing why this plan too was a wash-out. On top of the total lack of interest by passing cars, the county agent confiscated the sign and the booth as part of the then popular "Beautify America" program. How our little shanty came under the eye of Lady Bird Johnson will forever remain a mystery. Years later, when I was in Show Biz, working with Eartha Kitt, I asked her about her Vietnam 'do' and likened it to my 'C.O.C. booth,' but that comparison went undiscussed.

Undaunted, I made a new sign:

Free motel rooms. Free Meals.
Bonus $$ paid to first 1,000 cars.

I put on one of my fail-safe disguises, to wit: a Groucho Marx nose and mustache, and sat on the highway shoulder, trying to wave cars into the drive. Not one customer stopped. I had devised dozens of different disguises, including slouching hats, striped pajamas and a tutu. Nobody stopped. Of course, maybe it was the wrong time of day? Or year? Or century?

The Chamber of Commerce itself was never taken seriously. I was technically President of the White Lake and Kauneonga Chambers of Commerce of The Town of Bethel. The Kauneonga part refers to the Indian name for White Lake. I suppose that before the settlers went further West, they stopped off in Kauneonga Lake to kill a few natives, then headed for the California gold mines. Kauneonga replaced White Lake so that the local anti-semites could distinguish themselves from the Jewish hotel and bungalow invaders. The resort owners had their own reasons for reviving the Kauneonga name. In the 1920s Murder Incorporated, an alleged Mafia group, used the lake as a repository for old juke boxes chained to people they had "eliminated" from their social and business scene. The resort owners on the west end of the lake rebirthed Kauneonga, to make sure no one would associate them with this unsavory piece of White Lake history. It was all a moot point since nobody cared a hoot either way.

We each had our own agenda at the sporadic meetings of six citizens concerned with establishing a world-class cultural center and international elitist Shakespearean study retreat, where literary giants like Kafka, Pinter, Shaw, and Frank Sinatra, could come and enjoy the fresh air and take the waters of the lake. That failing, renting rooms in the few broken-down hotels and rooming houses was high on the priority list. I was trying to create some reasons for people to come to the Catskills, and kept generating ideas for music and arts festivals, conventions focused on special interest groups, such as baseball-cap collectors or tsetse-fly therapists. Whatever the focus, it would all take place at the elegant El Monaco. Other members had other suggestions, none so lofty.

"I need to find four families to rent my two duplex bungalows. No kids, no pets, no cooking, no cars on the lawns."

"We need some way to force city people to come to White Lake whether they like it or not! We can't afford to be Mr. Nice Guy any more. My cousin Solly is a lawyer with the welfare department. For a small bribe, Solly could send certain welfare checks up here, and nobody would know."

"We need to create a one-way free bus service with curtained windows direct to the bungalows. The curtains will act as blinders to keep the customers from noticing the far more desirable vacation spots, such as Grossinger's, the Concord and Kutsher's, along the way."

"Our President should contact the Governor and get him to build a monorail from the city direct to Kauneonga. No stops in between. One train every hour, all year."

I, the President, was not a big hit with the committee members. I gaveled out of order "curtelach," the little curtains, and they looked on in abject horror every time I mentioned starting swinging singles

71

vacation packages. Swingles was the code name for whores, prostitutes, bums, and other types not welcome in White Lake. End of swingles. I suggested getting Paris to be our sister city and they could send us Frenchies and we could send them our overrun of bunglehole renters *(zero)*. Foreign tourists in White Lake? Never! There were vehement objections, particularly from Yetta Zubinsky, the Chief Executive Officer of Yetta's Lakeside Bungalow Heaven. Yetta's late husband Morris, may he rest in peace she would add, would have a third heart attack right in his grave if foreigners were to swim in the same lake water as the natives. Who could know what foreigners would bring, to further curse a cursed community? Delete foreigners, especially Paris.

Fortunately, the extent of this advocacy group's energy was limited to mouthing off at meetings, and all I had to do was promise buses with curtains and then do what I wanted anyway.

One such event was the El Monaco Music and Art Fair. I issued the Cultural Affairs Director of the esteemed El Monaco Motel a Music and Art Festival Permit! Yes, this turned out to be *the permit* that would later launch a new nation! Though the first seven festivals didn't even qualify to be called 'disasters,' I kept renewing the festival papers each year. No use to tell you that I would schlep up to the top of the Himalayas, where the grand Zooch or Guru told me:

"Elliot, renew your festival permit. Something big is coming your way. Don't ask what, why. I have spoken."

The several pathetic desperate little festivals were held on the motel lawn, right on the edge of the highway, replete with signage declaring them Festivals. The signage was necessary since the only life on the roadside was me with my Orson Welles hat, counting dirty linens, listening to Neil Diamond on the loudspeakers, and surrounded by my abstract expressionistic paintings. Quelle image! It still amazes me that some concerned medical person didn't pass by, take pity on me, and haul me off to some happy-days place.

What was the music of this festival? The music that would pre-figure Joplin, Havens, Cocker? It was Bach and Mozart on those big hefty black discs known as records via my ancient maroon-and-white-striped Webcor (everyone in the '50s had one of these hi-fi players), and a very major series of extension cords.

Those pre-Woodstock festivals, with their average annual attendance of 7.2 mammals, were basically harmless, so I didn't get much grief from the neighbors. The few faggots and dykes the townspeople did see coming and going from my hotel were, at most, distant harmless 'weird tourists' who spent money. If they hadn't bought groceries, beer, or rented boats, it might have been a different story. Nobody ever mentioned *gay* or *lesbian* anything. Except for the cursing, threats and insults I got from the year-round locals, the summer resort keepers, for the most part, got along with everyone who was a potential room renter. That was the value system in place. Even my mother never dreamed to breathe one questioning word about Harriet and Louise and Mary and Thelma, who rented a cottage for three years. These big-scaled Brünnhilde-type[1] women spent nights drinking in the bar, hugging Mom, giving her big tips for bringing beer and clean towels, then spent all day in the cottage. The fragile cottage on toothpick stilts rocked back and forth, dangerously close to collapse.

"Such nice Jewish girls. They don't let any of those drunk boys in the bar annoy them. I never see one bad boy go to their cottage. Not like that Mona Ginsburg. When Mona's mother calls, my heart is breaking. Ellinoo, talk on Mona. Tell her nobody wants a used-up cow."

Mother had such a refined way with words. Ideas, forget. Pop got along with everyone. He kibbitzed, joked, enjoyed telling stories and was much too shy to even think of people's private lifestyles.

The Town Council decided to demonstrate their great foresight and prescience when I proposed the First Annual White Lake Water Ski Festival. That's when I discovered that this bucolic little mountain town had skeletons, not in the town's closet, but in the lake. The Council members were immediately up in arms because they were deathly afraid that juke boxes festooned with body parts—if not entire bodies—might surface, thanks to Murder Inc. I tried to explain to them that 40 years had passed and that, according to modern science theories, any corpses would have long ago decomposed. Nobody on

---

[1] A Richard Wagner operatic character.

the Council had any faith in science. If science were valid, wouldn't the White Lake School include Science in its curriculum?

49 or 51 days and counting...
My motel for a horse...

Business continued to stink, season aprés season. And there were always out-of-work people coming by the motel office looking for, if not a job, at least a beer. Mother wouldn't part with beer, but she did part with portions of cholunt, her deadly stew, and advice. Sick to the stomach from her poisonous cooking, and suffering liquor withdrawal pains, these vacant souls retched on the downhill 17B, en route to the next barroom door. Each person who stopped by claimed to be the head something from Grossinger's or the Waldorf. Bob and Betty, who would bring new meaning to "the horsey set," were two such people who had a profound, though brief, impact on the El Monaco.

We weren't doing much business, but for the few days a week we had guests, we still needed help cleaning the rooms, toilets and, when my mother wasn't looking, the laundry. So when Bob and Betty,

In the back, my Pop and Mamma. In front, Granma Bertha,
Me, and Granpa Bernard, circa 1948, pre-Spike Lee Bensonhurst, Brooklyn.

looking vaguely normal, knocked on the door, I heard them out. Betty said she was the former head chef at Grossinger's, Waldorf, Paris Hilton, and all the Europa Excelsior Hotels in Italy and Portugal. Bob's only experience was that he came with Betty. They were willing to work in exchange for room and board. Mother said she rented rooms and sold meals. We didn't need a chef, we had Papa. Betty and Bob said they would lower their sights and do odds and ends. All we had was odds and ends. Bob then piped up with a marketing idea of horses. He said he had access to 25 horses that he would bring over. We could hitch them to the crab apple trees outside the bungalows and they could live off the apples and wild weeds.

Apparently the lure of a complete eco-system was very tempting to Momma. She was especially delighted when Bob said that not only would the horses be free, but that he and Betty would pay for their room out of the proceeds from the horse rentals. Further, The El Monaco would get a hefty percentage of the take. Papa had a different view. He said the last thing we needed was one more responsibility we couldn't handle. He said, no, no, no, no. Angrily. Loudly. With authority.

Momma agreed only if Bob and Betty paid for the apples too. And so we were in the horse biz. I had an inkling we were in for trouble when Betty immediately began to complain that there were too many "spirits"—you know, as in dead people—haunting our rooms. Then she began communicating with tourists from a spacecraft in our parking lot. I tried to have that spacecraft materialize for me so I could get on it and get away. Nothing.

Hours later, 25 real horses clopped their way into our driveway over the remnants of the tourist information booth, dropping brown doo doo poop on the steps of my Underground Cinema, leaving other doo doo poop on the porch of my pancake house, and made themselves at home under our apple trees, next to the cheaper bungleholes, behind the cesspool, next to the swamp where peculiar things were flying overhead.

The horses were real. Very real. Normal looking horses. They had saddles and tails flowing in the wind. I was amazed at our good fortune. I thought for a moment that perhaps the Teichberg Curse was lifting. I had visions of tourists coming to White Lake, if not for taking the waters, at least for the El Monaco horses. I was increasingly desperate to get out of that motel. I would have sold my soul—and some said I did later, when Woodstock happened—to pay off our mortgage and get out of that living hell and never see my mother again in this lifetime.

By the second day, Mom and Pop were already fighting about the 25 nags. Mom kept declaring,

"We can't lose, we can't lose."

Pop stalked around muttering,

"We can lose, we can lose."

I looked at one sparkling white horsey and was sure if I kissed him, like that frog prince, the steed would turn into something unrelated to cholunt and cleaning motel toilets. Perhaps this steed belonged to my prince and had come to augur the bright day when I would indeed escape? I moved as close to that big nag as I dared. It's eyes looked into mine. Nah. No way.

This bright bubble of hope burst within four days of the arrival of the horse business. I spent sleepless nights painting new signs to post along the highways and around the motel advertising:

Trail riding, Dressage, Equestrian Training at the World Class El Monaco Resort.

Bob had not lied. We now had 25 horses and they liked the crab apples by the bungalows just fine. However, Bob had omitted some key information. There was no market for our equestrian services. Also, if a horse eats a lot of crab apples, he will soon be depositing a lot of road apples. Horse manure is large. Sure it fertilizes, but we had very swampy land that needed no fertilizing. And horse manure adds up—quickly. Within two hours, our bungalow colony was waist deep in horsey brown gook. Pungent, steaming (remember, this was summer; remember, this was swamp), horse manure. And guess what comes with horse manure? Horse flies. Lots of horse flies. Millions of horse flies. I don't know where they came from, how they got there. I don't think I'd ever seen a horse fly in White Lake before. But now we had them. Buzzing and buzzing. It was a nightmare worthy of Hitchcock, but instead of birds, we had buzzing flies. Big, buzzing horse flies. I don't know if you understand just how big one horse fly is and just how awesome one million horse flies surrounding a small bungalow are. It was terrifying.

I wasn't the only one who didn't like the smell of steaming brown gunk and the buzz of winged things with flapping things. The few customers we had were fleeing the bungalows. Mama was furious. Now she couldn't re-rent them without cleaning. Papa was ready to kill and was turning the house upside down in search of some lethal weapon. And the horses were none too happy themselves. They promptly did what I hadn't yet figured out how to do for myself: They high-tailed out of there. Since they were tied to our bungalows, this meant that as they tore themselves free and took off for freedom, they uprooted 25 of our bungalows including the Marilyn Monroe, the Elizabeth Taylor and the Frank Sinatra cottages. They began roaming the entire county naked except for the El Monaco colors!

My insane idea, that glamorous names painted all over the place would bring the magic of Hollywood or Broadway to schlep me into some other world, was evidence enough for commitment. What the fuck was I doing up here at this beyond-hell lake catering to straight people's vacation needs, when my vacation needs could be easily met just two hours south, in New York City, in the tunnels and caves underneath West 12th Street.

I don't know what I was doing. If some kind stranger had only interfered and put me out of my misery, it would have been a mitzvah. Okay, now and then in 13 years, there were some discontented husbands (closet cases to be sure), who wanted to be comforted behind the pool shed. There were some gay men who were in White Lake under duress, to visit family, or worse, working as counsellors in those elite children's camps, who took their day off in the El Monaco. And some few of those strangers in the mountains made themselves accessible for a bit of leather games in Shack Number Two, next to the James Dean pavilion.

No point describing Jon X, who was six-feet-four, and a major sports figure who everyone recognized but me, since sports bore me. Jon took advantage of my desperate angst and we became instant lovers. That instant lasted a good three hours, or until I got panic-stricken at all his talk of moving in together in his digs in Minnesota. I wasn't cut out to be a football widower! He thought I'd prefer to be his personal groupie following his team around the country, staying in motels, instead of running this motel. I should stay in someone else's motel when mine is empty? He said he had money and could buy me my own motel in Florida or Biloxi maybe. I told him I had a bad headache and was hell-bent on partying in the sewers of Manhattan for a few decades before I settled down in Biloxi in my own first-class motel. Goodbye Jon, wherever you went.

Meanwhile, back to the ranch-motel and escaped-horse opera.

We now had 25 bungalows slanting in all directions, enough fertilizer to supply K Mart or Home Shopping Club, and 25 horses scaring all the hair curler-coiffed vacationers in the county. At least the horses were gone. But soon the Sheriff was at the El Monaco office explaining why he was going to arrest my mother. She was responsible for thousands of dollars of damage caused by those crazy horses destroying property. That the horses were making a bid for one last burst of free-form dance expression, carried no weight.

I got on the P.A. system and paged Robert and Elizabeth, but got no response. The Sheriff followed us as we went to their room. Except for two horse blankets strung up like hammocks and a hastily-hung mirror on the ceiling, the evidence suggested that the equestrian operation was closed for the duration. Mama was furious; they'd made off with the bath towels. The sheriff was perplexed because he thought we were making this up. Papa was muttering his battle cry of the week before: "We can lose, we can lose."

I suggested checking out Bob and Betty's police records. I assumed they had a blotter.

They were wanted for horse theft, bigamy, child abandonment, stealing coins from a Church poor box, scams, insurance fraud, selling stolen horses to dog food factories, and substance abuse. And so we got off the hook and started shoveling horse shit.

The horses were another example of right idea, wrong day. Only months away, Warner Brothers and the Woodstock organizers would have been grateful to have those horses—probably the only form of land transportation that would have been effective during those three big days in August 1969.

6

For Members Only, The Future Exclusive Headquarters of the Woodstock Festival

40 or 38 days and counting...

Had I any notion that Woodstock would be coming 'round the mountain any moment, I wouldn't have bothered with any more piteous attempts at veneration, and ways to lure paying guests. I decided, much the way the Wizard of Oz decided that all the scarecrow was missing was a diploma to certify his intelligence, that all the motel was lacking was membership in something to qualify as a place to rent a room. El Monaco had no "self-esteem." People often called inquiring as to whether the El Monaco was a member of AAA, Mobil Travel Guide, American Motel Association, or some such group. I applied to all the above at one time or another. As soon as one of their inspectors rented a room, he sneaked away before dawn, never to be heard from again. At least this resulted in a good five rentals over a one-year period. Salesman's rates of course. Salesman's rates were the same as the other rates; whatever traffic could bear. Literally. I felt as if I were missing a heart when asked about membership.

Mama was smug about the economics, but was stung when she read one inspector's report that summarized us as a disgrace to the hospitality industry, and added that the proprietors should be imprisoned—that was too much. He noted the stained sheets, questioned whether they had been laundered—I had put on fresh sheets for him, but only my mother knows what he really found in his room—and that there were no towels except at extra cost, not to mention the empty TV shell and inoperable phone, lack of key, absence of soap, and having to pay rent for the parking space in front of his room. He saw no humor in my signage and reprimanded us for claims to "Deluxe" anything. Mama was crushed. Papa wasn't. The report had none of the downer effect it had on my mother because he'd given up so long ago that he could be driven no further down than he'd already arrived on his own.

This was bad enough, but then, before departing, he asked for a refund. Momma resolutely pointed to a hand-painted sign:

No Refunds Under Any Circumstances including sudden death, murder, runaway children, earthquakes, weather, or serial killers from Mars.

So, Mr. Triple-A added to his report that the motel had an improper policy of no refunds even for guests who find their accommodations wanting before using them. He didn't fight for the refund. I guess he knew a crazed look when he saw one, especially when mother started in on the Cholera/Potato/Minsk speech and the extended family curse.

I was temporarily inspired. Voila! A new source of brief rentals! And thereupon the El Monaco solicited inspectors from every approval organization, listed and unlisted. Eventually we ran out of associations, and this new source of income, a whopping $34.74 in toto, collapsed like last month's party balloon. Ah, but all was not lost. The Teichberg Curse eventually got a reprieve via a truck that sailed into the drive. The driver, an entrepreneur of quality and integrity and quiet desperation, earned his daily beer and pizza by offering classy gold decals that said "Approved Member." They came in ovals, rectangles, squares, circles. They looked swell. They cost only 20 cents apiece. For another 50 cents, he had a sign that said, "Official Approved Member." I went for the whole nine yards. I bought a dozen to stick up in every driveway and one to make into a necklace for Momma to wear. This later proved to be very useful when a camper's mother, who fancied herself too fancy for our motel, marched into the office to shrill,

"There's no air conditioning. I live on Sutton Place. And I wouldn't let my servants live under conditions as vile as these. I demand to know your Membership Number!"

At this point, Mother stepped in and, mustering up an elegance I had never suspected she had, said,

"Vee don't rent to your kind of people. This is an exclooosif muttel! You vant a number? You can have any nombah you vant. Pick a nombah, any nombah, and God will punish you for aggravating a mother who walked here from Russia in 40 feet of snow after midnight, alone in the world. Pick a number and complain to the membership association!"

The woman broke down in tears. Her wig tilted, her false eyelashes drooped. All that was missing was W.C. Fields and a camera.

23 Apparitions, 2 UFOs, 47 Phantoms sighted today

7

Let's Convert the Barn Into a Theatre With a Construction Budget of $1.36

In spite of the improbability of anything at all working out in White Lake, I ventured forth to establish a pre-Broadway tryout theatre. It didn't phase me that the Shuberts had Philadelphia and Boston tied up for these efforts. I didn't own downtown Philly or Boston, but I did downtown White Lake. I began with the barn.

The barn—as were most things in the Teichberg family history— was born out of adversity. Next to the cesspool and three feet this side of the swamp lay a deserted barn with slanted walls and floors. No heat, water, roof, or protection from the elements, this barn enclosed a space that could hold a stage and 250 seats. It needed to be thrown down, and the empty land hoed under. The cultural climate of White Lake, 5000 percent below that of the rest of the county, which had no need of cultural anything, did not demand a live theatre. Even a dead theatre was not on any priority list.

Pop used the barn to house his White Lake Roofing Company. That, of course, folded; no surprise there. So here I was with a decent roof on a barn, with no faded glory in its history to capitalize on.

Paul Revere rested his horses in the White Lake Summer Playhouse Barn. Dolly Madison was inspired to come up with 53 flavors for her ice cream while Martha Washington entertained the troops in this former barn, now the future home to Broadway Hit Musicals and Dramas.

Pop managed to dance around the roof repairs, plumbing, fixing and making do. The barn however, presented me with a smelly situation, even before performances began months later. The cesspools for the motel and bungalows, and for some neighbors whom I could never locate, flowed directly onto the grounds in front of, underneath, and adjacent to the new White Lake/El Monaco Barn Playhouse. And there was no place else to send this sewage, since the town refused to provide us with facilities. Pop fashioned an invisible pipeline to run down the highway and deposit its mother lode someplace near the Nazi encampments in Mongaup Valley, some four miles south. Mongaup, fortunately, was all downhill anyway, and the only people from there I had met were of German extraction, mysteriously deposited there in 1946. How they got a U-boat to landlocked Mongaup Valley is still a mystery.

Ever since I was two, performing naked on the roof and falling in love with the fireman who saved me, I had had this fantasy about having my own theater in a big barn. So here we were. Me and the barn sans stage, seats, lighting, actors, audience, or hope. I'd write, direct, and star in my own material. And presto, live theatre in White Lake. Oh, I knew that I'd have to include plays by others also and, so long as it wasn't Shakespeare, I was open to suggestions. The city was full of starving actors. They'd be thrilled to come up here, act in exchange for room and board in the country and be discovered. I'd be discovered, too. All that failing, maybe they'd rent rooms?

Undaunted by the foul smell of success and cesspool overage, I engaged Ollie to paint the barn. Ollie was a big-time movie art director who was having a streak of bad luck, and was fired by Grossinger's for being drunk when he was supposed to be designing the stage for Mitzi Gaynor or somebody. Here was his chance to do pre-Broadway theatre. To reinforce the belief that my barn would become the focal point of the Shuberts' envy, I painted one more sign that I nailed on a dead tree facing the highway:

Coming soon on this site:
Pre-Broadway Barn Theatre with parking for 5,000 cars.
Also: For Sale or Rent

Stage one of the White Lake Cultural Theatre Center. Anybody know a plumber, a director, a house manager, a cast and crew?

Since any fool knew you had to have a disco next to the theatre for actors and audience to hang out, I redid the motel-linoleum lobby ex-coffee bar and ex-office into the first disco in White Lake. My expertise as a color and design consultant for Fifth Avenue stores was nowhere to be seen. My budget didn't permit me to engage my professional self, so buying cheap unlabeled gallons of paint, I slapped colors at random on the plywood walls, pasted any old movie posters and photo blowups I could find on the walls.

I did an ugly (is there any other kind?) Jackson Pollock floor with the leftover paints, and drew a neon square which was now the 'dance floor.' A hollywood agent on bad times, now the owner of Lakeview Antiques and Furnished Roomettes, begrudgingly sold me Mae West's personal bar. Mae got this bar from Clark Gable, whose very own bar stools—that Jean Harlow had sat on—were on sale next door at the White Lake stool store.

Volunteers from the local Porno Parlor Supply Store and Nail Salon donated an assortment of graphic quasi-porno tchaktzas to fill to capacity every square inch of space. By overwhelming the eye, it would be possible to make the public think this was some kind of fantasy land. To use the horror phrase of choice back then: 'A Fun Place.' Yeeuch!

Mom, Pop, and I sat there, looking over this creation. From dust to dust, or to gold. Who knows? I made the mistake of inviting my sister, Goldie, up to have a look and give an encouraging word. Goldie, the Cassandra of the twentieth century, told us to walk straight to the bank. Hand them over the whole gesheft.

So, here I was. A barn theatre cultural center complete with the mountain's only Underground Cinema; an ugly Disco with an ugly old juke box; Mae West's questionable bar; a still seedy motel that was an approved member; a mini pool; plenty of swamp land; rooms and curtains with shower in hall or outside when it rained; and a crazy Russian mother cooking vile cholunt. And no customers, just more bills to pay. All this and still nobody came to put me away in some Happy-Days Homette? "When you're alone, you are with the only one you can depend on," to quote a play of my own that has never been optioned for Broadway or a film deal.

I couldn't possibly handle all there was to do. I put ads in the *Village Voice,* then the bible for my generation:

"Free rent. Barn Theatre. Theatre group wanted."

"Swinging Singles? Forget Fire Island. Bored with the Hamptons? Would you believe White Lake? Shares arranged. Free parties!"

"Free theater. Free disco. Free cholunt. Linens and towels extra. Lots of Doctors and big-boobed bimbos."

My ads in the *Village Voice* did net a theater troupe. Dozens of hastily-formed actor groups came to look. More went than came. They came up in droves; actors, set designers, directors, dogs, monkeys, writers, and who knows who or what. But there was activity and movement, ergo, life on my grounds. A bit of civilization according to me, shuffling along my swamp paths, looking at bungleholes, the barn, the apple trees, the Disco, and the lake. The sane ones moved on to hot spots in Buffalo or Hooterville. The process by which I selected those whom I allowed to take on the task of establishing this Broadway house behind the cesspool was complicated.

"Are you guys handy? Can you build your own seats? Box Office? Stage? Dressing rooms? Do you have a following? Do you have connections to book Katherine Hepburn or Zero Mostel in an original comedy that I will write if you can get them to come up here? Can anybody here cook? Anybody in the company have a rich Hollywood relative who would buy this place without seeing it?"

They fixed the barn, danced in the Disco and, since they were always hungry, loved mother's cholunt. They even put on some of my comedy plays. They quickly moved to classics. My plays didn't attract flies. The classics didn't attract flies. Flies, we didn't need. Customers we needed but were not getting. Pinter and Albee were the only playwrights worth considering, according to my sister Goldie. I agreed that perhaps a "name" would help draw audiences.

We did Pinter's *The Birthday Party*. Only Elaine Grossinger and entourage showed up. I went out on the highway and offered free tix, but nobody knew what a Pinter was, and nobody wanted to see any off-off-Broadway group in a barn that stunk from the cesspool.

I shouldn't have attempted to run a disco any more than I should have attempted to run the theatre or even the ice cream concession. A nationally-known accredited interior designer hung neon beer signs by the dozens in the windows, each one flashing to a different beat. Christmas lights everywhere in July. He called it kinetic art. Then it was cheap and free. Years later, he proved to be a visionary and it was called Kinetic Art and sold for big bucks in Soho galleries. We installed shills in the windows, and the people finally began to come. Then I got some beefy body-builder types to wear nothing on top. I hung signs:

Topless Waiters!

And the crowds came. Lots of women from all over the county to see the topless boys. Hungry housewives whose husbands were playing poker. Horny housewives whose husbands were playing golf. Hot men looking for other hot men. Cold men looking to see how hot men kept hot. Cold women looking for revenge against cold men looking for revenge. They all bought drinks and some rented rooms. So, I had a two-figure income that month.

Most wanted the boys to be bottomless too. This was the first Chippendale's, only I didn't know how to market it in the real world. The more crowded my bar became, the less money there was left over to pay bills.

A vital part of my successful management of these hot new ventures was schlepping ice from Monticello, seven miles away. I'd drive to town, load big hunks in my Buick, and speed back hoping the fucking stuff wouldn't melt completely before I could chop it up and shove it in buckets under the bar. We couldn't afford an ice machine. Period. I was cautious in counting how many cubes per drink. Momma would sell cubes to guests in the rooms. Cup free. If they complained that motels normally gave ice cubes free, she exploded loud enough for drunks in Kauneonga to hear:

"Come in winter, you can have ice for free! You think I'll let my unmarried son—just in case you know some nice Jewish girl—should break his back schlepping big hunks of ice and then chopping them into tiny cubes, while he is cleaning toilets, mowing lawns and ironing dirty pubic hair sheets, all so that you can have a free cold drink? A plague on you and your children! Kebayneyamatzera!! Pfooey!"

The Kebayneyamatzera was an ancient Russian curse, roughly translated: *Go fuck your own mother!* My poor Buick and wobbly legs were both ready to give out. I painted one more mural in an optometrist's waiting room, took the $2,000, (a fortune then), and bought an ice-making machine. That or die on the barroom floor.

When the machine arrived, Momma nearly broke into a severe seizure on the spot. The shocker came when she saw the receipt. It was a cash sale. No deals. No cholunt. No discounts on the deluxe rooms in our Presidential Wing, just cash.

This was a serious infraction of her rule, *never* spend money unless the Cossacks are at the door. She developed appropriate machine-specific ways to recoup thrown-out money, since the machine wasn't returnable. Momma charged for the cups that held the ice, plus electric tax per cup. People in the bar assumed the price of the scotch on the rocks included the rocks. Wrong. Iced tea carried a ten percent ice cube tax. Dad had nothing to say about any of this. As early as the 1950s, he was too worn out to argue with her. He didn't even try for a compromise. He'd hear her shrieks of injustice or cries for revenge, and he'd go do a roof, any roof.

Business began to pick up. The Disco attracted peculiar people who had agendas that were not on the usual White Lake menu, but who cared? They rented rooms, drank, danced, and did sexual encounter stuff, (which Mamma never saw), and were encouraged to do anything (legal) as long as they paid cash. All the increased income permitted us to pay the electric bills, linen bills, and back payments on the swinging singles paper plates and kosher chinese takeout dinners we dolloped out for them. Swinging Singles will not take kindly to cholunt three times a day on a three-day weekend. Fussy those singles, and good riddance to them. The topless waiters were bumping and grinding and selling drinks and working the room. The barn theatre was doing stuff back there; what exactly, who knows? I had no time to check that out. Someone complained to me that our theatre was doing porno! They handed me a flyer, to wit:

An Evening of Brecht in the Buff.
Pinter in the Pink.
Shaw in the Saddle.
All performed entirely in the raw by nubile Virgins!
$1. Admission.
Free Excelsior-of-Rome towlette.

My credibility as President of the C.O.C. was eroding, but times were more and more desperate.

"Madame, are you suggesting censorship? Legitimate theatre takes risks! We are a pre-Broadway house here!"

I defended my theatre troupe's rights and artistic integrity. I also admired their bartering towlettes with the hotel supplier. At least they had someone in the audience.

The bar needed a new look, a new gimmick. As any follower of trendsetters such as Ian Shrager of Studio 54 fame can tell you, last season's image is history. Last week's novelty is boring.

I gave serious consideration to ways and means to add new zest and life to the bar. Ah, but my budget was limited to whatever was laying buried in the muddy basement under the pubic hair-covered linens.

I handed out cheap paper plates (Stalin Memorial Hall), to patrons. They could write poetry or love notes or whatever on these elegant platters, and hang them on the walls and ceilings. Today they would call that "interactive marketing." We were actually ahead of our time. The poetry, however, proved to be ugly. The love notes turned out to be nasty. Not a terrific idea. It was popular with the low-lives and uneducated pack that called our bar home, but it was making me nauseous. Ah, the men's room walls were still available. The men's room, which was actually my parent's bathroom, (it had two entrances), needed a provocative theme that would attract a clientele to buy drinks. The reason behind the plyboard faux wall nailed across the toilet entrance to the boudoir was the liquor authority's disapproval of bars that had passageways to bedrooms. We couldn't afford to build a separate toilet for the bar, so we did the practical thing. After 4:00

a.m., Mamma could go pee. Yeeuch! Graffiti was the popular choice. Mamma didn't look. Poppa was nauseous. I started snorting white stuff without labels that Tia di Bogata gave me in tiny Tiffany-blue gift boxes.

I supplied colored markers and charged women five dollars each to come in and add to the poetic expressions over the toilet. Then, as an inducement to attract swinging single women, at midnight I'd auction off the key to the men's room door for a 10 minute private session to read the graffiti. Who would think this junk would have appeal to anyone? But it did. This was a successful enterprise. One that did not please some of the local church-going women. What were church-going women doing in my men's room anyway?

Some of the neighboring colonies began to get nervous as the El Monaco parking lot actually began to fill up. The women loved it, and where the women went, the redneck beer-guzzling men followed. The only problem was that it worked too well and was soon a standing-room only event. The neighbors were furious.

Sure enough, a few weeks later there were complaints filed against us by a consortium of bungalow colonies claiming strange and unnatural practices and other perversions at the El Monaco Disco. We refused to give serious consideration to these faux charges of prostitution, drugs and sexual deviations.

4.3 UFO'S, 486 Claims of sexual neglect, 13 Rapes alleged.

8

The El Monaco's Last Gasp

92 or 41 days and counting...

The last effort I made before Woodstock was to focus on those people who were lonely and without natural resources of their own to meet potential friends.

It didn't work out too well. We mostly attracted people who wanted to meet people under 30 who, of course, were people over 50. So, we mostly got what is called a crowd of 'losers.' We got left-overs, passed-overs, has-beens and never-could-have-beens all desperately looking for someone not like themselves. The few self-proclaimed trendies and under-75-year-olds who showed up took one look at El Monaco and its pathetic Disco and Mamma's meals from hell in paper plates yet, and swamp lawns, and flew away to the other cultural centers such as Grossinger's, Yeeuch.

Still, it was some business, which is better than no business. And by 1968, I was beyond humiliation.

90 days and counting...

In the spring of 1969, ever desperate, I advertised for the last time. My back was aching from painting Birds of Paradise on dinette ceilings in Forest Hills and Bethpage just to pay for those ads. My new, ahead-of-its-time, campaign went:

New Age Revivalist Summer Retreat.
Over 75, under 40, over 41 and under 27.
Spiritualist Sessions. Past Life Adventures.
Free Cholunt. Dance Lounge Sing-A-Long with Mitch Music.
Barter Backrubs, Mutual Massage Moments.
All-you-can-eat, Greens-only Health Menu.

El Monaco—Under New Management.
If you were here before and hated it, try it again.
If you were never here, a place you could love to hate.

So, I had yet another new theatre group that came up and took the free rent deal. (Nobody ever came back a second season; how come?) This time they were educated and sensitive artistic types, not dopey. They called themselves The Earthlight Theatre ensemble. Lively, alive, with assorted monkeys, dogs, performers, producers and groupies. You had to love them, and I did. They were 'family' to me. What I was to them, who knows? Go depend on a group of actors to tell you anything real.

Pop was ill and too weak to do much of anything any more. Mom was getting stronger but in all the wrong directions, and crazier by the second. I lied to her and said I got paid rent by the theatre, by the cinema, by the room, by the hour, by the monkey. I gave her the cash they paid, figuring I put it in the kitty anyway. My city jobs were suffering since I was totally used up and wallowing in stress.

The motel compound looked so busy and alive. That was comfort. Filled with actors, cars, drifters, poets, musicians, drifters, hangers-on, misplaced coast actors looking for someplace to hang out in the summer, and drifters. And no money coming in. As the family got deeper and deeper into debt, I was getting deeper and deeper into a desperate fantasy that the motel would find a clientele. While I searched the heavens for the phantom of the motel or the New Age seekers to arrive, I hung fresh New Age-type posters.

In 1969, nobody knew from New Age. I thought I made it up, as opposed to Old Age, which was quickly finding its way to White Lake. I had to make up my own New Age posters. My Bachelor of Fine Arts from City University of New York, and Master of Fine Arts from Pratt Institute, would now come in handy. I sketched bizarre symbols and odd colorful images with brief poetic notes at the bottom to explain what it was all about to the illiterate and novices who were sure to buy a weekend in White Lake. The *petit bon mots* included these explanations:

Kvento Lemassine en route to Nirvana.
Guru Lleywiller communes with Zabars.[1]
Vyeshtikomee rises from the wheatcakes.
Rice descending the stairs.
Nude pomegranate ascending the stairs.

These New Age images and messages seriously weakened my Pop's ability to cope. I was without visible strength. Only Mamma seemed to get stronger and more vibrant. The more Dad and I declined, the more energetic she became. Every month we'd get menacing notices from the Sullivan County National Bank, which was now done over in the Howard Johnson-Colonial-America look. A look that depressed me even more.

I dealt with my stress by redecorating the poolside with sixteenth-century torture devices, replicas made by a carpenter trick I met in a sex club who got off on creative torture-device building and drooled at the chance to install his visions in public. Poppa coped the old-

1965, Joyce(?) and me. The girls wanted me—I could care less.

[1] A famous New York Jewish deli.

fashioned way—he got sick. And Momma also coped the old-fashioned way, but instead of taking it out on herself, she focused on me and my ever-present bachelor status.

At 34, she felt my clock was winding down. She was determined to see me married. She still is. She's 93, living in a nursing home, and still looking for brides for me. I've told her I'm gay. She's known about my companion and friend, Andre, for 20 years. And she's still haranguing me about getting married so "I shouldn't be alone." Back then, in 1969, the more this woman, whom I detested but attached myself to vis a vis Jewish guilt above and beyond, the more numbers and tricks I made it with. The newly-gained freedoms gays and lesbians had fought for and were enjoying, were not yet marred with fear of immune system breakdowns or AIDS. I indulged in love and sex assignations by the dozen or, more accurately, by the gross. I couldn't tell her then. I should have, like so many of my brothers, but I was *trapped in the closet.*

Even if I had been straight, finding me a suitable wife in White Lake would have been a challenge of mythic proportions. If chickens had teeth, who cares?

Momma was lucky to have another stress-reduction hobby: counting her sheets and devising methods to keep the few guests from demanding refunds.

Meanwhile, Papa was getting weaker. What began as colitis turned out to be colon cancer which would slowly eat him alive. His once strong construction worker's hands were thin and bony. His once bulky frame shrank by the week. Somehow though, his hair stayed black and his eyes kept their fierce and shiny humor. I think he knew how hopeless was this mess we were in, but he kept on working as best he could, devoting his last energies to this strange enterprise.

The Earthlight Theatre was bravely rehearsing in case an audience emerged. There was a full house, once. A summer camp had bought out the theater for one dollar a seat. The camp director insisted the price include ice cream. Max Yasgur, of the dairy farm up the road—who later would host a far greater full house—made his first donation to the arts in White Lake by providing the ice cream. Earthlight spent weeks building bleachers out of scavenged and donated wood scraps. Borrowed lights, scenery bits and pieces, props, and even a ticket booth of sorts helped make it look like there was going to be some kind of show. Dad knew they'd never earn us a cent, but he encouraged them and snuck them food behind Mom's back. He must have known I needed some friends, and here were 20 people about my age and with similar interests. Mama was ever the hard-nosed businesswoman trying to extract rent, trying to charge for every item—soap, electricity, water, air. So what she charged, Dad and I tried to give back in cash when possible. And, when Mother wasn't looking, we often gave away batches of sandwiches and juice.

Then two European film-makers who had access to prints of European and New Wave films came up and took advantage of my free rent offer. From Czechoslovakia or some Eastern Bloc place, they were looking for creative freedom, and hoped to find it in White Lake. The deal was we'd share the box-office in exchange for the cinema hall and living quarters.

59 or 47 days and counting...

Mother was offering people 90 percent discounts if they booked for the season and paid cash. She gets points for trying, but even that didn't work. We were in the wrong place at the wrong time. Why go to the Catskills when for the same money you could be in Acapulco, the Alps, Paris? We offered fresh mountain air, but people wanted air conditioning. If I'd been as clever as Club Med, I would have advertised our lack of amenities as a positive. Obviously I wasn't clever in the world of resorts. But somehow, I don't think we could have pulled off an "antidote to civilization" ad campaign. What we offered was exactly what civilized people wanted to escape from.

The Sullivan County National Bank demanded loan payments by mid-July. Charlie Prince seemed to delight in his hinted threats of foreclosure.

As far as I could determine, we had two months before we would have to give up the nightmare. Prince, an over-fed upstater, smiled a ruddy upstate smile and said if the bank didn't get the money he certainly recommended bankruptcy.

Earthlight Theater troupers spent long days and nights in the bar/disco and tried to dream up ways to bring theater-goers to the summer rep they were still valiantly rehearsing. My bar became, even if only for a few weeks, an artists' salon. Okay, so it wasn't Paris. It wasn't the Algonquin. But considering this was White Lake, New York, it was high culture indeed.

Decoration Day, otherwise known as Memorial Day, is the hospitality industry's official start of the summer season. In 1969, it brought maybe one or two errant bookings to the El Monaco. The Earthlight troupe was ready with its summer repertory. All the linens were washed and ironed, so Momma and I had nothing to fight over yet. She decided to bring up God, religion, and the importance of prayer. She was getting ready to be certified.

42 or 45 days and counting...

July Fourth weekend came and went with less of a bang than Memorial Day. The mid-July deadline of the bank's threatened foreclosure of the El Monaco was only ten days away. It was difficult to believe the bank would take over this enterprise. What could they do more than we had done? The Earthlight troupe actors were adding lawn clippings to their food instead of salad leaves, which they couldn't afford. Money was non-existent and the actors considered going to The New School to take up secretarial studies. Others were considering hooking, but that was in direct competition to the bungalow ladies' free giveaways whilst hubbies worked in the city.

It looked like my dream of getting out of the Catskills was coming true. It wasn't the way I had dreamed—being kicked out by the bankers, broke and broken. But, the good news was I'd be out.

Desperate optimism still counts as positive thinking. And I was still thinking. No more dreaming, but conniving with myself trying to unearth some untried scheme to sell the compound to some lunatic or wealthy benefactor whose brains had dried up. There are those people, only I didn't know how to access them. Any day now something would turn the dire situation around. A ton of something would droppeth from the heavens like the gentle dew that...

9

Out of the Woods

59 days and counting...

Tuesday, July 15th, was D-day. I sat in the Disco at the former 'Joan Crawford' table, renamed the 'Omni' table, (we were now a New Age Bar), which was a table that slanted in the opposite direction of the floor. My ears and hair were flapping from the steam from the surplus half-priced coffee machine. The *nouvelle vague*[1] black smoke of burnt chemical-free muffins wafted through the thick gloom of Le Temps Purdue.[2] What a glorious sight we must have been to the non-existent crowd of over-75s and under-40s that didn't subscribe to a New Wave El Monaco Star Gazing Weekend package that included a free folding chair under the White Lake Stars.

A few Earthlight Theatre members were nursing tall glasses of something in a pale lavender-leaning-towards-beige liquid that mother was serving free of charge. I won't attempt to guess what that liquid was, but it was New Wave. If it was free, there were good reasons, none of which I care to recall. The troupe's director was reading the local *Times Herald Record.* Suddenly, he got upset and read the paper to us all:

"Guys, the Woodstock Festival is being thrown out of Walkill. After investing more than two million dollars in getting the stage set up and putting in toilets, water lines, roads, and stage structures, the town supervisors decided they don't want the dirty hippies to ruin Walkill! Blah blah. The Walkill community will not permit itself to be overrun and destroyed by thousands of drugged-out sex-crazed rock music nuts, blah blah. Those fuckfaces!"

[1] French for 'new wave.'
[2] French for Proust's 'lost times.'

They canceled the permit. The Woodstock Festival was not to be! Festival producers were going to sue to recoup their investments, and if they didn't find another suitable site within 24 hours, the whole enchilada would be nada. Hundreds of trucks and trailers from every point in the country were already en route to Wallkill with materials and supplies. And thousands of techies and crew would be left stranded.

My brains began to dance in a convoluted pattern previously reserved for fits of illusion in fantasy places such as my leather sex clubs, Amsterdam's red light district, and along the Siene in Paris after midnight. I felt the messiah was knocking at the motel door. A festival needs a home and a permit! I had a home. I had a permit. They could have mine.

The Festival certainly wasn't news to me. It had been in the local papers for months. It had upset me to know that civilization was coming to the Catskills, but 50 miles south; too far away to help me. But now, it was possible that an angel from heaven was sending the Festival my way.

I called the producer, Michael Lang.

"Do you know Michael?"

"No. I don't know him and he doesn't know me. I'm the President of the White Lake Chamber of Commerce and owner of the El Monaco International Resort in White Lake and I have a valid permit for a music and art festival and fifteen acres of land that Woodstock may have. Immediately if not sooner."

The Earthlight troupe, quivering with excitement, gathered 'round me. Mike Lang got right on the phone—or the horn, the 1969 name of choice for 'phone.'

"You have a fucking permit?" he said. "Where the fuck are you baby? What's the deal?"

"Route 17B. White Lake. It's in White Lake. I'm about 25 miles up the highway from where you are."

"Do you have a fucking lawn?"

"Yes, we have a lawn. A big lawn."

"Do you have some white sheets?"

"What? Has someone in Walkill said something nasty about our sheets? Of course we have sheets. We're a motel."

"Put the fucking white sheets out in a cross on the lawn, baby, and we'll be there in 15. I'm looking at the map. You have a landmark there? A sign? Something we can identify in the air?"

I mumbled that we had signs. El Monaco. Yenta's Pancake House. The Route 55 intersection. I don't think I was very coherent. All these years I'd been begging for something big, but now I was shaking. Whatever I told him, it seemed to be enough. And I ran to the basement to get sheets.

Mother started screaming when she saw me racing to the lawn with her prized sheets. She became apoplectic when the Earthlight troupers and I started laying them out, weighing down the corners with stones, shoes, whatever we could find.

"You're putting a cross on my lawn? Oy gottenu,[1] a sin on us all! And with my good sheets! Those are *clean* sheets!"

Her screams grew more convulsive as the Earthlight troupe decided to strip to their birthday suits. Perhaps in 1994 that doesn't seem so daring but, trust me on this one, in White Lake in 1969, they were taking their freedom and liberty and placing it in harm's way. And they began painting slogans on their bodies with lipstick, mud, whatever. The monkey and the dog got into the act.

Soon Mama's screams were drowned out by the thunderous clapping of a helicopter. The sheets billowed as the chopper approached and, not having any experience with these things, I didn't know the right landing procedures for sheets. My only 'landing' experience to date was the aliens from Atlantis who took me up somewhere and experimented on my brains. There was no sexual abuse involved, however. So the copter was billowing up the sheets and I was trying to hold the corners down like it was some hospital bed. The Earthlighters dragged me away from the sheets so I wouldn't get decapitated by the helicopter blades.

Mom thought Jesus was arriving in a big silver and white bird on her good sheets, the ones without pubic hairs ironed in! A cross on her Jewish lawn?

Poppa watched all this in quiet and stunned amazement.

---

[1]Yiddish for 'Oh, God!'

Neighbors instantly surrounded the entrance driveway watching this silver bird alighting as if it had discovered a nesting place.

The naked Earthlight troupe burst into a spontaneous dance.

Mother did not cope well with this display of idealism and hope. Neighbors and passersby were attracted like bugs to a street lamp to this bucolic scene. The Earthlight troupe was sincerely mystic in their dance. They were communing with nature and the cosmos and whatever galaxies were out there tuning into the 1960's peace-love-freedom message.

Unfortunately, the local cosmos of White Lake, which was now fast approaching the El Monaco lawn, wasn't similarly attuned. This esoteric rite was being performed to ensure a successful Woodstock Festival and bring us luck. So far, all it was ensuring was that the police would be after us. In fact, my mother was among the first to think of calling them. Luckily, Dad didn't listen to her orders and just stood there, watching the scene. Whatever was going on, he, too, must have realized it was better than mowing the lawn, better than being on roofs, better than cleaning toilets. The state troopers could wait.

As for me, my heart was beating to the rhythm of the chopper's twirling blades. It hovered above us and then dropped to the ground, the sheets spinning away from the landing site. I remember the rest as a silent movie. The blades stopped spinning and a silence set in. I couldn't hear my mother scream. I couldn't hear the neighbors shrieking at the nudity. I saw the great wordless dance of the Earthlight troupe, and a big silver bird sitting on my lawn. A door swung open and a young man who was mostly a mop of wild, curly long hair, stepped out. He was wearing a vest, no shirt, a pair of bell bottoms, and his feet were bare. Somewhere in that hirsute mess was the sweet boyish face, with its signature beatific grin, of Michael Lang.

Following close behind Michael was a young woman with a tiny hairy thing with two shiny black dots that looked like eyes, and another single black dot that looked like a nose. Its entire demeanor was that of a pocket Yorky. There were two others, very hip looking, also on the copter. I was fixed and focused on this Starship when suddenly, I was snapped out of this daze by Lang who called out: *"Elli!"*

I was puzzled. No one called me Elli except family. I'd changed it to Elliot the minute I graduated from Midwood High School in

Brooklyn. I figured that if my schoolmate Stewart Konigsberg could change his name to Woody Allen, then I could change mine to Elliot Tiber. After all, we sat together in the sickroom at the gym—that was the only way to get out of the miserable class—neither of us could climb the damned ropes to the ceiling. The only time I climbed those ropes was when I was forced to, if I wanted to graduate. I still remember the excruciating pain as I grasped those bending ropes and clawed my way to the top while the other kids jeered and laughed.

Who was this mop of hair with the big smile and bare feet that he was calling me Elli? Who was this big mop of hair with the big smile and bare feet that he was hugging me?

"Do we know each other?"

"Bensonhurst! Seventy-third Street! We grew up together. I lived across the street from you! We played stick ball together! I'm Mike Lang. You're Elli Teichberg."

To this day, I still don't remember Mike Lang from across the street. Of course, that was lots of years before. I had done my best to forget Bensonhurst, so maybe I forgot Mike and stick ball. He was ten years younger than me, so he must have been pre-young when and if I knew him. For sure, though, no long-haired hippie lived across the street from me then. Then again, I looked pretty much the same. Then again, I never played stick ball. So how could he have had time to do a D & B on me in the short trip from Walkill? Was he such a terrific con man or was my memory totalled?

He put his arm around me as his right-hand *femme avec chien*[1] gave me a hug too. We went into the Disco Bar, with half of White Lake following close behind, pressing their noses against the window panes. Lapenis and an assortment of rednecks surrounded the copter to try and find out whether we were being invaded from Swan Lake; five miles up the road was the stretch of their imaginations. Tourists thought Chitzen Itza or Russia maybe?

I locked the door for some audio privacy.

"So, how have you been, good buddy?" Lang asked, still smiling. We chatted about Bensonhurst, and how remote it was from "reality." We talked about the old neighborhood, the other kids. Stuff like that.

---

[1]French for 'woman with dog.'

Through all this, I still couldn't place him, but I took his word for it. Meanwhile, the thought of our being foreclosed the next morning kept beating on my brain. I was afraid to mention the Festival business because I didn't want to seem overly anxious, so I mustered up calmness and subtlety and asked:

"Can we lose all this Bensonhurst stuff and talk about music festivals?"

Lang asked to see the permit. The permit, which was perfectly legal, said specifically that Elliot Tiber of the El Monaco could hold a music and arts festival in White Lake during 1969.

I quickly added that I was also the President of the Chamber of Commerce and would gladly assure the cooperation of the local business community so that a repeat of the Walkill debacle would not occur. The weight of the entire Chamber, no small matter, was behind the Festival.

"After I spread out the white-cross sheets, there were 132 seconds until your copter arrived. I held a majority meeting of the White Lake/Bethel C.O.C. on the spot, literally, and we voted to approve the Woodstock Festival and everything you need plus 10 percent! Just do it." (I didn't know that phrase would be stolen 23 years later by Nike sneakers. There were no Nike sneakers in 1969.)

Lang asked to see the 15 acres of land I had described on the phone. We left the Disco, with Pop close behind. Momma was busy trying to cover up the naked Earthlight troupe. When they refused her shmattas and danced around the copter, she began renting lawn chairs to the instant audience.

By now, some limos had arrived and Stan Goldstein, the security chief, and some other members of Lang's entourage joined us in this virgin trek into the swamps behind the cesspool.

Poppa waved his cesspool-stirring stick at the nosy neighbors, discouraging them from joining the tour of the meadow. The Yentas couldn't be blamed since the number of times a silver bird with whirling wings landed at the El Monaco were zero. Momma gave up her 'rent-a-chair' biz and started charging admission to the Earthlight ritual Woodstock preview dance. It was the first paid performance of anything at the El Monaco. A historical moment which I have on film!

We walked past the rooms with the Miami Beach multi-colored doors. Mike and Co. stopped to look at the questionable signage:

Jerry Lewis Wing

They said nothing. We then strolled past the Presidential Wing, and they looked up at that signage:

Presidential Wing
formerly Moulin Rouge Wing

Nobody said anything. I was not sure if I should explain my signage or, as I've learned since but didn't subscribe to back then, let the spirit of the 'art' speak for itself. I said nothing because I didn't want to scare them away.

We slid down the gravel and sticky tar path past the tiny pool and down the hill towards the collapsing bungleholes.

Again, this brave group, rapidly losing confidence I was certain, stopped to look at the sign above the less-than-Olympic pool:

Elvis Presley's Blue Suede Shoes Pool & Cabana Club.
For guests only.
Outsiders will be sent to prison forever
unless they pay the daily $5 fee to Sonia the pool savant.

I dared not look at their eyes. They were likely thinking I was totally mad, but they didn't turn around to escape. They were desperate. I was desperate. We were getting engaged.

I wasn't entirely able to count on my own sanity either. Who knew if this was actually happening? Were these people here? Did a copter just land on my white sheet cross? Would the state troopers come and arrest me and my naked improv theatre and dance performance group?

The grounds were soaking wet. I don't remember if it rained, but no matter. Between liquid ooze that sloshed out from the swamp forest surrounding the compound and rain and dew from the whispering pines, every step was a slosh.

"Don't you have any open space?" Lang, the beatific, asked. The rest of Lang's entourage started whispering.

I explained that there was an open meadow-like area just below, not to be discouraged. With the disappointed and rapidly depressed expressions on their faces, they kept following. By now there were six or seven additional Woodstock people in our caravan. They must have thought I was some Florida shyster selling land under water. I was trying to make it clear I was donating the use of the land, but their feet told them there was a lot of damp stuff hiding the land. Oy, I worked that crowd trying to sell the idea of a festival on that dopey little 15 acres. I kept reminding them that I was the president of the C.O.C. and, unlike Walkill, was welcoming them with open arms. Mike continued smiling. I couldn't know what the others were whispering and thinking. From reading some of their books years later, I found out. Oy. But then, as we passed more signs, I was rapidly losing belief that my nomenclature *sur les* bungleholes would defeat me. If that happened, I would promptly set fire to the entire compound, and go to prison, gladly, for arson.

We passed the "International Cultural Information Booth" next to the "White Lake Summer Barn Playhouse," next to the cesspool. We passed the last building before the potential festival 'site.' My heart sank as they all looked at the knock-kneed, slanted-floored and peeling "Hollywood Palm Plaza" tourist rooming house, a.k.a. where the Earthlight Actors lived *en commune.*

We were just shy of twenty feet from the site. I felt relieved that my sign orgy was over. How could I explain to these strangers, whom I hoped were my saviors, that my sign therapy was an advance preview of my absurd, twisted, comedy courses I'd give at The New School some 20 years later.

I hadn't been down at this end of the compound in months, so the directory sign swinging like a hammock between two huge whispering pines with fake palm leaves (stolen from Lord & Taylor's windows) even shocked me:

Coming Soon on this site: 200-story Convention Center. Gambling Casino, Health Spa, and space for 2,000 cars.

I didn't dare look at their eyes or faces. I thought it would be 100 years before we finally reached the 'site.' In three seconds, we were trying to stand upright in this sodden and soggy clearing below the El Monaco compound.

"This is what I own and can give the Festival. You can cut the trees down. Level the land. How many people do you expect? I have a permit right here in my hands!"

Lang turned to Goldstein and said, "Couldn't we get a dozen bulldozers in here and level it? He's got a *permit!* He owns the land. He's the president of the C.O.C.!"

Lang was still smiling, a gesture that I would eventually realize was a permanent facial expression. Better than the sour dour grim White Lake expressions I was accustomed to, for sure.

Goldstein and his associates weren't pleased. They said the ground was too wet. I said they could drain it. They pointed out they had less than 30 days to set this thing up. Draining it was impossible. I think I panicked and made a variety of pitches that included hanging a stadium from sky-hooks, filling the entire El Monaco compound with cement which wouldn't be wet. Perhaps I crossed that thin line of sanity when I thought to tell them they could nuke the whole fukkin place to oblivion and put Woodstock on atop the ashes?

Then I remembered my milkman, Max Yasgur. As my entourage was heading back towards the copter and out of my desperate life, I blurted:

"Hey, Mike. I have a neighbor who has lots of open space. He has a big farm. Hundreds of acres!"

"Where? Who?"

"Just up the road. He's my milk and cheese man. His name is Max Yasgur. He has the best cottage cheese and milk in the county. He's a swell guy. Maybe he'll rent you his farm. He just has a lot of cows grazing there. There's plenty of space for a concert. In fact, the land slopes there so that it's much like an amphitheater. I'll call Max."

This was my very last chance at having the messiah rent out my fucking rooms and save my life. Not to blow it, I tried to look a bit cool. Hah. Not since my pre-1949 days of whine and Moses at the hardware store and Yeshiva in Brooklyn, had I sweat so much.

Lang looked cool. Goldstein looked cool. They all looked cool. And I, hotter than hell, was standing in a swamp surrounded by very cool, hip people. I tried to be cool, but I lost it and ran a Gold Medal sprint through the swampy forest, past my naked theater troupe and straight to our one working phone. I reminded Max how much he liked music and art and how he'd helped out with the ice cream for the Earthlight theater.

"If we can have our music festival on your farm, it would save me from giving the El Monaco to the bank, and my folks having to take in wash someplace in Miami Beach. I could even triple my milk and sour cream orders. Max? Say you'll do this."

"Sure Elliot, August is so quiet here. You know me, I love music. Come over with your friends and we'll talk."

We had been buying Yasgur's cheese and milk for some twenty years. For me, Yasgur's cottage cheese in particular, "the finest of its kind in the free world," was one of the few redeeming features of being stuck in the Catskills. So, with Lang, with the Woodstock entourage, (which included those two young men with millions and a dream; go know), we drove the four miles to Yasgur's. They went ga-ga the minute they saw the huge, open acreage of Max's farm with its natural amphitheater. The slopes and spot for the eventual stage were custom-made for a music festival.

"Max, these fellows need the land for a three-day concert. We need to get started tomorrow because the Festival is August 15, 16 and 17 and there's so much to do and so little time to do it? Okay?"

My heart pounded in my throat. I sucked up to the God I don't believe in, and prayed the Teichberg Curse didn't follow us the four miles to Yasgur's. I clenched my fist, my teeth, my face, my tail, my breath that this has got to happen. I knew if this didn't happen, I'd set the fucking motel on fire, and flee to Mexico and become a sex slave in Bangkok or the dunes in Tunisia where the hot running boys catered to big American men for two Lucky Strike cigarettes. If this dream evaporated, I'd punish God and the whole Jewish race by using my bar mitzvah[1] *tallis* and *tfillin*[2] for sexual abandon in some sex club in Greenwich Village. I prayed to God that these threats, and worse sacrilege, would be forthcoming if he were to forsake me just now. And I added:

"Next year, I'll spit on that wall in Jerusalem if you let these angels out of here without a contract!"

[1] A Jewish ritual for thirteen-year-old boys.
[2] Hebrew for a prayer shawl and religious leather strap 13 feet long.

"Think Max, you could have the exclusive for supplying milk and cheese and yoghurt to ten thousand music lovers!"

Max nodded in agreement. I watched his head nod up and down, and his smile. I watched Lang's face turn into sunshine, absolute 100 percent sunshine, and I melted. My feet were not going to support me if I didn't have a chocolate egg cream or chocolate milk—a Yasgur's chocolate milk—in a micro-second. But, I stayed cool. I looked cool. I looked hip. Okay, so I didn't look hip. Lang with his enormous mop of blonde curls was hip enough for everyone and then some.

We all went to discuss details at lunch at DeLeo's Italian Restaurant on the lake, across from the El Monaco. I knew better than to feed them Mom's dingbat stew in paper plates from The Hong Kong Raffles. I did not think this was the moment to show off the quality of the motel service, facilities, staff, or encourage close inspection of anything else. Better to let their imaginations fill in the blank spots about the struggle between two or four stars in the travel guides.

Yasgur waxed eloquent about my previous attempts at cultural events in White Lake. The sidewalk art shows, the theater, the nice classical selections on my Webcor record player.

"You guys are lucky to have Elliot here on your side. He has single-handedly brought whatever music and art White Lake has. He's a nice boy. His mother is a nice lady. His father fixed my barn roof, and it never leaked again. Nice."

"Would fifty dollars a day for the three days be okay?" Yasgur asked as he saw Lang with no shoes and looked into my desperate eyes.

"Elliot, I know how you've struggled so many years with your festivals and everybody knows you operated with a negative cash flow," Max waxed.

Lang and Yasgur shook hands. I was in shock. The Teichberg Curse hadn't struck this deal down even though we were eating traife.

As we left the restaurant, we heard the restaurant radio heating up. WVOS, the local station, announced a news flash:

"This just in. Mike Lang, Producer of the Woodstock Festival, is meeting at DeLeo's restaurant in White Lake with Elliot Tiber of the El Monaco Motel and Max Yasgur of Yasgur's Dairy Farm. They are discussing plans to move the Woodstock Festival to White Lake."

Yasgur smiled. Lang, as always, smiled. I tried to smile but all I wanted to do was return to the table and take back the tip they'd left for the waitress, who'd apparently leaked the story. I was upset about the radio news. For some reason, I thought it would make Max cancel the deal. To hedge the risks, I promised Mike that there were plenty of other neighbors with lots of good land who would help us if Max pulled out. I thought to myself that I'm worrying over nothing but the Teichberg Curse. Max is no redneck. He's nice, friendly, Jewish, loves music and could only benefit from an influx of people to the area. 'Jewish'? I don't know how many dumb years I allowed that faux notion that Jewish people would stick together or help each other because of that common Semitic root. It never helped me before, and I had no solid basis to think it would help me now. Still, when riding in an elevator without buttons, I always tend to grasp at any ring, brass or not. Mike, still smiling, told me not to worry.

The minute we got back to the El Monaco, the phone rang. It was Max. My heart jumped. Max said he'd made some calls and found out that there might be as many as 15,000, maybe 20,000 people or more attending the Festival. My heart, nose, ears, eyes, feet, nails, pubic hairs all sank. When Max reconfirmed he'd be delighted to host the festival, my eyelashes and heart leaped. But he wanted $5,000 a day, not $50.

"It'll cost to restore my farm after 15,000 people stomp all over it. Not to worry Elliot. I won't screw your festival. Trust me."

Trust him? I had someone else to trust? I was sure the Teichberg Curse was going to jettison this entire dancing with the angels to hell. I relayed the info to Mike. He was still smiling.

"It's okay, cool. I can live with that. I have to talk to some people, but it'll be a go," he said.

Max would sign papers sooner than later. It was a go.

The next morning, the Teichberg Curse was up at dawn. The local papers and radio were now saying that 50,000 tickets had already been sold to the festival. Max Yasgur raised his price to $50,000 for three days, with little add-ons such as clean-up guarantees, health and medical facilities, insurance and only he and they knew what for. $50,000 in 1969 is something like $400,000 in 1994. My brain mixed its metaphors and whirled around with the other strange flying creatures that were exiting the swamp. Our little trek the day before unleashed previously unknown 'things' that were now attacking everyone and everything in the compound.

But Mike Lang kept smiling and saying "Yes," "Yes," "Yes."

Every time Yasgur added a condition, I twitched and retched and sweat.

And Lang kept smiling.

"Why so worried, man? C'mon babe. Whatever it is, no problem. Tell me what's happening. We can deal with it."

And deal he did. I had never before witnessed a handler such as Mike Lang. And in the marketing fields I moved in, with big honchos crunching big numbers in Macy's, Bullock's, Bloomies, and Popular Club Plan, their style was pale lemon next to Lang's hot pink and neon everything!

Still, I worried. I could not fully enjoy the victory celebration in the Disco. My other head was still certain it would all fade away and the drudgery of toilet cleaning and cooking for swinging singles would be my future, or my demise.

The Disco was one big love-in. Using that 1960s phrase, 'Love In,' now in 1994 feels a bit like revisiting Neanderthal times. Everyone kissed everyone and everything. The Earthlight troupe did some number crunching of their own. Their inventive improv performance art in those days before anyone knew from performance art was mind-blowing. Some played guitars, some sang, some did sexual mime, some did movement pieces that were indefinable then and beyond recall now. News spread like wildfire, and suddenly, there were many new faces wandering in off the road to witness this event about to happen. The news spread all over the county, and by four in the morning, normal legal closing time, the bar crowd spilled out into the parking lot and onto the highway. State troopers were hanging out along with others. Neighbors were still in shock from the helicopter, and were now keeping tally on the constant flow of cars, vans, trucks and limos arriving steadily at the compound.

Dad rigged up an extension phone for Mike so that he could make calls with some privacy. Mike was and still is a piece of work. Watching him dance around the myriad of coordinating that had to be put into action exiting Walkill and relocating to White Lake, was one of the most riveting phenomena I ever witnessed. It was the bonanza in my rapidly overfilling cup. That I was a vital part of this supernova, or whatever it was to be, engulfed me totally. And no matter what impossible obstacles arose to cripple everything, Lang never lost that smile, never changed his rhythm, and dealt with them. And for sure I fell in love with him instantly.

Momma and Pop didn't yet understand the full impact of this invasion of what was then commonly termed "dirty rotten hippies." But earlier that day, Lang said the magic words:

"We need to rent some rooms. You guys happen to have any available? I think we need ten maybe 20 rooms? Maybe 30?"

Suddenly, this man with the Jesus Christ haircut and bare feet was acquiring messianic qualities for them, too. When he took a plastic bag of cash out to pay the bill—in advance, no less—Mr. and Mrs. Dysfunctional El Monaco began to think maybe their nutty dysfunctional son, who mystified them both since day one, wasn't so crazy after all. Maybe this was a Second Coming!

No maybe, 30 rooms in one shot? Maybe it was time to franchise?

10

The Teichberg Curse Fails

58 or 62 days and counting...

The Teichberg Curse had failed. This fact was announced in every morning paper in full page ads placed by the Woodstock people. That's what I read as I leafed through all the papers. Newman's Drugstore in Kauneonga, the center for garlic-breathed WASP old-school anti-Semitic retailing in the village, had a mob by the newspaper counter. I entered the shop, ordered the one decent item that Mrs. Newman had, a crisp bacon and egg salad on toast, picked up one of each paper. The crowd just stood and stared, mouths open. And there was the full page ad, blaring out at me:

"To insure three days of peace and music, we've left Walkill and are now at White Lake, New York."

The text went on to explain the political fights at Walkill, informed people there would now be twice the space and their old tickets would be good at White Lake. It closed with,

"See you at White Lake for the first Aquarian Exposition, Aug. 15, 16 and 17."

I was actually trembling. The local crowd, ugly as always, seemed a blur to me. I wasn't noticing any of them as I headed out towards my Buick. I had to stop because I suddenly was aware of them shouting at me,

"You did it this time you goddam Jew! Who needs these fucking drug and sex perverts? We'll get you, Teichberg! Your fucking motel won't be there for long!"

This was before Act Up, before Larry Kramer, before self-esteem and self-worth programs had been accessible to teach gays how to stand up and gird themselves against hooligans. My instinct to lash out that instant was so overwhelmed by the raving newspaper stories

110

confirming that I baked one of the biggest pieces of the pie in my life, that everything else was mush.

I can't recall all their exact invective. I do remember that a few stood up to defend me and assure me they were behind the whole Festival. I remember Ester, in her seventies or nineties, and owner of a relic hotel on the square opposite the drug store, hugging me. She said she already had people early in the morning rent all of her 30 rooms in spite of their previously being sealed by the multiple occupancy bureau. And Al something shook my hand and shouted down the rednecks. He was championing the good fortune the entire community was going to have for the first time in 50 years. But, these two were definitely in the minority. I had the good sense to get the hell out of there, and swiftly drove back to my little bit of heaven.

My hands were shaking worse than fall leaves in the first sharp blasts of winter winds. Even the fall leaves in White Lake were subject to the whims of the winds. I turned into our La Playa del Mar Cote D'or driveway on Route 55. It was difficult to find a place for my Buick, something that had never occurred before on the sinkhole parking lot. I thought I'd better paint some signs to allow for reserved spaces. Nah, enough sign painting for a lifetime.

Momma and Pop were dancing the phone which was now ringing non stop. Since this was still the only line into El Monaco, the only way to sort through the barrage of urgent calls was to take immediate executive action. I gave the phone to Mike Lang and said that until his lines were installed, simply hang up on any incoming calls that interfered with his high-wire juggling act.

From that frenetic moment on, the serious wildness didn't stop until two weeks after the festival was a memory, three months later!

89 days and definitely counting...

Lang's magic juggling had phone trucks there within hours installing the banks of phones he and his people needed. Outside pay phones miraculously appeared out of an army of communication trucks that kept coming and going around the clock. For 13 years I couldn't get the phone company to even consider giving us one phone booth without up-front guarantees and cash payments.

Our micro joke of a registration office now boasted six phones, all of which were ringing non-stop. And this madness of ringing where there was always silence was sheer delight. When Momma manned the phones, people from the world over got her oblique advice along with her abstract confusing brand of housing and room reservations.

"Dollink. Vee don't know from credit cards. Vee don't reserve no rooms with air conditioning. Some rooms have running water, some are under running water. Dollink, this is no good time to talk. You come, and we will find place for you. If not, so you'll have some cholunt. No, don't send checks. We can't afford to take bum checks. Just send cash. How much? Who knows? Send $200, and we'll work something out. Be good to your momma, she is the only friend you will ever have."

Lang and his terrific right hand, Lee Mackler Blumer, thought Mom was 'cute.' Okay, it wasn't the time to negate cute. I simply suggested they take her with them on a 'no return' policy.

Meanwhile, hundreds of Woodstock Festival staff members, crew, tech people, food management and waste management people, along with the press, plopped down into our compound. Pop enjoyed directing traffic, answering questions and, mostly, explaining to the growing mob of inquiring locals, that his son was the messiah!

Momma stood at the front desk taking money, pretending to know what she was scribbling on those little useless registration cards, and, after explaining the key system, handing out keys anyway. For the first time ever, on a weekday, the El Monaco was fully booked. And "No Vacancy" was our new permanent status! It was as if extra-terrestrials had landed on that first Woodstock helicopter. And more helicopters came and went from what became a temporary landing field. I abandoned the white cross sheets for some hastily-placed whitewashed stones and boards. Now the land-based attack began with caravans of black limousines. White Lake hadn't seen so many limousines, except perhaps in the 1920s when Murder Inc. reigned there. It was a peculiar scene to take in. If I had any presence of mind or brains, I would have engaged someone with movie equipment to just sit there in the compound and film everything, and we'd have a hell of a movie! Go know, and I didn't.

Things got a little awkward as the extra-terrestrials flashed credit cards, pieces of plastic that had no clout at the El Monaco. We were, of course, "Approved Members," I said, pointing to the shiny decals on the lawn signs. No, Visa and Master Card and American Express and Diners Club didn't take us, so we couldn't take them. I took out vital time from juggling people in and out of rooms, tents, shacks, and sleeping bags to phone the major credit card companies. I explained to the twits who took my calls the explosive situation. Not one of them could provide anything like instant credit card services. The normal routine investigations and approvals would take weeks, maybe months.

"You fucking idiot baboons, with an apology to baboons!" was the only educated response I could muster up. And then I realized that I didn't need them, not now. Everyone was paying cash. Why should I drop a percentage to those sharks? Fuck them. Sweet revenge came by itself weeks later when some biggies from the credit card companies called to reserve rooms. And their secretaries were sure to announce that Mr. X was the big stuff at Diners Club and they wanted deluxe this and that and to put it on their charge cards!

"I can let you have ten deluxe luxury suites in our Mata Hari and Douglas Fairbanks Wings. Diners Club? Oh, no, man. We won't take D.C., too many complaints about Diners. The worst. Lose this number and don't call here again!"

And American Express? I had such nachas to tell these bippos:

"Sorry, your credit card number is invalid. Oops, sorry, but your credit card is listed as stolen, I'll have to warn you this call is being recorded and will be used against you in the White Lake Court of Law. Oops, sorry, but we have no vacancies, and go fuck yourselves!"

For Lang and his entourage, it was, "Like no problem, babe." Cash flowed like water in the El Monaco "meadow." And cash, in an economically depressed town, bespoke miracles. You know, in Hebrew, Bethel, the town White Lake is a part of, means *Beth Elohim*, which means "House of God." For years I had understood that God/Damned were redundant. I was in the "House of the Damned" and this was the first time I felt blessed, but not by God. I felt blessed by those miracles happening to me moment by moment. I was getting more than my share. If there was any God, he would have been named Lang. Man-made miracles, Mike Lang-made miracles, definitely.

Every few minutes another vehicle pulled into the El Monaco. A technicolor selection of types from sharp to secretive, money-making to music-making, movie-making to cooks and bottle washers, it seemed like the UN. Shakers and doers, all with important missions, duties, agendas, arriving and departing, to and from Lang's and his peoples' rooms. To and from the bar to refill, the office for rooms, and the pool for a giggle. Porches, Corvettes, vans, busses, motorbikes, and assorted vehicles hard to define from coast to coast, roared into our lives, and they were joyfully welcomed.

The sour faces of my neighbors, especially Mr. and Mrs. Lapenis, added to the joy. That wore off in 24 hours, since we became the dispatching center for bus loads of hawkers and preachers of one kind or another stopping by for information. I had a daily supply of beers of every nationality being dropped off. Our usual Schaeffer or Bud wasn't enough to satisfy the variety of regional and international tastes our new guests had. Our New Age policy was dropped due to the Now Age requirements. Our Zen lounge reverted back to the Disco bar. All day long, the bar and pool areas were being used for impromptu meetings as Joel and John conducted various logistic sessions with their staff. Until they could get set up in trailers at the farm, our variety of slanted shacks served heroically as quasi-board rooms, financial centers, media conference rooms, and supply depots.

For the first time in 14 years, there was traffic in White Lake other than Yentas and vacationers. A welcome change. A relief. My folks and I were acting as traffic wardens as well as trying to keep atop the demands of a full house. The usual assortment of drunks from Rose's Monticello Employment Agency just wouldn't do. Fortunately, among the thousands upon thousands of young people pouring into White Lake in advance of the Festival, there were many who needed work. As the days and nights grew more hectic, I had as many as 20 on staff, cleaning rooms, doing laundry, making sandwiches, working the bar, mowing lawns, and keeping the machine functioning.

These people were from another planet. Everyone, male and female, seemed to have long hair. In addition to long, there were a variety of mixed colors that, even as a color marketing expert in my designer mode, I had never seen, decorating head and body. It may sound positively naive now, but multi-color neon-lit hair was a shocker and on the cutting edge. We didn't have that expression then; we had Groovy, Cool, Oh Wow, and Man. Clothes bore colors not yet available in nature. Male and female alike wore beads, jewelry and unidentifiable objects dangling from leather cords 'round their necks, waists, ankles, and from places not previously thought of as being able to benefit from decor. Up Tight was the expression, and to show that one wasn't, one hugged and kissed everyone. Androgyny was the majority sex. Now in the 1990s, TVs, crossdressers, sexually ambiguous, and gender benders are prevalent in most big cities. Way back in 1969, it was mind blowing, as we said then.

Not fitting into the majority norm of brain dead, a.k.a. mindless boring America, was tantamount to heresy and could qualify one as being a traitor. And everyone sang. Everyone laughed. And laughed. And giggled. And then laughed again and again. I never heard so much laughter in my life. Not complaining, just mystified. Until I found out.

The continuing laughter was sometimes chemically based. No? Yes. Grass. Hash. THC. And, of course, coke. I didn't know about drugs. It never occurred to me that all this on-going "happiness" might have had some encouragement or basis on anything else besides freedom from blandness and hypocrisy. But then, since I've been confessing my stupidity and dopey decision-making up to this time, the reader will likely not be dismayed by this naivete.

I was drowning in a sea of mediocrity, meaningless rituals, warped parental-ghetto-induced values that had absolutely no connection with any part of me. I now understood that my family support system was all peripheral nonsense based on 5,000 years of religious idiocy that did not meet any of my needs.

I didn't understand it while it was happening. It took at least six minutes to digest the then phrase of choice, "Whazhappenin brother?" But my gut reaction to replacing bubble-bouffant Yentas from the Bronx and Long Island enclaves of Jews, with these multi-colorful hippies, cool and hot, was that I was being born again. And that was, like, hey—Wow! However, my brains and guts were gradually making some educated redefinitions of who and what I was. For the very first time in my life, a new assessment of goals was in order.

It became apparent that there had to be aspirations aside from success and making money. I was encouraged by the kindred souls now enveloping me. Even Momma was sidecar material, at last. People were stirring me towards an appraisal of possibilities I hadn't known existed. My limited range of tenets were fucked up due to the misinformation blasted at me from my parents. And I bought into the psychobabble of the moment that, after all, they too were victims.

Observing Michael Lang up close was no casual thing. It was a rare opportunity to learn from his repertoire of laid-back life values. I attempted to apply some of his methodology to restructure my own messed-up systems.

Nobody native to White Lake had understood the Christmas lights and kinetic neon beer signs in the Disco. No one understood my preference for black walls. Certainly not my own parents. No use giving psychobabble about the soothing restfulness of black. You do black, people freak out thinking of funerals. Limited-visioned dopes that I never should have gave a second thought to overwhelmed my decision-making processes. When I recommended a black main floor for Bloomingdale's and Bullock's, I was fired fast! Five years later, Bloomies stunned the retailing world with their chic black main floor. Black boutiques opened coast to coast. Later in the 1980s and '90s, black-colored merchandise of every description. In the 1960s and '70s, I was being dropped from my free-lance color marketing work because I was recommending black for home fashions and product merchandising. The intensity and richness of black as a color for me was never in doubt. Nobody else seemed to understand it. When I was being let go from Macy's, I had handed in a 25-page report outlining in precise detail how Macy's, the institution it was, should be using their position and square footage to do theatrical, cultural, and socially significant events so they would indeed be part of the community they were selling to. I was judged too way out, and summarily dismissed. Within two years, every phase of my programming suggestions were established and the credit and monies went to those in power.

Now here were people who knew what an underground cinema was, who went to "art" movies, who'd heard of Edward Albee and who sensed the kitsch in Yenta's Pancake House's menu. Here were people who were not watching baseball games, beating up on people who did not look like polyester graduates of K Mart and Burger King University. Here were people who were concerned with environment, music, gentle living, and an entire agenda of humanitarian concerns. I'm not oblivious to the enormous number of baseball boobs and jerks who invaded White Lake, it's just that I didn't have time to devote to any of them. And, of course, a good number were fucked up on drugs and sex, and had no afterlife; but not everyone was.

And since my sexual dysfunction, according to the world of those heterosexuals and religious fools in power, was borderline madness, I would be the last person to criticize the so called promiscuous sexual perverts roaming White Lake and Yasgur's farm. Contrary to reports in the press at the time, I personally did not see even one instance of sexual perversity or deviant behavior. Granted, the sex world, according to me, had parameters that those in power would label highly improper.

White Lake's night life offerings—redneck bars where men gathered to celebrate the day's slaying of Bambi and other innocent game—were the standard by which I misjudged myself all those painful years. El Monaco suddenly seemed to be the exact center of the world. After the long days of Woodstockers working their butts off getting Yasgur's farm into shape, they descended en masse to my little ugly beer neon topless Disco for R & R. In addition to tech and crew and groupies, a variety of Hollywood and big-city music types hung out looking for deals and stuff I had no notion of.

Mike, Stan, Lee, John and Joel and some assistants sat at a Disco table with me. We were half unwinding from the hectic events happening hourly, listening to some of the Earthlight actors singing, and making out "things yet to do" lists.

Mother brought everyone bowls of cholunt which this group said was, "like wow, great vegetarian stuff." I was going to tell them about the meat and chicken fat and pull the bowls away from them and stop her from doing her schtick, but they all thought she was cute. And then Mike asked me:

"Elli, what do you want out of all this?"

"I want out of all this! If you could rent my rooms, I could pay the bills, and take off for parts unknown after the Festival."

"That's it? That's what you want? You're not going to hold us up for some big numbers? Rooms? Can do. You got rooms, we need rooms. What are your rates? How many rooms do you have? How many people can you accommodate?"

"If you use every inch of space—not all of them legit rooms, you understand—we could hold 250 or 400 depending on who counts. Of course, if you need more, all of White Lake is empty. In fact, all of Sullivan County is empty. Except of course for the big guys like Grossinger's and the Concord."

"Why don't you add up the total amount of money you would need for all your rooms for the rest of the season?"

I added up the normal rental prices of the rooms, the bungleholes in the place, the shower-curtain-divided spaces and multiplied it out through Labor Day weekend. I was amazed myself at seeing numbers that added up to a small profit. Of course, we had never seen such an income, nor any profit, since we were never filled. While the Hilton and Mariott chains talk of 80 percent or 74 percent occupancy rates needed to turn profits, I could never mention my 12 percent minus 11 percent occupancy rates with a serious face. Mike looked at the figures, showed them to Lee who showed them to Joel and John. All looked at me in what must have been disbelief, then nodded. I must have been perceived as the village idiot of all time. Money was being tossed every which way. This was big time, and only I didn't know about that. I knew they were my saviors, and whatever legit income I could glean was life-saving.

Mike smiled.

"That's cool. We'll rent all your rooms and curtained spaces. We'll move out a week before the Festival because we have to be on the site for the three days. And then you can re-rent the rooms. We'll pay for the whole season, but you can rent out the rooms a second time. Maybe after the Festival a few of us will need to come back to our rooms to wind up stuff. Okay? How about the Bar and the Pancake House and the Coffee Shop. We need to feed our staff. And what about the Theater and the Cinema? We need office space and meeting space. Can we rent those too?"

I was in shock. I agreed to give them whatever they wanted. Even Momma knew enough to be quiet for the first time in her life. Poppa was stunned, but so pleased and proud as he watched me and my new dancing partners talk over the upcoming live-action soap opera.

We shook hands in agreement. I did my best to keep looking cool while sweat did a pas-de-deux on my forehead. Lang then sent one of his many gofers to his limo to retrieve a shopping bag. He then handed the bag to me. It was filled with cash. Mike told me to take out the rent now because they preferred to pay in advance. And then he asked if I'd be interested in doing some public relations for the Festival.

"Can you coordinate the locals, the town officials and all? We'd really appreciate it. How about that job for $5,000?"

I indicated that I would make myself available for the job as promotional coordinator, and Mike dipped into the bag for the extra five thousand.

"Oh, Mike, I have one last important condition. Can you hire my troupe of terrific actors and performers and artists?"

"No problem, man. We'll hire all of them. They can start tomorrow. They can organize improv and performances and strolling musicians throughout the grounds during the Festival. It'll be fucking cool, You're all hired. We'll work it all out," Lang said, still smiling.

The Earthlight troupe broke into one of their happy rituals. No more including ice cream with Becket. No more shows like: "Sex, Ya All Come." No begging tourists to pull in off the highway to see a show and have a cholunt din-din. This would be the big time.

And there was more. Lang kept going.

"Elli, I know you need to make a mortgage payment. So, here's like what we'll do. I'll announce that the El Monaco is the only ticket agent for the next two weeks. You'll get all the tickets you can sell and the regular commission. Is that okay?"

I had no idea what this implied or entailed. I was in a state of bliss, grace, and hysterics. Box office for tickets? Sure, why not? I'd been unsuccessful at selling horses, rooms that were not, and singles dating vacations, why not festival tickets? My dreams were already true. My prince on a silver copter had clopped-clopped into my castle. There was more? Go know. Besides, I had always wanted a box office for my theater, my cinema, and now, I'd have a real box office for fest tix.

For the next two weeks, I stood in our "box office," also known as our registration desk, a.k.a. the linen rental desk, a.k.a. the White Lake C.O.C. desk, a.k.a. the cultural center of White Lake desk, a.k.a. Tourist Information desk, a.k.a. big joke desk, and now the "Official Festival Ticket Office." And the money poured in. Ads in newspapers and on radio stations in the tri-state area announced that the exclusive

One of our five entrances, on Route 17B.
Our sinful films were boycotted by town Nazis.

place to buy tix was the El Monaco box office, open 24 hours a day for two weeks. Car after car drove into our gravel driveways and bought tickets by the handful. People, real and unreal, sane or nuts, walked, crawled, motor-biked, danced into our five driveways and bought thousands and thousands of tickets. $35,000 worth in those two weeks; that would be equivalent to $350,000 in 1994. My folks and I never saw so much money in all our lives. And the tickets looked just like real tickets. I examined them over and over, as did my Pop. I thought I was having the longest wet dream in the West. I thought El Monaco was now the gold coast of the Catskills. Then people from all over the country began showing up. Our phone rang and rang and rang—we still were too scared of all this collapsing around us and so we kept just the one phone line for ourselves although there were now dozens for the festival. I was totally crazy and delirious. I was certain that at any second some nurses were going to come in and restrain me so they could continue with the shock treatments.

55 days and counting...

As exhausted as I was, at 34, I still had youth and energy to carry me along. I needed to come down, just like the others. I didn't know what went on in the motel rooms and roomettes, and never thought to intrude on anyone's private biz. Nobody intruded on mine. Aside from those guests who invited me into their rooms for neighborly stuff and sometimes more or less, I had my hideaway where I could calm down. Shack Number Two.

What's a shack? It's a step below bunglehole. Number Two in particular was unrentable in spite of Momma's inventive curtain hanging. Hidden behind a bush in the rear of the "Mitzi Gaynor MGM" bungalow, it leaned about 74 degrees south by northwest when there was no wind. Originally built by Pop to hold lawn supplies and barrels of tar for his roofs, this shack just wore out and needed to be knocked down. Not more than 12 feet by 9 feet, exterior woodwork, handcrafted by a European craftsman (Pop) in the Austrian tradition, barely supported the meager whitewash coating. It was at least seven feet high in the center where the support two-by-four held up the slanting roof. It got down to six feet on the sides. However, during strong windy storms, one could add three feet in any direction including up and be correct mathematically. No need for windows since the space surrounding nail holes permitted some light and lots of air.

Mom had shoved a Salvation Army-reject foldaway cot in there and stapled her curtains onto the wooden slats. She decorated the single hanging bulb with a dozen wire coat hangers so that it looked a bit like a Lipshitz sculpture, and named the roomette "Sonia's Nest." There were occasions she rented this nest. Over five years, during parent's camp weekends, when there were virtually no rooms to be had anywhere for 35 miles, at 2:00 a.m., if it were raining and foggy and Route 17B was washed out, (courtesy of one of her personal signs), a whopping eight dollars was earned. And I mean, that *was* earned!

But an unusual happenstance, well, happened, and that discouraged her from keeping Sonia's Nest on the room key rack.

One camp weekend night, after every space was filled, and the bar closed, and everyone tucked away, her mind kept spinning. She refused to shut out the lights and made sure the "Vacancy" sign was properly tuned in. She waited by the roadside huddled under an old shower curtain, since she had rented out the few umbrellas she had in storage. I had given up trying to convince the madwoman that enough was enough, and the fucking eight dollars was not worth staying awake for. Plopping into bed was essential, since the next day always began with rushing to have breakfast ready for a couple of hundred people, and getting linens ready for re-doing the rooms. Energy and strength were in constant demand but in constantly short supply.

My pop had long since gone to hide between the faux panel in the men's room in the bar and their bedroom—which was rented out during parent's weekends. Poor man, it was the only quiet hidden spot where he could grab a few hours of precious rest. It was desperate and I had to take desperate measures. I climbed the whispering pine tree that the shack was kind of nailed to for support, and hid away atop the meager roof. I began making spooky sounds, little hissing noises with my teeth and light whistling. Nothing too way-out, but just enough to get Momma to notice. Knowing her devout belief in dreams and spirits, I seduced her to come close to the shanty.

She saw whatever she saw, which I had to assume was her usual group of memories from old Mother Russia. I didn't have to do much theatricalizing because she was totally in concert with signs from other worlds, other beings, and especially from her mother's spirit. Her mother had a habit of warning her of impending troubles over the years, so one more warning, albeit this nasty shack in the rain, was not improbable. She shut off the motel sign, and went to sleep under the office registration desk.

In the morning she removed the Nest keys from the rack. There was no discussion.

With Shack Number Two off the rental list, and clearly never to be looked upon again, I decided to provide myself with a bit of privacy. I installed a collection of leather toys and sex devices. I covered the walls with black rubber sheeting, hung a leather sling, a crucifix, some chains, and black outdoor grass carpeting left over from one of my imaginative free-lance installations from a model room I had installed in the prestigious National Antiques Fair at the New York Coliseum. "Prestigious" was their self-proclamation, not mine.

The ho-hum celebrities involved, all for a worthwhile charity to be sure, were busy playing House with the huge collection of baseball daddies who shared facilities in the hall, whilst the charitable society ladies did the selling. A good thing there were loudspeaker connections in the men's room to page those who were needed for photo ops, or else the annual antiques fairs in New York City might not continue. And after all, charity is charitable.

I never expected to find any like-leather-minded guys in White Lake, but just in case, being prepared couldn't hurt. (Those readers who think it's a pun when I say it couldn't hurt—please know, S & M has nothing to do with 'hurt.') Being an outsider all those years when people came up to El Monaco to play and romp about the motel while I was supplying fresh towels was not a terrific situation. Being outside looking in has also been known to increase panic and decrease self-worth, which can lead to brain damage and stimulate serious depression. It also can make you fat. Each time guests were moving the foundations of the Presidential Wing, I ate another Hershey's chocolate bar. And to realize that Marky Mark wasn't even born yet, so buying Calvin Klein wasn't any adventure!

Not to think I was lucky enough to have orgies nightly or long lines of boyfriends dropping in for fun and games. There were the rare occasional camp counsellors, lost souls, and leather bikers on the wrong route from Canada to New York City. And once in a while I would drag up some temp from the city for a mini-weekend. It wasn't easy wearing leather cap and chaps while renting rooms. I tried, though.

28 days and counting...

My track record in no way prepared me for what was destined to become a world-focused historical event. All I knew was what I read in the papers, and what Mike and the army of Woodstockers that came trekking through the compound ventured to guess. Numbers never went beyond 35,000. Then they stopped at 50,000. Only 75,000 tickets had been printed, or was it 100,000? Go know. I was addicted to chocolate, Pepsi Cola, and leathersex. When I went out, I swallowed a couple of straight up J & Bs, sung along with Ethel Merman, and psyched myself into believing that the earth was flat. I tried to have a party with whoever went along with my little playlets and allusions to illusions. How would this limited track record enable me to handle the parade of styles of sexual and mental persuasions that was now moving in rapidly? The stuff I'd done furtively in closets, I didn't consider outrageous or unacceptable. Outsiders did plenty of that without help from me. What was amazing was that many other closet doers would be shlepping to ugly downtown White Lake to do it in the open for the first time. That never dawned on me. I wasn't prepared for what was just around the next curve on rotting Route 17B.

Men and women, men and men, women and women, cross-dressers, tran-sexuals, tri- and bi-sexuals, hermits, celibates, straights, bulemics, obsessives, husbands, wives, issues, bikers, trekkers, and the full range of indeterminate everything were now en route to the farm. And they had to pass my front door to get there. Maybe others knew what was coming down, but not naive stupid me. Okay, many others didn't believe it was happening either, evidenced by the fortunes that were never made. Never was there such a peaceful assemblage that netted losses all round, if you are counting in terms of gelt.

Nobody knew. Okay, if there were some who knew, they weren't telling. Okay, there was no shortage of soothsayer types in what would be described as the Grunge look today, wobbling about the motel and the town, lecturing that the future was here and here was the future. They held on-the-spot religious meetings with fervor and zest. Their instant followers became instant deserters with every passing new oracle. Whenever I stopped to catch my breath, I would consider the momentous analytical declarations of whomever had stopped by for water or information or use of the phones. It was impossible for me to subscribe to most of the in-depth on-the-spot evaluations without the benefit of Barbara Walter's insightful remarks or Mike Wallace's sure-fire conclusions.

When I heard the theory that Yasgur's cows were reincarnations from some other planet, and it was recommended that the 'bashert' system of evaluation was the accurate one, I had to have renewed confidence in *Boy's Life*. Go know. We didn't know. I didn't know.

11

Working in Mysterious Ways

26 days and counting...

Lang's smile is difficult not to love. It's understandable why I kept calling him an angel. He was not only an angel, but an angel who had extraordinary access to extraordinary amounts of cash. To me he was the man who had dropped in from heaven to compensate me for past injustices. Heaven owed me; they sent him with the cash.

Mike was sensational. Everything he promised or hinted at happened. It was beyond fantasy. It was so out-of-this-world that I now believed my own loudspeaker announcements that Liz Taylor was paging Jimi Hendrix and that Joan Baez was hanging out by the pool waiting for the free barbecue. Now when I paged Laurence Olivier, it was within reason to suppose he'd really show up. I got on my Navy loudspeakers and enjoyed myself, paging Kirk Douglas and Neil Diamond to move their stretch limos so that Janis Joplin and Sammy Davis, Jr. would have room to do an improv concert in the parking lot. To my surprise, nobody paid attention to my announcements any more. Of course, the fact that most everyone was stoned could have been the reason. Others were stoned and also had business agendas, so could care less. After a while, I was much too busy to continue my star-fucking-announcements. More urgent matters needed tender care, as I'll tell later.

And then the incredible happened. I paged Desi Arnaz and the phone rang. It was Lucille Ball. She booked some rooms for the Festival! Then she put Tennessee Williams on the phone—and he booked some rooms. I made the reservations. Hey, I spoke with Fellini, but Charlton Heston, the gun lover, him, no way.

It has since been suggested by those who were not there that either I was stoned out of my bird or people were pulling my legs, or not,

I'll never know. The Festival was such a jumble that most of the reservations we took never got through the traffic and we filled the rooms with people wandering in off the road. But who knows? The zillions of phone calls on lines that were so fucked-over and crossed, I could have been talking to the Pope or Stalin and not have been certain. Maybe I really spoke to Lucy and Tennessee! Why not? I spoke to phone voices until I lost all ability to get a sound out of my throat. Maybe they spoke to me? Ten years later, Tennessee Williams would be my neighbor at Manhattan Plaza, an apartment complex for theater people. When I asked him if he'd been en route to the El Monaco, he fell over drunk.

25 days and counting...

The next few days brought an ever-increasing onslaught of cars, vans, trucks, 18-wheel trailers, mobile homes/offices, and hundreds of Woodstock staffers.

Sam Superbowitzky, the former head of Methuselah Movie Studios, with his mega-powers and connections, took time out to be with me at the El Monaco. I didn't know who he was, nothing about his status as anything or why he found it profitable to hang around me for a while. He wandered in during a short lull in the havoc, and stared into my face. Go know why a handsome stranger decides to stare. I was getting used to stares that were chemically-based and meant nothing. I was used to having men and women stare at me, follow me around like lovesick puppies, and even, on many occasions, pant for me. Being born so handsome, I had to learn early on to chase these people away with a broom. It was hard to determine in White Lake if big honchos were after me for my exalted position as president of the C.O.C., or simply went bananas from being close to my chemical makeup.

But to end all rumors here, Sam Superbowitzky and I were not shacking up in Shack Number Two. He wandered into the bar. He had mistakenly eaten a huge portion of Mama's cholunt and was a bit green. I gave him a spoonful of apple cider vinegar in water, and he just missed being dead from lack of oxygen. He asked for water, and refused to pay for the cholunt. Mother went to get a state trooper from the corner, while we shmoozed. I advised him to sue her and have her put into a Lithium program at Bellvue. He laughed at my jokes and tousled my curly hair. (Now that he is gone and so is my hair, I'm getting legal advice as to whether I have a hair-damage case against him). I asked him outright if he was toying with me or if he was serious about settling down and reforming his bent ways. We laughed.

But these days, in retrospect, my memory is fading on this stuff, so if it wasn't Sam Superbowitzky, it was his look-a-like. Whoever he was, he wanted to know insider stuff about stuff that only insiders knew about. I asked him what he did at Methuselah, and if he had some connections to get me a starring part in a movie that didn't require me to audition and that would be a guaranteed box-office bonanza so I could fly to North Africa and play in the dunes with the Arab boys. He said he was the main man and if I wanted the moon, he was the one who could get it for me. Okay, why not? I asked him to either pay for the cholunt or make room at the bar for a paying customer. After all, there were hookers from Monticello who were paying me five dollars per stool. It took me only two and a half minutes to blow a big connection to Hollywood. Ergo, I live in a subsidized apartment. Sorry.

25 or 32 days and counting... (Who is counting?)

Within a week of Woodstock's invasion, Lang asked me to arrange for a news conference with the local papers. Rumors had started making the rounds that White Lake would be as much a fiasco as Walkill. Rumors were circulating that 90,000 hippies would devastate Bethel beyond reconstruction. Instead of awarding a Nobel Prize for this, they again wanted to stop the Festival!

Press conference? Sure, routine for me. I, who for fourteen years had been sending press releases to the local rags and successfully getting write-ups about my little Festivals, Cinema Openings and Art Shows, had no problem here. Just a routine, seasonal announcement. Easy. Piece of cake. But there was a big difference this time. My past announcements never drew an army of press people. Nobody ever showed up to personally inspect my Underground Cinema, Art Gallery, or Music Festivals. It would have been too chancy to let someone come and see the reality of my operations. El Monaco definitely looked better on paper. Every paper and local radio or TV show had been very happy to report the unusual cultural upheaval in downtown White Lake. It was something to fill the Arts and Leisure sections, which had nothing to report on. My press releases must have saved many a job of arts reporters in territory where there were none. I wasn't expecting much live response. So, when the press cars started arriving for our "conference," I was shaking. Mahler and Bernstein on the lawn and a discreet selection of my paintings was one thing, but this time I was pushing big stuff. Like, Wow, Hey, Man! Groovy.

Hell, it was a wonderful sight to see not only local press but journalists from the foreign press and major New York publications. Momma checked their credentials at the door and handed them a hastily scribbled menu description of her homemade cholunt. Pop stood by a "PARKING $5" sign and made up for the past droughts.

The reporters had questions. Lots of questions. No one had ever asked me so many specific details about anything before. They wanted to know about the hippies. How many? Who are they? When were they coming? Would there be drugs? Where was my permit from? Did we follow all the rules and regulations? Did we have enough drinking water? Toilets? Did we have Board of Health approval? Hey, lots of nasty specific questions that had no place in my press conferences! So rude.

My quick wit was at the ready. What hippies? Who hippies? What drugs? What Health Department guidelines? Of course, we have a permit. Here's the permit! I am the President of the Chamber of Commerce! Would a leading civic leader such as myself go ahead with a festival without the needed permit? I was insulted!

Then they wanted to know what our provisions were for moving 150,000 hippies in and out of White Lake without adequate roads and evacuation plans. 150,000 hippies? I was still trying to sort out keys for my Presidential Wing reservations! Handling 140,000 hippies? Where did they get these additional hippies? I apologized for Joan Crawford's rudeness on all levels. Nobody cared.

More questions. Was Yasgur's farm zoned for music festivals? What kind of sanitation system did we have? Were we insured for the Festival? What about security? White Lake had one policeman. What about housing? Were the Sullivan County resort owners backing this? Would they provide accommodations for 150,000 dirty, rotten hippies on drugs, those social outcasts who were out to destroy the moral fiber of Sullivan County? And what about me?

"Are you on the payroll of certain mob organizations? Isn't it the case that you have sold out your own people?"

"My own people? White Lake people are not my people! Native White Lakians cannot be considered people, mine or anyone else's!"

I was clearly out of my league here. I did what intelligent people do when they're out of their league: Keep it simple. The noise of the reporters simultaneously shouting their questions made it impossible for me to speak and be heard. So Pop dragged the mike to the Navy speakers and I made a simple announcement:

"There will be a Music and Arts Festival held here on August 15, 16, 17. It is just one more summer Festival, part of my ongoing yearly Music and Arts Festivals that have made White Lake the truly international cultural center it has become. Evidenced by the fact that you wonderful ladies and gentlemen of the press are here to report about it. I've been proud to be the artistic director of these Festivals for the last ten years, and hope that..."

A reporter asked my response to accusations that I'd been paid big bucks to swindle the county. What was the scam? How much bribe money did it take to sell out the county?

"Distinguished ladies and gentlemen of the press. Yours is an honorable profession, the second oldest one, I'm told. To settle some of these wild rumors and accusations, let me make it perfectly clear. (Nixon stole this phrase from me. I know I saw him and that horror Pat sitting in the corner booth next to the graffiti wall.) The Festival has rented the El Monaco for the remainder of the season and the motel will function as headquarters and field offices. Since you are all assembled, I'll take this rare opportunity to announce that next year my momma will build a 200-story skyscraper with revolving health club and United Nations conference center on the 85th floor. And you are all invited to inspect the proper press room we'll have available there for occasions such as this. However, since I've got to make up about 30 more beds and clean a dozen toilets, today's conference must end."

Lang and his associates looked on while all this was happening. As they'd arranged with me, for reasons they never explained and I didn't need to know, I did not identify them nor introduce them to the reporters.

Later that day, or maybe the next, or maybe the one before—I wasn't sure then and I can't be sure now of course—the press increased the number of people coming to the Festival at a rate of about 10,000 per day. It didn't take more than 24 hours for the number to pass a million dirty, rotten thugs, ax murderers, serial killers and music lovers who would be coming to Yasgur's farm to devastate the good people of Bethel, rape their daughters and wives, pillage and plague. No mention was ever made of the men getting raped.

I don't know where they got their numbers, but the more they broadcast, the more people drove in to buy tickets. We worked 'round the clock selling tickets, renting rooms. The El Monaco never had such volume business. Neither had anyone else in the county. None of us was prepared. I saw the handwriting on the wall, or thought I did, and ordered truckloads of supplies; hot dogs, canned foods, bottled drinks, sheets, tents, et al. Only, none of the suppliers had the faith I had. Normally, a motel ordered, the stuff got delivered, and you paid in 30 days. Now I had additional problems to juggle. My three hands were juggling my four other hands when suppliers refused to fill any orders at all.

This new wrinkle had two sides. Ethically, many refused to deal with the man responsible for dragging Sullivan County through the mud. I had become the "Satan of Sullivan County" and was not to be trusted with deliveries of soap, paper towels and toilet paper.

Reason number two had to do with the money being tainted. I did find a supply house in Monastir, Tunisia, that would airlift all the toilet paper and hot dog buns we needed. A call to the White Lake International Airport made it clear there were no flights scheduled in from North Africa. My pleas to the Pentagon went unanswered.

"I know who you are and what you are! I have no intention of permitting any aircraft having anything to do with you and your drugged-out hippies. Just you try and land one fucking hippie airplane on my nice clean tarmac, and you are dead meat! And I'll fire on any psychedelic school busses that try to drive onto my runway! Drop dead you fucking Jew Faggot Commie!"

I knew right off the top that the public service image of our airport was going to suffer. It didn't occur to me that the North African drummer who had recommended the Tunisian Toilet and Hot Dog

Bun Company of Monastir as a supply source, was flying in and out of airports without benefit of aircraft. Go know.

Smooth Sailing? Hello?

The physical layout of the El Monaco was a big terrible awful vicious problem in terms of people movement, placement, and servicing. My master plan was based on mayhem, Hershey chocolate bars, and nausea. The motel had "developed" at random over the years. The deluxe main rooms were literally on the highway and amplified any sound of passing traffic through the cheap walls. Light sleepers were in hell. The Presidential Wing was in the rear by the pool. Any conversations whispered there bounced off the water and directly into those glamorous suites. The construction was the cheapest possible to obtain using government-rejected supplies, scab labor, (there were no unions anyhow), and left-over rusting and weather-decayed materials the carpenters lifted from their money-paying contracts with the Hilton Hawaii and Excelsior Roma.

The Cote D'or and Palm Beach Guest Houses by the pumps and cesspool systems were squeezed in between noisy motor sheds and facing makeshift parking lots. Their little windows opened to permit flying things with green and vicious orange eyes and wings to buzz into the five by seven roomettes. Yet other buildings containing two to seven bedrooms with community shower and toilet—sometimes in the hall, other times outside on the porch—were not easy to identify or locate. Room numbers were a creative puzzle with the prize being check-out time. We couldn't afford a real architect, and used the bank President's son-in-law instead, which guaranteed the loan for the faux brickface from New Jersey. Since most of these outhouses were there for a half-century but were part of different properties and shifted about by wind, mud, and time, the only unifying element was the melange of pastel Florida colors on the doors. This hodge-podge of slanted cottages was located, helter-skelter, wherever the swamp was least likely to swallow them.

To make it easy for me to show rooms, especially at 3:00 a.m. on stormy dark muggy scary nights, since most accommodations were nowhere near the registration desk, we bought a yellow four-seater golf cart. The flapping fringed awning and its colorful signage above was intended to accomplish two purposes: First, to let the prospective renter think this was some Hawaiian resort. Second, to not frighten the renter into thinking he had to walk through swamp-bog and snake-infested gook to some dark dank bunglehole. It might have worked out except Momma would always insist on charging three dollars up front for the ride, (many balked at this), and the choice of signage on the striped awning was questionable:

County Undertaker's Convenience Shuttle

If we took a brand-new cart, it would have cost double. It was a matter of value. I painted out the signage 12 times, it always shone through. I was not superstitious, but some renters were.

We recycled one outdoor platform that had served as a cover for a no longer functioning well into a share/suite for five by slapping together discarded row-boat boards as walls and plastic sheeting for a make-shift roof. I used it as an outdoor platform for the first White Lake Motel Danseuse Performing Arts Theatre way back in the early days, before we became the dreaded El Monaco. My doctor's daughter, Marian Dombeck, and I, in love with each other, (so long as no sex reared its head), danced away to all the Fred and Ginger recordings we owned. We tried to sell tix at one dollar to cover the cost of taps for our shoes, but without crowd-control techniques in place, people watched for free. Yet we, dancing fools, kept up that fine Hollywood tradition which says something I never could remember. Our performances were unfortunately interrupted when Dr. D. needed his 'nurse' and the motel needed another toilet unstuffed.

Now this outdoor dance space had a tar paper roof, two-foot by two-foot stall shower and micro-toilet in a narrow dark hallway that had an air porthole on the roof, and 6.2 bedrooms. The sign over the entrance declared:

Fountain Who Towers

Every room had a skeleton lock, since skeleton keys were a dime a dozen. Thus I was able to comfort fears of intrusion during the middle of the night that some picky guests had of being raped by some madman with a key to the room. Each key came with a tag that said, to wit:

"When you go to sleep, chew some gum and stuff it in the keyhole and anyone trying to open the door will get stuck, giving you enough time to holler for help. Don't look for a window under the curtains stapled to the blank wall. There are roof vents you can scream through by standing on top of your bed. Thank you, the management is not responsible!"

The key phrase was: *The management is not responsible.*

I always dreaded the looks on the faces of the unlucky renters of the bungleholes and shacks that were in the far-flung corners of our property. "Is it far?" they would ask, innocently. I tried not to make eye contact when I answered them and ushered them into my trusty black Buick convertible. The flags and balloons I had strung up on the car, like for a cheap low-life wedding, did not encourage confidence. That they had to get in a car made it clear this wasn't good news. It was terrible. I felt like a purser telling passengers on the Titanic that their rooms in steerage were convenient in case of hitting an iceberg, albeit in this case an iceberg named Teichberg.

But what could we do? It was all we had. Knowing what I know now, what I could have done was to dump the whole mess into the bank's hands, and disappear with a new identity in some third world place. Instead, I kept dumping hard-earned salaries after bad money into the bottomless cesspool a.k.a. White Lake.

While Lucille Ball, Tennessee Williams, Greta Garbo, and Cecil B. De Mille had yet to show up at the motel doorstep in these first few days of Woodstock, I did get my first taste of what was to come when a bright red Lincoln stretch limo drove up.

Its passenger was as conspicuous as his vehicle. He looked like Humpty Dumpty, but in omelet form, after the fall. I had no idea who this strange and massive protoplasm was, but he did present a business card. All I remember was that he was the Senior Vice President of something. I apparently did not look impressed enough because he loudly volunteered the extra news that he was Senior Vice President of the largest recording company in the world. Humpty claimed he had reserved five deluxe rooms and informed me that his security people would be along "momentarily." Seasons before, anyone who had reserved five deluxe suites would have impressed me. Now, I didn't have time to be impressed, and I didn't have five deluxe anything. And I was busy smelling the arrival of Eden. Since I had a weight problem to handle myself, I was always uncomfortable with people heavier than me. I always saw their battle of the bulge as a sure sign they were me, a few weeks ahead. And then he announced something new for my vocabulary:

"My *handler* will be here soon. My handler will handle everything."

This was the first time I'd heard the word "handler." What could need handling? Already, I wanted whatever a handler was. Was this a boy-toy? Something I could get into? The concept had such appeal. Oy, could I use a handler to handle whatever!

I didn't get a chance to ask, because Humpty was very in the now, and not in the moment that would momentarily come, and he wanted to know about his reservations.

"Who took your reservations? If you called on a Friday evening or on the Sabbath and a Russian-accented reservations agent was 'handling' the phone, forget about it. She doesn't write the reservation down between sundown to sundown. She just kept it in her head, which is not able to handle complicated items like reservations. Stuff in her head tends to be a permanent condition with her and the information would never get out of her head, onto her tongue, or onto a piece of paper. In any case, I don't have five rooms available now. If you want five rooms after August 19, we can do that."

Humpty did not take this news well. He started to sweat, like a reheated omelette, not a charming vision.

"Janis Joplin will be arriving by copter. She does not want to be annoyed by anybody. You must have some room where she can have privacy? Where no one can see her?"

And all I had left, in terms of housing, was "The Doll House" with its leaky ceiling and 4:00 a.m. shower-dripping restrictions. Hardly suited to my big idol, Janis. I would have offered her my room except I didn't have one.

There is a time for exaggerating, a time for omitting, a time for outright lying. This was none of those times. This was the time for telling the truth and kissing Janis Joplin goodbye. I told Humpty straight: "I have no actual rooms left. I have the "Doll House" and a community kitchen with shower curtains hanging from clothes lines that close off the hall and create five cubicles. These accommodations are not suitable for human consumption and certainly not for Janis Joplin. I can make a call to Grossinger's and see if Elaine has space."

"How far is this Elaine Gro... whatever?" Humpty asked.

"Nine miles."

"How far are we from the Festival site?"

"Four miles."

"I'll take the Doll House and kitchen."

Humpty paid cash in full. I was too ashamed to take him to his "accommodations" and sent Momma instead. She who genuinely believed these were acceptable, even homey, "rooms," could bring him there in good faith.

It was a brief round-trip tour. Humpty was back at the registration desk in a rage. For the first and last time in the history of the El Monaco, a customer received a cash refund.

"I told you it wasn't for Joplin."

I met Humpty again, years later in Paris. In the late seventies, I think. It was difficult not to recognize him. I'd never before and have never since met someone of his form. He was sitting in a bistro next to the St. Georges Theater where my musical comedy "Attention Fragile" was running. The cast and crew went there every night after the show. We were sitting at our same table in the corner, when Humpty rolls over and compliments Anny Duperey, the star of our show, on her performance. Anny's English is not too good when she doesn't have a script that she's memorized, so I stepped in and translated as best I could. When I finished, I gave him a handshake and told him I remembered him from Woodstock. I asked him if he remembered the El Monaco and our Doll House. He said he remembered nothing, explaining that he'd been tripping out on coke and a technicolor selection of pills the whole summer and Woodstock was just one big blur. He was functioning now as an advance man for a Queen Elizabeth-lookalike who had a magic monkey act that crossed international borders. In 1969? Joplin?

"I was a big fan of Joplin. But, I never knew her. Handlers? Woodstock? Hey, I could have been there but, then again, in those days, I didn't know where I was. Handlers? No, I've never had any handlers. Why?"

24 days or 33 days and counting...

The rooms were all rented. An army of my people were outnumbering the local Nazi bagel-makers and gay bashers. Music was in the air and I was having the time of my life! And Momma was so busy, she was off my case. For a while.

12

Prince of Bankers

23 days or 32 days and counting...

It was instantly essential that the Festival have a proper local bank account. Mike Lang came into the El Monaco bar late on a Friday afternoon carrying a heavy, bulging plastic bag. I was sorting out the overwhelming mess of bottles, glasses and leftovers from a party they'd had the night before. Mike gave me a peek inside his bag. I had never seen so much cash in my whole life. Hundreds of thousands of green dollars. Not Monopoly money. I thought maybe he was going to leave a big tip for the beer party from the night before. But no, Mike had other things on his mind. He asked me to accompany him across the road to the White Lake bank. He needed to set up some accounts for payroll, purchasing and immediate check-cashing abilities to pay the staff.

We walked into the bank and saw the long lines of farmers chewing their cud and dressed in politically correct plaid shirts, overalls, and dung-flavored boots. This was real country. Ralph Lauren, then unknown, was sitting on the floor sketching the outfits for some mad illusion about being a fashion maven. Ralph was always sitting on floors with his sketch pad. We stepped over him. This was not your Republican horsey set, this was your Republican smells-like-horsey set. It was Friday, which is payday in White Lake. And even farmers need weekend spending money for whatever else redneck farmers do when they're not farming or killing Bambi and her mothers.

I and Mike Lang did not fit in. I was wearing black designer jeans and a black designer shirt; a vivid color choice I still favor today. And Lang was wearing his fringed leather vest, bell bottom jeans and no shoes. And, of course, Lang was wearing his hair. His big mop of light brown ringlets, cascading down his face, his back and along his shoulders like one of those big English sheep-herding dogs.

Banks are usually quiet, but this one got so quiet that it absorbed sound. Everyone was all stares. Naked feet? Bare chest? Long heavy hair? Huge hair? Hair that was alive?

The decor was the Rooster and Eagle school of Howard Johnson-highway Americana. The architecture was Neo; Neo-Gothic, Neo-Roman, Neo-Greek and Neo-Americana. Some political error must have been made because the lobby centerpiece was a painting of White Lake, by the abstract expressionist Elliot Tiber.

Charlie Prince, a puffy man in some variation of poplin or seersucker suit, quickly came out of his office and rushed towards us. A move which management consultants in the 1980s and '90s would call "damage control." Suddenly the farmers, frozen in line, in time and space, thawed and started mumbling:

"Filthy hippies. Drug trash! City trash! Anti-Christs! Faggots! We'll get you, Tiber and Yasgur, too."

Lang smiled. I cringed. Prince rushed over, red-faced, looking at his two odd customers, his eyes, however, darting nervously among his bread-and-butter customers.

"Can I help you?"

"We'd like to open an account."

"We're not doing... I, can we talk... in private?"

Charlie pulled me to the side. His beaded perspiring face and neck began to do a dance of death on their own. He whispered:

"We've been doing business with your family for fourteen years. The bank took an ad in one of your theater programs. The bank helped defend your movie house when the Mother's Committee attacked it. The bank even bought your painting of White Lake hanging there in spite of the consensus that it doesn't look like any lake anybody here ever saw. We try to help our customers. But this is going too far. I don't own this bank. I'm only President of this branch of the bank. Not the whole bank. I just work here. We don't deal with subversive anarchists!"

Lang motioned to me. I shuttled back to him. He whispered: "Tell this dude I have $250,000 in cash in my shopping bag."

I relayed this information as coolly as Mike did: "Charlie, my associate, Mr. Lang, would like to open an account and deposit the $250,000 he has in his shopping bag."

Lang opened his bag just enough so that Prince and I could see stacks of green bills. Prince reached into the bag, took out a packet of fifty-dollar bills, and pulled one out. He held the piece of paper up to the light. His hand trembled, and the bill fluttered like Old Glory in the wind. Liquids oozed out of his pores and traveled down his neck, making him now both a figurative and a literal redneck.

"The bank is closed!" he shouted to everyone and no one. "The bank is closed. Everyone out, please! Now!"

Charlie Prince, President of the Sullivan County National Bank, personally ushered the remaining farmers out of his bank. A good ten of them were still on line and it was five minutes before three.

"Out!" President Prince shouted. "Out! We're closed."

Prince locked the doors and ushered me and Lang and the shopping bag into his office. The locals were now outside the building, their faces pressed against the bank's rooster-eagle windows. Charlie got very nice and proper the moment we had privacy.

"I'm Charles Prince, the President of Sullivan County National Bank. How can I help you, Mister... ?"

Mike explained that we needed to open several accounts then and now. The Woodstock business manager and accounting team would follow on Monday and would want to set up the payroll, check-cashing and other services the Festival would need. Charlie looked at me, then back at Mike who was casually laying packets of fifties on Charlie's desk.

"Tomorrow is Saturday. We're not open on Saturday."

"Elli, isn't there a bank in Monticello? That's only fifteen minutes away, right man?"

Mike's gentle question spurred President Prince into action. Suddenly he reached the bank's headquarters and had someone lasso its manager who was making sure he wasn't in the bank any later than 3:02 p.m. on a Friday.

"No, this is important, Goddammit! I've got Tiber here from the El Monaco with the Woodstock people. They want to open accounts and set up a payroll thing tomorrow. Yes I know tomorrow is Saturday you dope! Any city fool knows what day it is when a fool works in a bank. We have $250,000 here in cash for an initial deposit... Yes it's the El Monaco. No, not the bankrupt El Monaco account. He's with El Monaco. Are you guys a corporation? What is this cash? Who belongs to this cash? Where did all this wonderful cash come from?"

Mike Lang interrupted this barrage of questions with his beatific smile and a gentle suggestion:

"Elli, why don't we just go to Monticello? Isn't this the bank that's been threatening to foreclose the El Monaco?"

"Foreclose?" President Prince blubbered. "Foreclose? No, no, no, we've never thought of foreclosing on the El Monaco. We've been doing business for twenty years with the El Monaco. We're neighbors, Mr. Lang. See that painting on the wall in the lobby? The bank purchased that at one of the first annual White Lake Music and Art Festivals at the El Monaco Motel."

This highly picturesque President threw the dopey phone onto the floor and his hands did a Lambada as he futzed around his desk searching for account-opening forms. It took him four Sullivan County National Bank-embossed black ball points until he found one that wrote. Then he started scribbling information down, and kept asking for references, something concrete about the source of these funds. Mike rattled off the names and fancy titles of men on Wall Street, Beverly Hills mega-names, Hollywood and points west mega-corporations, and showed annoyance at having to continue since he was bearing big cash in his shopping bags.

As he handed Mike the forms to sign, Prince prattled on and on about the extensive banking services that were now at the instant disposal of Woodstock, not to mention his undying respect, admiration and support for the El Monaco and the esteemed Elliot Tiber, not to mention God and County. Oh, and the bank would provide free security, escorting him across the street to the El Monaco. In fact, Prince himself would do the escorting. I don't know if Mike heard a word, because Mike, for all his long hair and bare feet and his endless smile, was checking every form he signed, reading every word. This was no babe-in-the-White Lake-woods we were doing business with. And Mike knew what was what, which way was up, and if he had to

140

balance his Porsche in one hand and Joplin in the other, I was certain he could do it, with ease.

For the next 30 days, Charlie Prince honored his word. Prince and his minions did indeed escort large sacks of cash back and forth across Route 17B to the Disco men's room. Now I was using the graffiti hidden door as a hiding place for cash.

There were several apparitions reportedly emerging through this graffiti door during this period. No serious investigations netted any proof of phantoms or other-world creatures.

2,956 yenta kvetches alleged they were being stalked by bikers.

13

The Greatest Economic Wisdom
Ever Disgregarded

23 or 32 days and counting...

I grew up on movies. My fantasy was to make movies, write movies, direct movies, star in movies. Hollywood was my wet dream. It was an American sickness for a large portion of the population. As it turned out, just five years later I'd be making *High Street*—my first feature movie—in Brussels, which is culturally about as far from Hollywood as you can get. Go know. I didn't know. I hardly knew about that day.

The upcoming frenetic events as Woodstock took over the El Monaco were more than a stroke of good fortune—this was the embodiment of a lifetime of years of movie fantasies of a young boy in Brooklyn whose only effective escape from the hardware store from hell was to be found on a big silver screen. Whatever Hollywood fare played at the Marboro movie house in Bensonhurst, as long as it was Betty Grable, Maria Montez, Marx Brothers or Mae West, (as long as it wasn't about hardware stores), it was better than reality. This is not the place to go into the sex stuff in the children's section or the S & M stuff in the balcony. Enough to mention I was under 12 and none of that stuff had any identifying labels. I didn't initiate movie sex, they were doing it to me. And it did help me in those delicate formative years in ways and means that the Yeshivah of Flatbush didn't.

And yet, 20 years later, in 1969, it seemed that Hollywood was getting closer and coming to me. Almost. Go know that in just six years I'd be in Hollywood, an official Academy Awards film entrant! That is just one more direct ramification of Woodstock. If not for the threats of being sent to prison, I wouldn't have run off to live in Europe. If I hadn't been in Europe, I'd never have made that movie.

I'm asked about what I got out of the Festival. A new lease on life, which is a whole lot. It's been everything.

Hollywood came to White Lake in droves. In addition to the snow blizzard falling in August, there was the allure of money, music and deals. There were executives from Warner Brothers, NBC, ABC, CBS and Paramount, most record label execs, managers of rock stars, agents, would-be agents, wannabe rock stars, wannabe stars, fuckers and fuckees.

The local population, as some of the newspapers would later write, was equal to the size of Oklahoma City or Phoenix. And while the media reported on every hairlip and belly button of every aspect of Woodstock and Bethel and Yasgur, not one included a single breath about the approximately 100,000 gay men and lesbian women who were there to help build the Festival and, later on, to hear, live, and create the music. So, being a part of that closeted group then, and as one who came out in 1979 and has been out and kicking since, I want to set the record *straight* here and now! We were there, everywhere, then; we're here and there and everywhere, now.

Local land owners with sharp business minds refused to rent space to hippies. Police hassled those roadies who tried to park on the roadside instead of providing help. I rented out spaces to all comers, provided water and electricity hookups, and juggled according to the flow. But ultimately, there was no more room at this inn.

Prepping the land at Yasgur's to accommodate all these arrivals would be no mean feat and would take time. The stage and support facilities that had yet to go up would require the logistics of building an instant city.

Lang asked me if they could park trucks and store equipment on the El Monaco lawn until the farm site was ready to accept the heavy arrivals. He promised the Festival would restore my lawns to their original condition.

"Lawn? Restore our lawn? We don't have a lawn. We have a bog! You don't have to restore it! If you kill our bog, you'll be doing ecology a favor! Please, take our bog! Use our bog!"

Mike indicated he had a budget for such expenses, and was paying others so it was only correct to pay rent for ours.

"Park anything, anywhere, for as long as you like. If you knock down a bungalow, don't worry about it. Any destruction of my bungleholes will not only improve my property but be an ecological gift that should be recognized by the Fullbright Foundation or the Nobel committee. I'm happy. My rooms are rented. I made my mortgage payment. I'm socking away a bit of extra. I'll earn a salary for the first time in 14 years! Park and pay whatever you want. Do whatever you want. You want I should kill God? I'll do it!"

And again he gave me cash. He got on the horn and gave instructions to others on horns who, in turn, got horny too. Oy.

Within hours, vehicles representing the breadth of the entire automotive production lines of the 1960s roared up Route 17B and into the three El Monaco driveways.

All this action was a tonic for Poppa. He took on a new zest and found strength despite his failing health. He had been moping around the compound bent over, stooped in disappointment and pain, but now, suddenly, he graciously guided trucks into a maze of impromptu parking spaces. Using a naked broom handle to direct the steady flow of people and machines, he looked like a symphony conductor—albeit in baggy beige trousers and a wrinkled buttoned-down shirt that wouldn't stay tucked in. A pre-Ralph Lauren look for only three dollars per bag of Salvation Army shmatas.

And apparitions and phantoms were sighted here and there.

Mamma was happy because she, in her own words, "likes to floit" and had found young people who, unlike her beloved son, thought she was cute. Her cholunt, dreaded by all her relatives with the lone exception of my father—who was rather indiscriminate in his gustatory impulses—was a big hit among the cognoscenti who saw this as an ethnic variant on *cassoulet.*[1] I was delighted to see Mother distracted and focusing on anybody but me. At first I issued gastronomic warnings, and scurried around frantically trying to beat off the Ex Lax movement, but she was too fast for me.

On top of my new role as field consultant for the largest outdoor event in the world at that time, there was additional handling that needed to be handled—fabricated by snakes from under the rocks.

[1]A meaty, beany, fatty French dish.

Jealous neighbors filed complaints about every minute occurrence both real and imaginary. They called the state troopers every hour on the hour to demand immediate investigations of the proprietors of the El Monaco. Complaints included wholesale prostitution, white slavery, drug rings, child abuse (before that term was popular, so it didn't get much attention), violations of state liquor laws, violations of multiple housing occupancy limits, and a host of real and imagined obstructions of American patriotic responsibilities. All this at the El Monaco, and committed by the hand of a Jew, also a pervert and a city fella to boot.

Bella Menifelli, a big woman with wire hair curlers surgically implanted in her skull, who was a perennial in a nearby rooming house with a window facing the lake, personally dropped by to express her immense displeasure directly to the CEO of the board of the offending local establishment—to wit, the El Monaco. She was very big on adjectives. She called us communists, kidnappers, liberals, Christ-killers, mother fornicators, faggots, bus-pass abusers and, of course, the worst adjective in the informed dictionary of her brain was that three-letter special: "Jew." She claimed that her son was a big judge in Hoboken who lived next door to Frank Sinatra's cousin.

"I'm calling my son collect if you Jews don't stop this Festival! I have connections! Ask anybody in White Lake what my word means! It's my last warning! We don't need any more Jews in Sullivan County and we certainly don't need no queers!"

Unfortunately, that wasn't Bella's last word. Nor was it her first. For a good five years, she made our bar a weekly stop on her list. She'd buy a bear and a Stewart's Infra-Ray authentic Italian something parmigiana hero and settle into the bar stool nearest the entrance. In between mouthfuls she'd bad-mouth anyone who passed by and her closing speech was always the same:

"I am here a witness to everything you Jewish hotel owners are up to. Prostitutes in the bar! Prostitutes in the bedrooms! Prostitutes out on Route 17B, non-stop. I'm calling my son the judge who lives next door to Frank Sinatra's cousin. And when I tell him what's going on here at the El Monaco, they'll close you down and burn you up. Why don't you people go back wherever you come from? Wouldn't you all be happier in a land where big noses are considered attractive?"

She would then exit to great applause from whoever happened to be in the bar. And she usually flopped onto 17B, giving her index finger a good workout en route to her slanted flowered wallpapered roomette. Quelle classe!

Route 17B, a simple two-lane country road, had transformed itself into a four-lane highway. State Police were stationed at the intersection's only traffic light, a yellow blinking thing that had its own meaning. Too high for drivers to see until they passed it, the troopers now installed temporary stop signs and red stop lights in every direction. None of it made any sense, but it was getting so mobbed, it wouldn't matter. For the present, it was essential some kind of scarecrow or animated dummy give directions to the farm.

Health inspectors, fire inspectors, water inspectors, air inspectors, anyone with a license to inspect anything, knocked on the El Monaco door. The neighbors complained to every authority they could find, accusing us of breaking any minuscule ordinance they could dream up. We were trespassing, we were fire hazards, we were moral hazards, we were health hazards, we were even permitting Royalists quarter as the Revolutionary soldiers were attacking Fort Sumner or whichever British enclave may have been in the vicinity of the Hudson, 70 miles away.

More current at least were the hippies swimming in White Lake without paying the illegal entry fees. And after swimming, these perverts began washing themselves with soap, and were fornicating other persons in the lake. Surely this was polluting the waters. We were generically hazardous to the local health. Vasmer, the dimwit grocer, complained that hippies came in to make purchases and were scaring off the regular customers. The Ritz movie house manager complained that the hippies loitered in front of the theater, and were scaring away the respectable cinema crowds. He canceled *Finian's Rainbow*. He had to board up the salle because hippies showed every intention of sleeping in the seats and squatting in the aisles. When the rains came later on, the manager could have opened the doors to let the kids find shelter, but he didn't.

My first line of defense was to act within my rights and order Bella, the inspectors, and the hordes of wannabe litigants off my property. My useless pleas about freedom of expression, the right of all people

The Holy Waters of White Lake,
1969, during Woodstock.

to use public facilities which included roads, public bodies of water, and stores that were "open to the public" accomplished nothing. Liberal or democratic principles were not in the lexicon of White Lakers, Bethellers, or Sullivanites.

My legal quotations had no impact other than to provoke these brain-dead non-persons to hurl an assortment of threats towards me and my family.

But where I was flustered and angry and outraged, Mike Lang was a solid rock of strength and calm. Like, wow, man, cool:

"Hey, it's no problem. Relax. Enjoy. We've got everything under control. We'll have our people deal with it. Not to worry."

Lee Mackler Blumer, Lang's right hand and security administrator, enlisted my help coordinating housing for the Festival staffers and scores of other people who needed housing. El Monaco of the slanted floors and dubious accommodations was booked solid with Woodstock staff and administration through the end of the Festival. So, all the Festival performers would have to be housed elsewhere. My fantasies of The Who, Joan Baez, Blood Sweat and Tears, Santana, Jimmy Hendrix, Joplin, and my great passion, Barbra

Streisand, parading through the Presidential Wing and joining in the post-performance audience discussion groups in the Underground Cinema, would never come true. In my heart of hearts, I knew that air conditioning, blinds that closed, door knobs that turned, toilets that flushed, floors that were level, and rooms that had room, not to mention walls, were amenities that would be considered necessary by the performers. Stars, after all, can be so fussy. I called Elaine Grossinger. She cursed me out and told me that Grossinger's would never host hippie filth trash. I was offended that this woman, the mother of my former art students, would treat me that way. I foolishly was overwhelmed by her and who I thought she was, and so I was wrong to try and appease her ignorance by begging for housing only the artists, some of the great musical talents of our time.

"Elliot, are you mad? I have all the world's greatest musical talents of our time here all the time. Your filthy shoddy schleppy collection of dirty drugged-out hippies have no hope of stinking up my beautiful hotel!"

I assumed that was a 'no.' I told Elaine that one day I'd tell the world that years ago she had served me shrimp salad. Shrimp in any form is not kosher. Grossinger's entire foundation was built on kosher everything. On the over-rated kosher grounds, in her kitchen, in her house, with her own hands, non-kosher shrimp? On the hallowed glatt kosher grounds of Grossinger's, shrimp, not only non-kosher, it is unkosher, it is traife. It's a slap in God's face! And all these years, thousands and thousands of innocent Jewish guests have come to her kosher hotel. It's incredible to me now that any of this shit went on about such junk.

"Okay Elaine. Give me back my painting, and turn the page!"

I next called Phil Greenwald, owner of the famed Concord, (without the 'e'), Lillian Brown at Brown's Hotel, dopey home of the famed Jerry Lewis Room, (who cares now, nobody, but they cared then), and a slew of other lesser-known, but equally dopey and unglamorous hotels of the Catskills. But the answers were the same. No one wanted to house hippies, drugged-out rock stars and their groupies. Klein's Tophill Cottages, Klein's Hilltop Cottages (no relation), Klein's Mountainview Hotel (no relation), Klein's Lakeview Hotel (no relation), Goldberg's Lakeview, Warshinsky's Mountain

View and Lakeview, were equally appalled at the very idea of defiling the mountains and memories of their parents with these infidels of the long hair and loud music. Almost every mountain-top view and view top-mountain house/hotel/bunglehole colony/rooming house did not wish to pollute their dumps with Woodstock trash.

Desperate, I went for the bottom of the barrel and called establishments of the El Monaco variety. I called far-flung relatives of the long-deceased owners of the many defunct little bungalow colonies and hotels. I sent runners to the cemeteries to look up names of the long-departed owners so we could contact their heirs. Cash offers to these surprised inheritors of tax-closed hotels met with delight and joy. They had long ago given up hope of any income from their slanted multi-occupancy buildings. So this once-in-a-lifetime opportunity brought activity and the smell of paint and noises of Woostockers hooking up water, electric and, in short, noises of life. It was springtime in the mountains once again. Former resort owners were stunned that people were coming to the Catskills, and ready to rent these flophouses. Their minions quickly got things running, doors and windows unboarded and readied the places for spartan but usable living.

And I enjoyed so many different aspects of all this 'do.' Nobody bothered to fill out applications for permits for anything. Hotels, bars, eateries, facilities of every description with long-ago invalidated licenses, were being enlisted to join the new nation rapidly emerging in this flowerless pit. The best part was watching White Lake come to life, like some kind of Jewish Brigadoon. I knew these weren't going to be fit accommodations, but the welcome mats were certainly more humane than the obnoxious remarks and attitudes of the big guys. Grossinger's was a relic and a fossil, only Elaine didn't know it. Now she does. Years later, her clever insightful marketing netted a bankruptcy, and her hotel was leveled to make room for condos.

Still, with all this activity and renting and fixing-upping, it was still impossible to house everyone near the farm. Every available room within a 50-mile radius was booked. And still there wasn't enough to meet the needs, evident by the eventual sleeping under the skies of hundreds of thousands of happy hippies.

Meanwhile, Pop guarded the El Monaco grounds as he had since 1955, but this time with zest, pride and joy. He didn't care what nasty junk anybody said, or about the names called him or his son or his wife. His natural high was seeing 'his' 20 years of hard work a success. A success that might not last more than 60 days, but one he had given up all hope of. When local hoods drove by to taunt him, he proudly pointed to the over-full compound, a sure sign of income. Success by any of the Jews was a sore irritant to the native boobs. The rednecks screamed and complained about their long list of grievances, some of which are indicated here:

"Jack, you and your son Elliot are destroying this town. The roads are impassible for the decent and God-fearing Christians. You are housing the anti-Christ! There are depraved goings-on in those flower-painted school buses. These aren't our upstanding citizens! These are communists! Reds! This is America's heartland. There is sex going on in this town! This is indecent!"

The rednecks continued harassing Pop and me during and long after the festival was over and gone. The odd thing is that it brought my Pop and me closer than we'd ever been. I can't remember more than a quartet of times that we'd ever laughed so much. I can't remember any other time when Pop put his arm around my shoulder.

I can still hear those scratchy redneck voices screaming, particularly about the yellow school buses that had been defiled into whore houses on wheels. For some reason, the neighbors held Pop and me responsible for the desecration of this hallowed icon of innocent childhood—the yellow bus. And that sex might be occurring behind the little curtained windows of these flower-festooned buses was a concept that was un-American, pink, red, and definitely communist.

While the rednecks' stance may have been a prescient pre-cursor to the more successful moral majority movement of the early 1970s, it was, in the balance, ineffective. So, the locals upgraded their schtick into threats:

"We'll close you down, Jack Teichberg. The El Monaco is violating every law on the books. We'll get the judge in Monticello to take away your operating license. We'll have your fucking faggot son Elliot, arrested. We'll have all those cars impounded."

Pop responded with an imagination and energy I had never imagined his quiet, gentle demeanor could produce: First there were the tar tastings. Pop backed up his Teichberg White Lake Roofing Company truck next to the main entrance of the El Monaco. Sitting in the truck bed, he heated up his tar kettle and stood there stirring like a witch out of Macbeth. I love the smell of hot tar. Still do. He graciously offered tastes of steaming jet-black tar to every town jerk who passed by and hassled us. After a day of tarring, Pop got bored and got on top of the motel roof—and you thought roofers didn't have a sense of humor—with a big garden hose and cooled down an assortment of town jerks and misfits. Another day it was apple pitching, like a scene out of the wild apple orchard in the *Wizard of Oz*. And his final play—which I really didn't believe he'd do—was the cesspool trick. I am not able to detail the cesspool trick. What I can tell you is that it was quite effective in keeping low-life trash from messing with us. The news of Pop's prowess in the plumbing arts spread quickly by word of hose, nose and mouth.

22 days or 19 days and counting...

The locals demanded to see me and "the wild-haired man with all the money." My Pop stood his ground on the back of his roofing truck, which by now he outfitted as if it were a tank. I was twice the height of my father, and joined him on the back bed of the truck.

While these local outbursts were occurring on the El Monaco lawn, the Woodstock worker bees were busy building the Festival superstructure; the scaffolding, stage, food and sleeping tents, toilet facilities, and so on. Staffers scurried through the El Monaco, doing laundry, cleaning and all the other things necessary to keep an organization moving forward, all at a dizzying pace that is best summed up as "just to the left of out-of-control."

When I wasn't involved in riot control, I shuttled back and forth with Charlie Prince and the bank deposits. Pop was having the high time of his entire life. His weak frame and condition were overshadowed by the glistening sparkle in his eyes. I was exceptionally happy that he was getting some hard-earned rewards which, up to then, I had been certain that he'd never see in this lifetime. Momma was in heaven counting cash, hiding cash in her secret places, so much so, that she didn't even notice four entire Sabbaths. These were all drastically new experiences for us. Depositing cash rather than begging for loan extensions. Six hundred and fifty percent occupancy was totally new. As for Mom, her religious experience of this new prosperity was so intense she saw no religious conflict here. She has always been into a nightly prayer thing; a nightly showdown with God, a lengthy discussion of everything going on in her life, her children's lives, and any other lives that affect her life. Her new closing lines, which I overheard night after night through the matzo-thin plywood office wall and quote as best I can, were approximately:

"God, I know you will excuse me for handling money on these few Sabbaths as this is my desperate time of need. I know you wouldn't have sent this festival if you didn't want to help us, so I am working every day to show mine gratitude. Did Noah not work on the ark every day for forty days? As soon as this festival you sent us is over, I will make a nice donation and I'll make Elli go to shule, say Yizkor, get kosher, find a nice Jewish wife and in general act normal again! Thank you God for saving us from ruin."

24 days or 20 days and counting...

Early one morning, angry as hell and deciding they weren't going to take it anymore, the cranky town elders, oblivious yet irritated at the same time to my great economic import and the sudden new breath of life in this former dead thing called Le Lac Blanc, called a meeting of the Town Board. The subject? Cancellation of Elliot Tiber's Music and Art Festival permit.

My gut reaction was total panic! These dopes were going to kill off this golden goose. They were going to choke the few gasps of air the entire county had experienced in decades. These jerks were going to toss out the biggest economic boon to a resort community possibly of the century! I had proposed Bethel establish, with Woodstock Ventures, some kind of annual festival 'do' according to the style of Tanglewood in nearby Pennsylvania. Such an annual event would draw national respect, year-round business, revitalize the dead economy and, of course, raise property values. The tax base would be so overflowing that the local schools, facilities, and lifestyles would be enriched beyond their imaginations. Nothing doing. They didn't need Kikes and Fags coming into their secluded preserve and allowing dirty hippies to have sex in their lake and rape their wives and children.

Again with those rapes? There was not one rape or even complaint of actual rape for the entire three months that hundreds of thousands roamed them thar hills.

So this new meeting caused me to do what I knew how to do best. As an Aries and a pragmatist and a pessimist, fighting off my usual Aries optimism, I panicked. I called Lang. He listened, smiled, and did not panic. I looked for some trace of panic or despair in his hazel eyes (were his eyes hazel?), but saw only serenity and comfort. He picked up one of those new 200 working phones at the El Monaco, and punched in his people. Mike assured me that he was in control and he knew who to call and what to do.

Within two hours a helicopter whirred above the motel. Its passengers included two "definitely non-local attorney-types" and a lithe blonde woman who looked like Faye Dunaway. Well, if she wasn't Faye Dunaway, she sure looked exactly like Faye Dunaway, sounded exactly like Faye Dunaway. Besides, it made perfect sense to me that Faye Dunaway would be on our side in this battle against the Teichberg Curse. I will have you know, however, that I did not embarrass the Teichberg clan by dribbling all over Faye Dunaway. I was restrained, polite and quietly led them all to Mike's room in the Presidential Wing. I maintained whatever dignity I could, considering that Faye Dunaway was a hair's-breath behind me. People all around us were staring and whispering. I knew the fascination was with Faye. Yes, she asked me to call her Faye.

This was a key strategy meeting, and nervous and apprehensive as I was, I also was on-the-spot in love with Faye. Though F.D. wasn't one of the many silver-screen stars I'd been paging on my navy loudspeakers for so many years, she *was* a bonafide silver-screen star. More important, she was here. I was here. It was bashert we'd go off into the future together. With my new-found value systems struggling to replace the old ones, I still plotted asking her to pose for pictures by the pool and endorse the motel for the following season's singles weekends. Was I a fool here or what?

Faye, your entire life will take a bizarre turn or something, if you take me home to Hollywood with you forever. If she didn't want to take me to Hollywood, I'd settle for any location she named that didn't have a motel or a Yenta within a thousand miles.

Everyone discussed strategies and operative plans. I am certain I was asked stuff and that I replied stuff, but so starry-eyed was I, that I can't recall anything. No doubt Lang or Lee or the others would recall, but I don't want to ever chance it that they would shatter my fond romantic memories of F.D. by telling me that wasn't actually F.D., but Sheila Slotnik or some such other person. Anyway, I had trust in whatever they were going to do.

And I had no confidence in anything I would have thought of doing since the entire gesheft was beyond anything I'd ever done or thought of doing.

At eight that evening, the attorneys, Dunaway, and Lang piled into one of Lang's limos and rode one mile down Route 55 to the schoolhouse in Kauneonga. The thinking was that I should arrive there in my own wheels. I hated the thought of being separated from F.D., but it had to be done. The fate of Woodstock was hanging in the balance. The fate of El Monaco was hanging. I was hanging. The town was ready to make earrings out of my testicles, so it was the time for serious stuff. It was a bumpy mile along a pot-hole riddled country road, past faded houses in various states of neglect and disrepair. The mile-long stretch seemed deserted. Not a house light was on.

When we reached the schoolhouse, however, there was no shortage of signs of life. Everyone within twenty square miles seemed to be there. There wasn't a parking space available. This was certainly not going to be like the meetings I had attended for fourteen years, where four or five cranky old men showed up to vote "No" to anything except busses with curtains.

It felt like we were about to attend a Salem witch trial, with the bad news being we were the witches. The cinderbox building was packed horizontally and vertically. Those who hung from the ceilings only missed using nooses, which would have been a decided improvement. There were no seats except for the four rusty wooden folding chairs saved for us in the front row. I never did understand how wood chairs could rust, but the rule of thumb I found useful was that if it was in White Lake, it could rust. New wooden pool-side chairs, when unwrapped, rusted instantly. God worked his wonders in White Lake.

On a platform in the front were the town supervisor, the no-neck postmistress (his wife), a couple of Board members and other undistinguished scum members of the town government. The noise level in the room was painful. The sounds emitted by so many witless boobs all in one small room were enough justification to declare the entire band of nitwits out of order.

The good news was that half the hall was filled with friendly faces among the enemies. Owners of the dives that we had rented, which had been empty for maybe 50 years, were there. They understood the economic blessings of the century and were most grateful. Those store owners who had stocked up with supplies at my suggestion were also reaping the early rewards of Woodstock and were naturally on our side. Then there were rednecks and people who came out of the woods and swamps who had not seen electricity or running water in decades. They too sat and stared into my face. They couldn't speak English, but their faces spoke volumes about hate! Wonderful. A terrific feeling.

The bad news was the other half of the hall was filled with the enemies, a frightening group of men and women, their necks glowing red under the harsh light of the fluorescent fixtures. Lang, the attorney, Faye Dunaway and I sat up front at a small folding table. The attorney had a folder with papers. Lang had a folder with papers. F.D. crossed her legs and the room looked. I had no folder. No papers. I was just now trembling as I felt my life was over. So naive. Lang told me to be cool. He was cool. The Woodstock people were cool. Everybody else was not cool. I got the feeling that F.D. was a smart plant by Lang. Okay.

The Town Meeting got underway according to rules of procedure unknown to civilized man. One by one, each Board member on the podium spoke to the destruction, devastation and degradation the Woodstock Festival and Elliot Tiber were visiting upon their fair town. Then they cited a litany of laws and ordinances which they claimed were being violated. And finally, there was a call for the rescinding of Tiber's Music Festival and Art Fair permit.

When Lang nodded to me it was time for me to speak, I asked for the floor. There were shouts of "Out of Order." The friendly half of the room shouted down the unfriendly half. The third half stared. A definitely-not-a-Rhodes Scholar type called upon Lucifer to do his stuff and, with a crack in his voice wailed, "Visit thy rancor and punish these long-haired demons and give Elliot Tiber a double dose of your most gruesome curses, Amen!"

Then one of the leading ladies of White Lake Society said something about exterminating that fucking permit, Tiber and his Chamber of Commerce, arrest every person in White Lake and at Yasgur's farm who is not a resident. I thought surely this was the appropriate moment for me to ask for the floor, slanted though it was. Someone shouted that I was out of order, but the friendly half of the hall shouted back and I was granted three minutes to present my case. This is sort of what I said:

"As president of the White Lake/Bethel Chamber of Commerce, and owner of the only motel that is an 'Approved Member' in White Lake, I have been advised by legal counsel that my permit is legal and valid and that there is no proper legal cause for cancellation of this Music Festival. I have been running my Music and Art Festival for almost ten years..."

At this point, I was rudely interrupted by vicious cat-calls and shouts, not to mention a series of rude and scatological remarks. But I persevered.

Town Meeting, Bethel Chamber of Commerce,
votes "Yes" for our permit, 1969

"What is wrong with you people here? All of White Lake is on the brink of annihilation—or haven't you noticed? There is no tourist industry here—or haven't you noticed? There is no traffic, no business, no people paying taxes for badly-needed town facilities. We're dying! Or, haven't you noticed?

"A golden goose has mysteriously landed on Max Yasgur's farm. And there are enough golden eggs to feed us all. This Woodstock Festival is putting us on the map. We will have ten, fifteen, maybe twenty thousand people coming to our dead resort town. That's ten or fifteen thousand live people with cash in their pockets, buying, renting, spending. Maybe this is a one-shot deal and if it is, it's income for all of us. But better yet, maybe this could be a permanent, annual festival like Tanglewood and Edinburgh. Every year, we could have tourists and income. We could nourish the arts! How can you stand there spitting curses on a miracle! What are you scared of? Long hair and new music?"

The booing and hissing was recorded and later used as a soundtrack for 'Killer Tomatoes Eat Giant Chicken Aliens.' I gave up and gave the floor to Lang. Wildman Mike Lang introduced himself, and with his transcendent smile, coolly outlined the Woodstock Festival's plans to abide by all the laws and how they would work alongside the community to restore any property damaged after the Festival audience left.

He also added three magic words: "twenty-five," "thousand," and "dollars." (A huge sum in 1969, worth ten times as much in 1994.) This sum would be given to the community to be used in any way deemed suitable by yet another town hall meeting.

At the mention of the money, the booing and catcalls briefly subsided. Mike continued speaking, dryly and without emotion. He listed potential benefits of the Festival to the entire White Lake/Bethel community. He noted that the Festival was building an international telecommunications center at the El Monaco and Yasgur's and that the Festival would reach audiences around the world. This was, he said, again uttering more magic words, publicity worth millions of dollars to White Lake, Bethel and Sullivan County. This was publicity that could bring new businesses, investors, tourists. This was an opportunity for rebirth that any other resort community would pray for.

Hecklers drowned out the rest of his speech with shouts of: "Corruption! Mafia! Commies! Degenerates! Perverts!"

Finally, a Woodstock representative stood up and outlined the legal parameters of the situation. He pointed out that Woodstock had a valid legal permit which gave them specific legal rights. Further, the Festival had procured additional permits from various health and public assembly departments in the county. The Festival was meeting sanitation, health and security requirements. The bottom line was clear. The Festival organizers were acting responsibly. Any twit could see that. And there were plenty of twits there.

Max Yasgur stood up. The room fell silent. Yasgur described his experiences with the Festival organizers. He said they were ethical and straight-forward. He stated the obvious; that he owned his farm and had a right to lease it as he pleased. There were no laws on the books outlawing or limiting public assembly in White Lake that month.

The twit part of the crowd booed and hissed. The supporters booed and hissed the hissers and booers. Accusations of Jewish greed and calls for boycotts of Yasgur's dairy products ricocheted off the cinder-block walls. The slanted floor creaked under the thundering stamping feet. Clark Gable and Myrna Loy left the schoolhouse in utter disgust. Apparitions and phantoms left the schoolhouse due to nausea.

The meeting on that sweet gentle summer night in an innocent schoolhouse in the Catskill Mountains accomplished nothing. There was no vote taken. The Lady's Auxiliary lost its social graces. Not one ginger snap cookie or glass of lemonade was offered. No one asked us out for a beer blast, not even a clam bake. No one asked how my hunting season had been. For a moment I felt guilty for personally ruining the cultural and social traditions of this former Kauneonga American Indian community that the benevolent white animal killers and beer drinkers had liberated a hundred years before. But that guilty moment quickly passed. Everybody left the schoolhouse more convinced than ever of the position they had taken when they had entered hours before.

That week the town power brokers met secretly and voided the El Monaco Music and Art Festival permit. While they were at it, they created an ordinance that limited public gatherings to fifty people. The local papers dutifully reported these legislative actions, but no one seemed to think that this fifty-person limit would apply to the annual firehouse picnic or Sunday church services. The White Lake grapevine was now quoting unnamed sources that 400,000 people were coming to the concert and that the Governor was putting the Army and Navy on alert. Navy? White Lake is major-league inland!

14

Meanwhile, Back at the El Monaco...

20 days or 30 days and counting...

Meanwhile, ticket sales went bananas at El Monaco. They were bought by music stores, concert bureaus, shops, newsstands, and wherever people of good taste congregated. Not in Kauneonga, however.

The enormous crowds of tens of thousands were now at the site, milling about outside the hastily-erected fences; things were getting very uncool. Skirmishes and arguments and totally inadequate security began to get serious. The fencing wasn't going to hold, that was clear. I wasn't there, being overwhelmed at El Monaco, so all this is from hearsay. Those in charge had no way of knowing in advance that the crowds would swell to the hundreds of thousands. The control systems they were preparing would certainly have been enough for the expected 50,000 or 75,000. The population was exploding so rapidly that it was only a matter of time before the wire fences would give way.

Arguments about price gouging, inadequate toilets, drinking water, food service, prices of staples, and all sorts of unforeseen logistical needs were taking over, escalating into very heated dangerous situations.

In order to prevent the situation from turning nasty and becoming lethal, Lang sent out an announcement to the TV news media. All entry to the Festival would now be free. This wise and intelligent action by Woodstock Ventures was the responsible thing to do under the treacherous circumstances.

20 days or 19 days and counting...

Somewhere in the middle of all this, I juggled quickly diminishing supplies of food and beverages. By this time, the newspaper and television reporters were citing figures of 200,000 to 750,000 people expected in Bethel.

I couldn't get the wholesalers to send trailers full of snack foods and sodas. I attempted to purchase supplies from other counties, but without standing credit, and with rumors rampant about chaos and mayhem, no companies would deal with me. I couldn't ask Woodstock Ventures to bother about my immediate needs, since they were in over their necks just trying to stay afloat. Mike was commuting to financial centers to raise more urgently-needed funds. Rumors were in charge, unfortunately.

Suppliers ridiculed my requests for dozens of trailers of Coke, hot dogs, soap, bottled water and other essentials. When I insisted on my quantities, the suppliers insisted back that I pay up front in cash. The more they laughed at my estimates, the more scared I got—I knew I needed all that food, but what if... I'd be stuck with a life-time supply of hot dogs and Coke and my whole nest egg gone. Pop and I talked about it all and we concluded it would be safe to invest in two trailers of Cokes and hot dogs with fifty more trailers on standby. So we paid for two trailers and we got two trailers. As it turned out, we could have sold five times fifty. But the fifty on standby would never be able to get through the crowded roads. For the first time in our lives, we caught up to the bills. If we extended ourselves on any risk, if it rained, which we assumed it wouldn't, if the town managed to stop the whole thing, if the marines or national guard sealed off the entire county, we would have to eat twenty million hot dogs or go to prison. We decided on the safe route.

Meanwhile, out back at Yenta's Pancake House, the big boys arrived. The summer before, I had painted it red, white and blue, naively thinking the frenchie colors would permit passersby to think they were in Paris. I filled our sad-looking outdoor tables and umbrellas onto the highway out front, and played Piaf. The menu boasted misspelled french crepes which were still my screwy pancakes, but thinner, smaller-portioned, and with Gallic names replacing American names. So if there were any people hungry to experience a bit of Paris outdoor cafe life, they didn't stop in. I had the same number of travellers I had with the Streisand and Redford stacks with maple syrup. I didn't understand that people accepted the International House of Pancakes as international and not El Monaco's Yentas! Was a 20 percent increase too much to expect in White Lake? Twenty percent of zero being as much zero as two percent was, this corporate identity make-over was not a brilliant marketing move. So, as far as Yenta's was concerned, even I, the stubborn optimist, had given up.

Now, this forgotten jewel of White Lake real estate suddenly became the beneficiary of that old real estate saw: Location, Location, Location. Offers piled up to rent Yenta's Pancake House. This was another opportunity I didn't get quite right.

I was so excited that anyone had any interest in it at all, that I rented it to the first cash offer. It was two thousand dollars. Again, a lot of money in 1969. More than we ever netted in a busy season. A whole lot of money for a business that, in all the years I'd been painting and repainting it, naming and renaming it, had never recouped the cost of my paint. You have to understand that three months earlier, for another ten dollars, this fellow could have bought all of White Lake. So to me, this two thousand dollars was astronomical.

Not only did I take the two thousand dollars, but I didn't sign anything with anybody. I was naive and desperate and so hungry for some income that I would have sold my mother to these people. I would have paid them the two thousand dollars to take her away with them and not to tell me where they came from. I didn't even get names, phone numbers, addresses, or any statement of intent. For all I knew, they could have been lying about coming there in stretch limos to sell hot dogs and sandwiches. For all I knew, they may have wanted to run a drug operation and a prostitution house next to Momma's kosher kitchen.

14 days or 19 days and counting...

Uncertainty grew painful as the new tenants occupied the premises. Their crew looked as if it had been supplied by Central Casting for a Chicago gangster movie. Truckloads of food, beverages, kitchen supplies, dishes, and normal restaurant things started to arrive, and thick-necked workers hauled them to the second floor above the restaurant. Then came the overseas shipping boxes and crates stamped "Bogota" and "Mexico."

Mom went over to a handsome silver-haired guy in a suit who seemed to be in charge to ask if they knew the rules of kosher cooking. The man politely listened and made notes on a small dead-lizard-covered pad. Mom wanted to go inside and check, but he wouldn't let her. Pop got nervous and, saying there was trouble with the plumbing, asked to go upstairs to work on the bathrooms. They refused his help, insisting that they were satisfied with the toilets as they were. In two weeks, if anything needed fixing, he could fix them. Meanwhile, the silver-haired gent said, they were trying to get the place together in time to open for dinner.

Later that night, a convention of expensive cars pulled in and parked at random across the muddy lawn surrounding Yenta's. It occurred to me that maybe we were getting in over our heads. They made me nervous. I offered them a full refund if they would get out. The thug informed me the restaurant was temporarily closed for redecorating and that if I wanted to have pancakes I should go fuck myself.

Nice. That was not how El Monaco conducted its public relations. No matter how vile our accommodations, we never did interfere in people's private sexual functions. I insisted that the proprietor who rented the facility come to my office no later than later. Sooner would be better.

Later that day the Yenta's manager, accompanied by a very tall, very wide, and very dense-looking male person, came into the El Monaco bar to "talk." They made it clear that they had paid in advance for two week's rental of Yenta's and that any assistance from the El Monaco staff would be considered interference and a violation of their rental rights. Pop insisted that we were responsible for anything that happened on our premises and said we would inspect the restaurant.

I didn't recognize these men and asked for the one I had in fact rented the place to.

"Oh, Johnny? He got called to an important executive planning session in Sicily. We bought out his lease. You want to see our bill of sale or what?"

"Johnny? He said his name was Tommy."

"No. We dunno no Tommy."

A few choice street remarks flew back and forth. The wide dense guy took a swing at Pop. I was no trained fighter. I knew nothing from karate or self defense. I couldn't even climb the ropes in the Midwood High School Gym in Bensonhurst. But I was 6 feet 1 and thirty pounds over the top and used my volume as best I could and swung at both goons. I saw Pop slip to the floor and I went wild. Mom heard the noise and rushed in with Pop's baseball bat and, being 4 feet 10, swung from a low but effective level. The two goons ran out cursing.

Fortunately none of us were really hurt. Pop had some minor bruises. We were all rattled, but whole. So we held an instant El Monaco executive board meeting and unanimously voted to put off inspection of Yenta's until the renters left. However, we did call the police. The police, two pre-*Terminator* storm trooper types with crew cuts and mirror glasses, informed us that any disturbances were entirely my fault, since I was guilty of bringing the hippie invasion to God's country.

So, for the duration, Yenta's would do whatever they were doing until they finished whatever it was that needed finishing, and then Monday morning, August 18, before dawn, poof, Yenta's would be returned to its former status:

Dead, empty, unwanted, and desperately for sale.

15

Fat Envelopes Talk

16 days and counting... (Or was it 18 days?)

One of our neighbors, the Cadillac Hotel, was run by a brother-and-sister team. Riva, a Viveca Lindfors look-a-like, and Victor, a tall, almost elegant man—the silver-fox type like Claude Raines in *Mr. Smith Goes to Washington,* but taller. Like his sister, Victor seemed refined and well-educated and a misfit in White Lake. Unlike his sister, he was a shrewd businessman.

Some years before the Festival, Victor bought some swampland at the foot of Route 17B for less than $20,000. Coincidentally, the very next day, the local Chicken-Flicking Contest Board chose that very swamp as the location for their new Bethel Bobsled and Olive Tree Competitive Sports Stadium. Reportedly, a surprised Victor, with luck shining down on him, sold the swamp for over two million dollars. Whatever the profit really was, it was an arbitrage move of proportions large enough to inspire the local power brokers to ban him from doing any further business in New York State. He hid twenty miles up 17B on the Pennsylvania side of the Delaware River.

Victor, however, apparently knew a big opportunity when he saw one, and determined that Woodstock was worth risking a border crossing. Victor dropped by my bar to buy me a drink. He made a few innocent remarks about the surprising number of people, cars, vans, trucks and yellow school buses strewn all over our grounds. He knew how to suck information out and, naive me, I was delighted to have such an over-abundance of news to share with this neighborhood big shot.

Victor quickly expressed surprise that Woodstock, considering all the tons of cash they were flashing, had not hired me to be their liaison and on-site international public relations office. A liaison team? I wasn't sure what this meant. I was already hired to do local public relations and was more than happy with renting out El Monaco's rooms. But when Victor pointed out that a local liaison office was imperative to ensure the continued cooperation of local power brokers, I began to get nervous. He explained in very seductive and polite terms that he and I could share a $25,000 fee to be the invaluable local coordinators for the Woodstock Festival. To me $25,000 was equivalent to the moon.

"What will Woodstock get for $25,000," I stupidly asked.

Victor then explained that the festival permit—my permit—plus the many subsequent permits from various county health and safety departments, could be instantly voided, revoked, canceled, whatever, unless—and this was a big unless—Woodstock had a strong liaison team featuring Victor. In fact, if the Festival did not hire us, he was sure that the state militia would be deployed to clear the entire Festival site. With that interesting tidbit of information, Victor finished his tall glass of Tab, flashed his Claude Raines smile, and excused himself.

I raced to Lang to tell him the liaison offer/threat. Lang, ever calm, asked me to arrange a meeting with Victor.

Less than twenty-four hours later, the Festival honchos, myself, and Victor met in a closed-door session in the graffiti corner of the El Monaco bar. Victor outlined the full range of liaison and public relations services now available to the Festival for $50,000. My cut was now reduced to $10,000 due to complicated mathematics that took into consideration unforeseen expenses on Victor's side, all of which would be dispensed directly to people in very high places in Monticello.

Immediately after Victor's proposal, Lang invited Victor into his private office (Room 2A, in the newly renamed Woodstock Manor, formerly the Ocean View wing).

Half an hour later, the two men emerged. Lang was nonplussed, Victor was not. Victor stopped in the Disco, where I was keeping a low profile, per instructions from one of the Woodstock people who looked like Walt Disney to me. He could have been Disney; he sounded like Mel Blanc, and quacked like Donald Duck, but that wasn't important just now.

"Elliot? You better advise Lang and his cohorts about the facts of doing business in White Lake. If they think that they'll cut out our liaison services, they're underestimating Victor. If there is no consulting fee, I guarantee there'll be no Woodstock Festival!"

I watched Mike's motel door that morning. His Porsche was in front of it, so I knew he couldn't have gone far. The curtains were closed, but the lights were on and I could hear music playing. Well before noon, a limo arrived and parked next to the Porsche but no one got out. Then Victor arrived. His expression was not especially friendly. He nodded to me as if I were supposed to understand something. I didn't. Mike then emerged with two business types. They all piled into the limo—notice no one invited me to go. Mike gave me a nod. They sped off.

Some hours later the limo returned. Victor stormed out, made a strange face at me, and headed towards his sister's non-existent 450-story future condo site. Mike emerged and gave me a victory sign. I ran over, we hugged and he said:

"Everything's cool. Nothing to worry about. We adjusted Victor's nose. Woodstock is going to happen. Relax, babe."

There were 14 UFO sightings that night. Six apparitions.

The Festival preparations continued at a dizzying pace. So did charming gestures from the quaint townsfolk. A brand new lawn mower walked off the El Monaco grounds one night. Windows in some of the bungalows were smashed. Healthy servings of horse manure were deposited in front of the newly-named Faye Dunaway Wing, formerly the Hollywood Hills Wing. Guests did not consider this abundance of fertilizer a sign of good luck. Tires on parked cars were slashed. Red dye gave the non-Olympic swimming pool an uninviting hue. Bags of household garbage were tossed like grenades from passing cars onto the El Monaco lawn. The police's stock answer to any complaints from the El Monaco was:

"That's what you get when you invite hippies and drug dealers to White Lake."

I wasn't privy to all sorts of behind-the-scenes arrangements that assorted unknown persons were doing deals to keep the Festival afloat.

It began with a late-night meeting on White Lake—that's right, on the lake. A certain person, on behalf of another certain person whose identity was not revealed to me, gave some other someone a list of names of some alleged officials of a townie politico. I wasn't told which town this townie belonged to. I was to use my non-existent crew experience—from the Ivy League college and prep schools I never attended—to row these certain, possible, alleged officials out onto the shiny nighttime waters of White Lake. One at a time, at 15-minute intervals.

I accepted the dubious honor of being the gondolier to escort all these alleged unnamed county-somebodies into the misty vapors of the Lake, far from the shores and their snake-infested lily pads. Another somebody hinted that there just might be thirteen number-10-size envelopes taped under my captain's seat. In fact, it was suggested that should I inspect these envelopes, I might notice that each envelope would have the code name of one of the alleged officials hand-lettered on it. I was terrified. I was confused. I knew whatever was going on was certainly highly suspect, bordering on "wrong." But by this time, my life was so upside down that if it meant losing the Festival and returning to my toilet-cleaning duties, I'd row that fucking damn gate. I'd do a whole lot to save this dream Festival.

Late that night, someone who may or may not have been a person whom I did or didn't know, and another someone who may or may not have been he or she who was supposed to be someplace else, walked through the dark wooded area that led to White Lake. And someone, likely unknown to me or anybody else, waited on top of a hill where certain prearranged flashlight signals could be observed.

The joy rides to the center of the lake were on time and scheduled intervals were respected. Eight out of thirteen persons showed up, took the ride and disembarked minutes later, envelope in hand. If Bogart and Peter Lorre were involved, nobody told me what happened to the other five. Their envelopes may still be in that boat for all I know. The guy who resembled me, doing all that rowing, was too dopey to keep the remaining envelopes. I personally don't know nothing, since I was having a manicure at Georgio's in Beverly Hills that very night.

What was in the envelopes? Whoever was driving the rowboat didn't peek. He kept his hands on the oars and his eyes on the snakes in the water. But whatever messages those envelopes carried, they had impact. Apparently, fat envelopes talk.

Lady luck was changing course, and the next morning the Festival permit was reinstated. The police became cooperative. The hate calls didn't stop, but they did become less frequent—for a few days, that is.

16

Drugs, Sex, Rock and Roll
Next Week

11 days or 9 days and counting...

Sorry this isn't precisely chronological. It's the best I can recall 25 years later. Suffice to say that I was in a purple haze through most of this Woodstock-prep time.

The best fix on the exact time I can offer is that somewhere between the end of one day and the beginning of another—July and August are good to talk about—I managed to take a quickie trip over to the Festival site. I had only some precious few spare minutes, thirty at the most, that I could be away from the invasion at the El Monaco. The roads were impassable for the four-mile drive without the use of the Harley Davidson bike that was driven by a state trooper. He smiled. I explained I was depending on the kindness of a stranger. He put me on the rear seat and forced me, brutally, to put my arms around his waist, while he flew through the winds and heavens and took me there.

The miraculous mini-city of the Festival was totally overwhelming. Lighting equipment, miles of wire and cables, scaffolding, stage constructions, hordes of tents, trucks, bikes, buses, horses, tractors and unidentifiable material engulfed the farm. The farm was unrecognizable. It used to be a meadow with an assortment of four-legged moo-moo-sound making milk-giving machines. Now it was a natural amphitheater where sheets of plastic covering equipment billowed in the wind. The moo-moo milk machines were not there. Instead, every square inch of land was occupied by sex-crazed drugged-out monsters making purple haze smoke. It was also a vast mass of energy, joy and life.

170

I wasn't totally sure I was seeing what I was seeing since I had no road signs or landmarks I could recognize to guide me. My state trooper, however, strong and confident, wise and all-knowing, was able to get me through otherwise impassable territory. Volunteers of every possible origin, every shape and color, every creed and sex, were helping build this mega-festival site, digging latrines, setting up crafts, arts and clothing booths. Tents, trailers, cars were scattered like pick-up-stix throughout what had been grazing pasture.

Hippies and Voyeurs at White Lake

It was breathtaking and invigorating and heart-rending all at the same time. Working side by side were what everyone was calling demented hippies but, who were, in reality, hard working kids from colleges, high schools, jobs; from everywhere in America and everywhere else across the world. And they were not all heterosexuals either, which was not reported but feared. There out in the open sunny fields were armies of lesbian women, working with straight women and men, and gay men, working along with senior citizens, over-40s of all sexual bents. I saw cross-dressers and drag queens and macho Hell's Angel bikers and vertically-challenged people and horizontally-challenged people. All, side by side, helping to set up food centers, emergency health stations, toilet facilities, and roadways in and out of this emerging city. Being a partially-closeted man, it was, as the apt 1960s expression said, Out of Sight Man! Literally! And I saw no evidence of any of this collection of dopers and perverts raping local women, girls, boys, men or infants in the two- to five-year range.

My trooper disappeared into the sea of madness. Not even a goodbye or let's take lunch real soon! I never saw him again, so good riddance to that rat-fink pig. I walked around, enjoying the guitar music, the chorus of mixed voices from every direction in every style and language imaginable, and then some. People were playing various strange-looking musical instruments that were fashioned from metals and woods and fabrics and twigs and found objects recycled. People were hawking all sorts of tskotzkas,[1] souvenirs, newspapers, political and social petitions, and unidentifiable items I don't dare to describe.

I passed a parked mini-van that had thousands of flowers painted all over its exterior. The sliding doors were open. Lanterns illuminated the interior, which was lined with multi-colored rugs. The sweet smell of incense wafted from within. A girl about 25 was swaying to music that only she appeared able to hear, a decidedly different beat from the hard rock music playing on the car speakers of a nearby vehicle. Lying inside the floral van, stretched out on a bean-bag cushion, was her companion; a swimmer's body surrounded by sandy hair and beard with a vacant smile on his face.

The couple invited me to join them. I poked my head in the van. The young man held up a tiny bit of paper with a dot on it.

"Just put it on your tongue, man. It's a trip."

"What? What is it?"

"No idea, babe. But it sure is the good times all packed into one itsy bitsy dot. Oh yeah, they call it 'instant travel package.' I'm feeling no pain."

The woman ran her hands on my neck while I licked the paper. The man reached out and helped his girlfriend get me down in the van. At first I didn't feel anything. I didn't feel the micro-dot dissolve. I was mesmerized by what I thought were his penetrating emerald green eyes. But go know what color they really were. I lay there, relaxed

---

[1] Yiddish for 'little nothings.'

on a bean bag between the two of them. Somehow, unannounced, the motel and all my suffocating responsibilities made a quick exit from my world. I dissolved into the music while the girl's silky hands did a number all over me.

"In a few minutes you'll get a real nice buzz. Relax. Don't worry. We'll be with you the whole time."

He started to run his hands along my legs and the two of them began to sexually arouse me. And who wouldn't be? Okay, there are plenty who wouldn't be, and I can name names, but what for? For the next ten minutes, ten hours, ten years—I have no idea how long, but it felt like forever—I was in some strange state of bliss, unlike any bliss I'd ever read about or fantasized.

Shapes and colors and moods passed through me with the silkiness of honey. I know they were talking to me the whole time, but I have no idea what they were saying. Sexual fantasies flickered through my mind, like some endless porn film starring the three of us. Only their faces kept changing, their bodies kept transfiguring. Sometimes they were just shadows with flickering lights where their eyes should have been. There were moments when I entered their bodies; I don't know how, but I was inside their bodies. It was as if I were plummeting into a black hole in space. I kept diminishing and spinning recklessly. Sensations of joy and wonder rapidly alternated with terror, unrelenting terror. Then colors started pirouetting and gyrating. I was overwhelmed as if space was moving through me. The physical softness of these two tender people was caressing me, erasing some bad stuff that was flying around my face. It was petrifying and wonderful at the same time.

That was my first acid trip. I assume I was in the van for hours, but am not sure. The couple "talked me down," a method I would become experienced with a thousand times over the next few weeks as kids bad-tripped all over the El Monaco. Meanwhile, the couple related the breadth and scope of their three-way sex—they called it a "mutual sexual journey"—and taught me some incantations they assured me would protect and guide me in the future. What could it hurt? Lauren Bacall never called me, if that means something.

I'm not sure what else happened. But I still remember their gentle and loving expressions. And gentle love was something of which I'd experienced precious little. Wild frenzy, that I knew about. Loving? For me, love meant getting a puppy. Later.

Somebody from someplace took me someplace and in ways and means I don't remember, got me those four miles back to the El Monaco. And the joint was jumping. Mom and Pop were dancing check-ins, -outs, parking, feeding, laundry, and in their spare mini-seconds, they made constant trips to hiding places in the sub-basement mud flats. I had no choice but to dive right back into work.

Knowing what I now know about acid, I have no idea how I managed to function competently after that trip, but I did. I didn't come down from that high until a few days later. And thereafter, when those itsy bitsy dots were freely offered to me, I was in control enough not to do any unplanned "travelling" for the remainder of the Festival. In fact, I only did acid one more time in my life, knowingly, and that was four years later in Brussels. George Peppard, for some unknown reason, was taking me down on the floor of a Flemish apartment overlooking the green market. Don't ask. Maybe it wasn't G.P., it looked like G.P.

No energy to count anything...

The reasons why the kids at Woodstock took drugs have been discussed and documented by experts and amateurs the world over. I won't attempt to add to that over-abundance of discourse on why people do drugs. Since I'm not able to add any new insightful analysis or advice, I'll stick to the part of Woodstock that I alone knew about. Suffice to say thousands of people I spoke to that week had one common concern: Life as it was presented to them by their parents just didn't seem to warrant accepting for themselves. The drive for money, better titles, better cars, better things appeared senseless, and getting high and checking out fantasies took on unreal appeal. And not to forget, there wasn't any AIDS or knowledge of immune system failures then. If the above is not clear, I can summarize it very simply: *How do I know why people do what they do? I'm not able to be my brother's keeper. Oy.*

While man landed on the moon that very summer, it was also the world of man in which two Kennedys could be assassinated in sharp succession, followed by Martin Luther King. It was a world in which people were coerced into fighting in wars that didn't make sense. These were people coming of age and finding that the world their parents had created for them was at once frightening and deadening. That's why they were at Woodstock. That's why their hair was long, that's why some—not all, not even the majority—experimented with drugs. Anything that would trigger them into a different mind-state and keep them from turning into civilized brain-dead twits, seemed the right way to go. Ergo, the expression then: Right on.

And she who might be he said: Let there be music!

17

The Final Countdown

8 or 9 or 7 days, and counting...

A week before the Festival. Tents everywhere, along the roads, behind buildings, between tress. Trucks, station wagons, mini-campers, motorcycles lined Route 17B, five deep. Portable toilets sprung up like mushrooms. The site is as complete as it's going to get, though nobody knows that yet.

Pop became jovial and sparkly-eyed as he worked our horrendous 24-hour schedule. The kids and workers came to talk to him as if he were some wise being, the grand proprietor of the El Monaco, the Woodstock official headquarters. The father of the son who owned the permit that made the Festival possible. And he got into this role. Suddenly this man, whose world had been limited to what was in a toolbox, and what orders Mother had barked at him, was a big shot. Suddenly this motel, which had been an embarrassment and albatross for everyone except my deluded mother, was a source of pride, not to mention income! This man who'd hoped to create the American dream for his beautiful fellow-greenhorn bride, but somehow never did it to her satisfaction, now felt like a somebody. He was beaming, and this was not a man who beamed much.

Momma underwent no such transformation. She was too busy counting money and making sure nobody cheated her out of her due. The notion that everyone was bent on cheating her was an obsession I grew up with. She counted and recounted every dollar that came in. Then, she decided she didn't trust the bank either, and hid money everywhere. Pop and I knew she was doing this and let it slide. When her memory slid, and her mental bookkeeping didn't jell with her totals, she would accuse us of being short and fools to smart types who took advantage and cheated us. Dopes that we were. Meanwhile, she was the one hiding cash in pre-Ziplock baggies, floating them in toilet tanks, in cabinets, under cabinets, behind loose tiles in the shower, under floor boards...

7 days and counting... (Maybe it was now 6?)

In the final week before the Festival the days and nights merged, indistinguishable from one another. The only hint I had of the passage of time, in the linear fashion by which most of us know it, was that some of the hours had light and some were dark. I spent perpetual immeasurable days and nights minding and monitoring the El Monaco's first aid emergency station, drinking water, non-existent food supplies, creating lost and found systems for missing kids and anxious parents, and defending the compound against local goons. These unending responsibilities all contributed to the blur.

I remembers using up in an hour more first aid kits than I had in the past fourteen years. Thousands of pairs of bare feet met shards of broken glass, splinters and other debris, and I did the best I could to patch up the wounds that stumbled my way. Many casualties were more serious. Victims of bad drugs lay on the walkways and road shoulders. I got every blanket I could find in the motel inventory, such as it was, and rushed to wrap shivering bodies. It was getting impossible to even use the phones. All the circuits and lines were busy 24 hours a day with outgoing collect calls. Incoming calls from anxious families and friends made communications a disaster. I used my Navy speakers to beg anyone within earshot to bring over dry blankets and first aid material.

An ongoing and central concern was water and the chronic lack thereof. Pop and I set up improv spigots for drinking water by placing a series of hoses, linked in a serpentine pattern, from the pool pump in several directions for as far as we could. We opened the pool shower to everyone and kept it flowing for those desperately in need of bathing. Soap was now a luxury nowhere to be found for miles. Sheer luck that our four deep spring water wells kept functioning. We then converted the non-Olympic swimming pool into an Olympic bath tub and invited everyone to bathe in it.

We dug trenches in the crawl spaces under the motel buildings and created emergency "beds." Teens and adults appeared out of nowhere to help us get whatever meager aid we could to the continuous flow of humanity coming into our compound. It was a violation of local ordinances to house people under buildings, something that never came up before. Celia Lungful, village fool with political connections in all the wrong places, butted in to tell Pop that she was going to file a class action suit for illegal housing of immigrants. I couldn't take time with that townie bitch, so I ordered her off my property. It was embarrassing to her, but funny to those who had to be there at that moment:

"I fully intend to report to the police that you are here illegally soliciting sexual favors from minors for money. El Monaco does not permit professional prostitutes to hang out in our muddy basement sleeping pits."

She flew out. We did what we could to take care of people. At least the pool water was wet. At least the crawl spaces were dry.

People kept entering the compound asking for friends they'd "lost" or never found. It was sad to see them, exhausted, miserable, usually coming down from a trip, and unable to move further. I went into sign-painting mode and made an ad hoc missing-persons center out of a table at the road. Two college students from Alaska pitched in and got the word out and, within hours, lines snaked down the road to register the names of missing friends.

Network television crews from ABC, CBS and NBC, who had a bank of rooms painted black and transformed into transmission studios, made the entire scene take on the look of a combat zone in some other country. This was no longer just a local concert. Suddenly it was an event whose gentle message of peace, love, and music was or would be reaching the world at large. That is, if the mad logistics of survival of the elements could be overcome.

When Warner Brothers arrived with their cameras and crews, word got out that they were making a movie. Instantly, any semblance of reality dissolved into fantasy. You know you're real when the news reports you. You know you're realer than real when Hollywood immortalizes you back into the world of fantasy where the story began.

Michael Wadleigh, who wandered over to me, never explained what he was doing or for whom or that it was a biggie. The director of the Woodstock movie looked like any of the other cool Woodstock people. He debriefed me. I gave him the lay of the land and some background about the Festival. But that initial conversation was all we had together. That he was slim and brilliant and so remote in what he had said to me, made me alert to my urgent need to vacate this fucking ugly motel ASAP and find another life.

As the Festival opening neared, Wadleigh rode to and from every place including in and out of my several driveways. There he was, hair flying in the wind, in an open convertible, a movie camera mounted to the hood, shooting background material that never made it to the big screen. Their loss. I never did see any shots of the El Monaco in the finished movie, though. So, somewhere at Warner Brothers there's a can with out-takes of this story. Later on, to be edited by a young Martin Scorcese. In addition to being in love with his movie camera, convertible, loose lifestyle, I loved Wadleigh instantly. He was slender. Anybody slender had my vote. If you've ever suffered fat, you know what I'm talking.

Every single room, nook and cranny was rented. Yes, it was a mantra come true: My rooms were rented and I might yet have a chance to get out of the Catskills.

18

The Closet Door

5 days or 4 and counting, but out of control...

With a few days left before the Festival, right on schedule, Lang and the Woodstock entourage checked out of the El Monaco and moved their operation to Yasgur's farm. The network people vanished after they paid extra to repaint their rooms white. I left them black because that is the only cheerful color in the world. For about twenty minutes, I was bereft. The hum of activity, the constant flow of staffers, had made the El Monaco a home for me for the first time. And for the first time in my life I felt I had family. Woodstock made me feel like I wasn't an alien.

My actual family had no idea what I felt. They all knew I was gay, but didn't have any inkling of what that meant. And they for sure never asked or were able to discuss it. Now I suppose they never wanted to know more. It was brotherly for me to celebrate their children, their events, their simchas.[1] Mine lovers, events, were likely disturbing to them, so they were ignored permanently. The safe way was that whatever I was about, it either didn't exist, or it was too embarrassing or frightening to get into. It's too late to define.

So, suddenly, even though it was expected, my new-found friends and family were gone. The change was kind of brutal and it hit hard. I'd sum it up as "overwhelming melancholy." As I signed out the last of the Woodstock staffers, I felt I was losing this new identity I had acquired. I knew I'd never see most of these new compatriots again. I was no virgin and knew how love affairs fade away quickly, still, it was upsetting. I ate a lot of Hershey bars. But the wallop of stuff that had

[1]Yiddish for 'happy occasions.'

180

to be taken care of didn't stop just because they moved onto the final phases of Festival prep. In total, I had maybe 23 minutes to devote to feeling bereft.

Hard on the heels of the staffers' departure came hordes of Festival ticket holders who wanted motel rooms. They descended upon the El Monaco micro-registration office. How they got there, where they came from, go know. People were trying for rooms continuously. It was just this moment, suddenly, the entire compound was empty. Oh, everything was reserved and paid for in advance. And then some. Like the airlines, we over-booked. Most of the room reservations weren't showing up because they couldn't get through the miles of cars as the world's "largest parking lot" grew and grew. For the first time in all the miserable fourteen years at this motel from hell, I had people not just asking to rent rooms, but begging and offering huge sums of money. I was in strange territory.

So, waiting till the 6:00 p.m. check-in hour, and surrounded by all those empty rooms again, we just started taking in cash and tossing unmarked keys to the long line of instant check-ins. I didn't dare think of how we could service these new people.

We had 500 people checked into our 250 people maximum-capacity motel. I had to foresee the solution to this problem before it went further:

"The rooms are rented on an as-is basis. We are completely out of linens, towels, soap, food, and other amenities. We do have running water and electricity. We are not responsible for your sharing arrangements or sexual compatibilities. The keys do not work and are only a psychological toy. We cannot be held responsible for anything. These conditions are almost the very same ones we offer when there are no Woodstock Festivals. Enjoy."

I shouted these new rules to the long line as Momma took the cash and Poppa lead them via the played-out golf cart towards the various buildings. It actually was a lot easier than our usual methods. People followed the golf cart like the piper. Pop simply pointed to a room or curtained space, and whoever would rush inside and be happy to have someplace dry. In two hours, we were filled wall to wall, top to bottom. The fanciful names of the various buildings may or may not have impressed the new guests. They never commented. Most got stoned on whatever and, within hours, fled by foot to the farm, never to be seen or heard from again.

With people everywhere—underfoot, overfoot, on roofs, under crawlspaces—it was no longer possible to discern where the slanted floors ended and the knock-kneed walls began. The drapes from Sloane's were long since stripped and used for emergency blankets and bandages. My assorted signs were barely readable because the constant onslaught of rain created a steam effect that dissolved the magic marker ink on eye contact.

They came to White Lake from all over the world. From Copenhagen, London, Paris, Rome, East Berlin, Los Angeles, Mexico, and Pretoria. They were from every state in America and from every state of mind, including some that the C.I.A. was still busy trying to classify.

Suggestions that people go home were met with incredulous looks. Pop managed to string lights through the El Monaco woods to help desperate campers find places to lie down. First they filled up the forest behind the pool. Guests were allocated places on a first-come first-served basis. Emergencies were put ahead of everyone.

Every square centimeter of bog was rented or occupied. Even fabled Number 9A, which had no windows and no bathroom, a roomette created by the inventive crash of my Buick into the front of the Garden State Brickface indestructible faux brick. Momma was parking the tank Buick, and pow, poof, we had a doorway to yet another minuscule room. This was the year before, and the only leftover wallpaper Momma could find in the town garbage dump was one with eagles perched atop something sinister-looking. There were three rolls, just enough to do this four by seven space, not including the four foot high door Pop bought at the Nazi lumberyard for $4.49, no returns. That door was intended for a tall doggie but worked out just fine for the remodeling budget we had. So in effect, our shrewd decorating ideas gave us a new motel suite to rent out for less than nine dollars. I renamed it "Eagle's Nest" to make it more poetic. No one knew it was also the name of a hot leather bar in Chelsea.

Room Number 9A, Eagle's Nest, served us valiantly. I want to make it clear that I never mislead anyone. When we were full, I'd announce to the desperate traveller, before taking money:

"We have no vacancies. That said, we do have our Eagle's Nest, which is not much of a misnomer. You have to bend down to get in the four foot high doorway. There is no standing room. The army cot without a mattress takes up the entire room. There are no windows. There is one light bulb that cannot be turned off unless you are immune to skin burn. There is no place to put a suitcase. You have to keep everything in your car. You have to use the toilet in the Disco bar. You have to shower out by the swimming pool. The rate is obscene for such a horror, but it is two figures. You have to pay in advance, and there are no refunds because it's late and I am exhausted and you have to have a sense of humor to rent this room in advance."

And it was always rented by me without aggravation. However, when Momma rented it, there was always upset and demand for refund and lawsuit threats:

"Dollink. We have just one last deluxe room in our deluxe Beverly Hills Wing overlooking the parking lot and registration office. It's a charming doll house, but since we already have another room named Doll House, this one is called Eagle's Nest. It is a bargain, would a momma lie to you? You'll pay me fifty dollars but you promise not to tell my husband because he gets crazy when he sees I rent such a room for bargain rates. My husband doesn't like bargain hunters. It's late, pay—cash only—and I'll give you a discount on my cholunt for breakfast. Oy."

People kept coming and coming and coming, however. Defying radio and television warnings of the disastrous conditions, they kept coming. When cars broke down, they hitched. When that became impossible, they walked. Some for 50 miles! One person in particular still sticks out in my mind. She arrived driving a school bus that had been painted over in psychedelic colors, with flowers that I had never known possible, intertwined with serpents in heat doing what serpents in heat probably do, but my limited experience kept me from knowing about. She pulled up in front of our Underground Cinema and stepped out. She was huge. A good 300 pounds in a June Allyson-type dress, with innocent ribbons in her shoulder-length hair. Her name was Georgette and she was originally from France, though she'd lived in the States for about twenty years. She sounded like Maurice

Chevalier with a Portuguese accent, filtered through a softee ice cream machine.

I immediately told her we were booked solid, not a square inch of floor space was available. But she said all she wanted was a parking space for the bus. It turned out the bus was a mobile Zen meditation and holistic center. Remember, this was 1969 before Zen was mainstream and almost every card-carrying yuppie studied Japanese in his/her spare time.

The only physical space left was behind the barn theater, adjacent to the back wall which, like the floor, was perilously slanted. I saw no reason why she couldn't park there for the month. In fact, the bus might help keep the wall up. Thus this "temple on wheels" procured a prime piece of White Lake real estate. Then out piled the rest of the Zen center staff. There were three more very large women, in the Georgette mold. Millie was wearing a frilly dress, with daisies and ribbons tied in delicate bows. Hank and Yo-Yo, however, were "tough trucker types" in overalls, plaid shirts and construction-worker boots. This may have been the first visible lesbian Zen temple to set foot, or, as in this case, park bus in Sullivan County. They were very open about their sexual preferences and gave lectures explicating their interpretation of the fairer sex. I was so overjoyed to have kindred spirits, that I instantly refunded their rental and invited them to shoot out their tires and stay permanently.

I was discovering that the gay closet I'd been in for so long had a door with a key and a knob. I was so roused and relieved to see other gay people in my face that I was waking up to the untenable situation I had put myself in for 14 years. And to coin a phrase, better late than never, after the Festival, this was my very last summer of this torture. That was one of the bonuses of Woodstock. My people came to hear the music, to give birth to freedom and to come out of the closet. These were not Yentas fixated on finding me some nice Jewish girl. These tough women whom I loved instantly were going to find me a nice guy, Jewish or not. My head turned 360 degrees as I juggled the grand possibilities of being out. I didn't know how or when to announce this to my parents, but I would figure it out.

Anyway, Georgette and her crew were instant "family" for me. I was particularly grateful when, free of charge, Georgette removed a curse that she was sure had kept me from realizing my true spiritual potential. Plus, Pop and she became instant best friends and spent much quality time together. It was great to see Pop have a friend. It seemed so masochistic of him to consider Momma his friend. She wasn't anybody's friend. Go figure, Millie was quite taken with Mom, but that relationship went nowhere as soon as Mom understood that no money would pass hands.

19

And Not a Drop to Drink

5.5 days and counting... (Maybe 5.1?)

Rumors ricocheted off the mountain sides. Hippies were rioting? Hells Angels were shooting people at random? 500,000 people? 750,000 already were in Bethel with maybe another million people on the way? All stoned? All high on something? I didn't know what to make of the rumors. People certainly were stoned and tripping—as was I. And with the highs came wild stories, erratic accounts, a great deal of fantasy thinking. I didn't want to believe that there were killings, but I was getting apprehensive. I'd never seen so many people in one place in my life. It was a thousand Times Squares on New Year's Eve, but for miles and days in advance of the event! What if there were problems? How could we handle this? I was no Leona Helmsley and I didn't run a tight ship, nor did I know how to. I was frenzied en route to hysterical.

When the going got frantic, I phoned my sister Goldie. Sometimes she yelled at me, sometimes she helped, sometimes she did her Cassandra routine. This time, she said a simple "forget it." She repeated *her* mantra:

"I have no interest in that motel. You should have gotten out of there years ago. I told you years ago not to throw away your youth on that rotten motel and Mom and Pop's garbage."

And she added that she hated rock music which was loud and just a lot of hollering and screaming by degenerates and I should take a bus in Monticello and get out of there.

"Get out of that snake pit. Mom and Dad will fail, and that will be the end of all that money-making wasted life and nonsense. No, I'm not coming up there to that lunacy."

186

Next I phoned my sister Rachelle. She was on overload herself. She was nursing her younger son who was, at the time, suffering from a degenerative bone disease. Adding to her unavailability was the fact that summer time was boom time for her husband Sam, an optometrist in another summer community. El Monaco's economics and Sam's practice economics were on opposite schedules. Traditionally, we spent the two summer months losing all we could. He spent those two months making all he could. In my heart of hearts, I couldn't beg him to come out and help us.

I called my baby sister, Renee, in beautiful celestial Marlboro New Jersey, now the home of the famed Marlboro weeping Madonna. Her mantra is "Yes." "No" is not a frequently employed word in her vocabulary. In my family, if you were ever moved to run away, Renee was a good choice of haven. In minutes, Renee was on the road. Unfortunately, traffic had gotten so ridiculous that she never made it to the El Monaco. Trapped somewhere just outside of White Lake for 37 hours, with her tiny baby, she finally gave up and went back home to future crying-Madonna country in New Jersey.

So, I just had to dig deeper into my reservoir of strength or stupidness as always, and finish up. Goldie's tunnel vision must have been in an elevator without buttons to think I'd just take a bus in ugly Monticello and walk out on the biggest event of my life! My misguided filial duty aside, this was an event of monumental proportions that outweighed her tennis mantra, which as far as I could understand was,

"If it's distasteful, I'll play tennis and it will go away. Whatever it will do, it will do it, without bothering me."

Hey, she was probably right. She was a tough cookie, though I didn't know it then. I know it now. We were on our own. But at least I wasn't the only gay person in the world, finally!

5.1 days and counting... (No longer able to count.)

Meanwhile, the local rednecks were heating up in those final moments before the Ides of August. The son of a local merchant, a God-fearing concerned citizen of White Lake, often drunk and one of the countless drag racers who used 17B as a track, sauntered up to me one night as I was checking the water level in one of our wells. A big muscle type—the kind you see today wearing "Gold's Gym" tank tops—he told me that he spoke for the town and was disgusted with our ruining Bethel and White Lake and that certain people would be poisoning our water supply. In fact, he said, the well I was checking had already been poisoned.

Then he picked up a lead pipe and started swinging it around his head like a lasso. I didn't know from lassos or lead pipes, but I quickly devised two plans. Plan A was to run like hell. Plan B was to kill or permanently maim this neanderthal who was doing a mating dance around my person, all in the name, no less, of the God-fearing Christians of White Lake.

I opted for Plan B. There I was, standing in a mud puddle in the dark surrounded by the whispering pines reserved for tourists. I looked around desperately for some make-shift weapon to defend myself. There was nothing but soggy twigs and branches and mud. My self-defense opportunities were limited. The mud looked most promising and just as I was trying to figure out some way of splashing him in the face before his lead pipe landed on my head, an angel from someplace made this menacing yokel slip in the mud and his pipe landed on his shin with a resounding crack. He let out a blood-curdling shriek. Not having done any training as a fighter, which I later corrected in a karate course at the New School, I stooped low enough to scoop up his lead pipe and give him a thwack while he was down. Got him right in the arm. It made a terrible sound. While he writhed in obvious pain, I had a couple of new choices. I could shove his sorry face into the mud and see if he could breathe under the ooze. I could kill him and prevent his seed from reproducing and making more like him. I decided to see how long he could breathe under the mud. I changed my mind when it dawned on me he could be dead, and killing someone was not for me to do.

The well tested clean. Drinking water in the county was drying up fast. Some avaricious locals were indeed selling water by the glass. Some creeps were demanding and getting a nasty five dollars a glass.

Just as water was scarce, so was food. When false rumors spread that we had a stash of Coca-Cola and hot dogs, mobs descended upon our two food trucks. It was a scary and potentially dangerous situation. Hundreds of teens and young adults, hungry, surrounded the trailers stuck in the mud on our front lawns. Pop opened the rear doors and it was obvious that the trucks were empty. But it took a long while to get that information passed among the upset kids. Most of these kids were stoned, so who knows where their brains were at? Grass makes you hungry, often starving. This time, the starving was physical in addition to the mental. It was a miracle that the situation didn't explode into a serious disaster.

Some young guy with a powerful voice and a guitar jumped up on one of the empty truck beds, and sang "On the Way to Woodstock," the hit song of the month that had taken on festival-anthem status.

Here I am with a truck used for housing on the El Monaco Motel's grounds, August 1969

It was one of those magical moments of the Festival days that will stay with me forever. The kids, some hungry, some full, swaying and singing to the music. It was a sweet eternity, and if someone had denied I was in the Garden of Eden sans le or la snake, I would not have believed them. I wished it would never end.

Pop and I instantly converted the food trailers into emergency housing for 150 happy campers. These trailers were big, but not so big that the 150 could sleep lying down. But still, when during the Festival the infamous rains began, we were all grateful for any kind of shelter. Any kind of music would do.

20

What Goes Up Must Come Down

4 days or still 5 days and counting...

Drugs. Ups, downs, blues, greens, whites, yellows, reds, pinks. They came in every size, style, color and description with some beyond description. Then there were the organics: baking soda, oregano, sage, paprika, aspirin and floral essences. There was the grass of choice, called Acapulco Gold, which, had it been the 1990s, would have been classified as a "designer drug."

Some you smoked, some you ate, some you boiled and smoked, some you licked, some you sniffed, some you watched sink into the mud. It seemed that under every tree, behind every bush, in every room, nook, cranny and shack at El Monaco, people were turning on, getting high, coming down, cooling out, getting hot, and the term of choice: tripping. It was hash, grass and coke, and a whole lot of UFO stuff, too. Reports of wild sex everywhere were exaggerated. There was certainly a lot of open touching and caressing and naturally, sexual activity. That it was so open and honest upset those brain-dead people who freaked out at the sight of nakedness. The same monsters that get off watching violent TV cop shoot-em-ups, war movies, and mobsters nuking everyone in sight. Love-making has always been a threat to many warped twisted minds, evidenced by the religious right coalitions that still threaten, in 1994, to take over America.

As for my personal excursions into sexual abandon, ah, those I remember well. My first acid trip and liaison with the two hippies in the floral van was the prelude to other Woodstock romances. A journalist from *Time* or *Newsweek*, (who can recall), had introduced himself and asked to interview me. I had trouble concentrating on his questions because he was my type. Blame it on his marine-green eyes. Blame it on his silky sand-colored hair. Blame it on his attitude. Blame it on his big heavy boots which I thought meant he was into leather and all the S & M stuff I considered the nectar of love life. Turned out he wore the boots because they were comfortable. I took that to be a tease because I needed him to be a card-carrying member of the leather fraternity. I was wrong. Despite this shortcoming, we connected instantly and spent time together doing many of the so-called unnatural things that so terrified my neighbors. We did it in my car, in the shower by the pool at night, in Shack Number Two—anywhere at all, as long as it was out of my parents' sight and could be done in ten-minute segments.

We had a good thing going there, and given some normal time we might have hooked up. But as quickly as he came into my life, he disappeared into the sea of humanity marching down Route 17B and I never heard from him again. Jonathan? Jeremy? I don't remember, but I think it began with a J. A good man is hard to find.

There were 37 UFO sightings behind my Underground Cinema today.

Meanwhile, the radio and TV news were reporting deaths, growing violence, and near-hysteria. Their juices were up and buzzing as they gleefully reported that the National Guard and FBI were on their way.

The media complained about the music, the service, the food, the decor, the weather and the hosts. We didn't know it would monsoon for three days in August, in particular, August 15, 16 and 17. We didn't know that bad drugs would materialize and be passed around to unsuspecting kids. We did know that freedom was a good idea whose time had come, but we had no idea a million people would come with it.

The press reports exaggerated the scale of every aspect of the festival and life in downtown Bethel.

Early on, police with handcuffs and batons arrived to move the impassable crowd along. Their unnecessary roughness provoked confrontations, which were a threat to the peaceful gathering. In front of the El Monaco at the intersection of Routes 55 and 17B, a trooper on a horse swung his baton at three colorfully-dressed kids who were smoking joints. He used his huge horse to scare the hell out of one boy, about 16, and leaned over and cracked his stick on his head. The boy dropped, bloody, to the concrete. His buddies and a group of adult vacationers hovered over him, trying to help. Ignoring the protests of the adults and kids alike, the trooper dismounted, cuffed the kids and radioed for back-up.

What frightened me more than anything was the look of pleasure in the trooper's eyes. His expression changed from pleasure to fear only when he realized his back-up wasn't arriving and he had an angry crowd of stoned hippies shouting "Pig, pig!" at him. At one point, he gave up, uncuffed the kids and got back on his horse. I suppose he would have galloped away if he could, but because of the endless jam of people, the best he could do was ooze back under the rock where he came from.

After several random rough incidents that troopers provoked, some arrangement was made from above and the police adopted a new attitude. The instructions were to keep the peace and not incite riots. The free-wheeling use of drugs, then, was tolerated for the duration of the festival.

I knew very little about drugs until Woodstock. I'd been chain smoking cigarettes—regular tobacco—since I was ten. I got into so-called "recreational" use of relatively innocent mind-altering substances such as THC and grass in the mid-1960s. Woodstock's currency was hash and coke and a good time. This was not a bad scene. We were playing with new toys. None of us ever dreamed that these new toys could kill you or damage your immune system. The experiences were astounding and wondrous. There I was, a driven 34-year-old, caught in the American chase after success—early, low-level yuppie, I guess—and I was smoking and licking and sniffing stuff that took me to the moon. It was instant dream vacation from the nightmare of a world I had created for myself. Today, it's called substance abuse. But what did we know? We were in wonderland. Nobody even used the word abuse.

There were 84 apparitions today, but no UFO sightings.

21

Sex, Surrogates, More Drugs, and the Baroness

Too high to keep counting...

I'm not giving out some proposition for intellectual discourse. When I say Woodstock was the womb of a new world, I know what I'm talking here. Close your eyes, spin around and point to anything at random in your room, or on the bus, or wherever you are reading this book. Whatever your finger has landed on, one can find its debt to Woodstock. My new computer, a Dell 386, outdated while it was being delivered, owes something to Woodstock. *Psychedelic colors on the monitor; that's Woodstock! User-friendly; that's Woodstock! Communication; that's Woodstock! Compatibility; that's Woodstock! Network; that's Woodstock! Family; that's Woodstock!*

Woodstock was the call to freedom that helped unleash the gays out of the closet. And out of the closet came leather suits and S & M paraphernalia. Look at Madonna's outfits! That's S & M clothing! Suddenly we're legit! Calvin Klein's ads push mean, sadistic expressions with vacuous eyes. Ah, the look of choice in the S & M sex clubs coast to coast. Even in the time of AIDS, major clubs such as Limelight in New York City, feature S & M-nasty as the lure for their every-which-way crowd. Bloomingdales' windows, toys, outfits for toddlers, all have some traces—sometimes major ones—of our gay and S & M lifestyles. If there were a million people at Woodstock—which I believe is the case—not the 700,000 estimates that have been cited in the press, then ten percent of that crowd was likely gay and lesbian. Nobody acknowledged that possibility at the time. Hey, lots of observations were only made long after, as the entire event settled into various perspectives. I was there and those three days were a revelation, a revolution, and a starting point for re-evaluation.

Among the heralds of this new age was Victoria, a woman in her forties, dressed in harem pants and a leather-fringed vest. Victoria presented me with her glossy purple business card: "Sexual Surrogate. $200 per session, with or without."

"Because it's Woodstock, I'm adjusting my fee, so talk to me, I can take you anywhere. Talk to me!"

Momma was at the wrong place at the wrong time. She glanced at Victoria's purple card and screamed. I wasn't sure if she screamed because she saw the word "sexual" or the $200 fee. Mama's relationship with the Almighty was not on such solid ground that she would chance ex-communication for openly renting a room to one who had the word "sexual" on her business card. While Mama screamed and chased Victoria out of the El Monaco, warning her to stay away from me, I stared at this purple card. In 1969, sexual surrogate was not an over-the-counter item. This was pre-Oprah, Phil, Sally and Doctor Ruth. I was at first amused, then intrigued, then realized that I was missing out on a potentially rich experience. While I wasn't naturally interested in the services of a Victoria, and would have vastly preferred Victor, the idea that such a thing was available and within reach was an eye-opener that was long overdue.

I watched Victoria leave and cross Route 17B. She didn't look too forlorn. This was pre-twelve-step everything, pre-self-esteem "issues," pre- any kind of issue. Any wounds to her pride couldn't have hurt for long because at the corner was a mounted state trooper who seemed very delighted by the purple card she handed him. I, personally, was less delighted. Not because my mother had chased away a female sexual surrogate, but because I'd had my eye on that very trooper for myself. A lot of good our proximity to his post did me. I never even got a wink. Had I known that the liberating effects of Victoria and Woodstock were going to lead to a proliferation of gay sex clubs and that, in less than a year, I'd be living in Europe having my pick of men in and out of uniform, maybe I wouldn't have been so depressed.

With a lot of help from hash cookies and other goodies which were being freely passed around, I became more gregarious, if not intrepid. The hash made every man seem like my type, even men who didn't wear uniforms. Shack Number Two, my leather salon, was finally getting used.

As for Momma, Woodstock was changing even her. You know, there was so much hash and grass that we were all getting a contact high. Mama was getting a bit more human. She wasn't so shrill, and she wasn't so tight with the money. Then again, we had so much money then, maybe it was the money that was giving her the high. Maybe it was just good vibes in the air. Vibes, in case you don't know, were the precursor to auras and the more scientific term "intuition."

Anyway, suddenly mother was being genuinely nice to people in need. And the profit motive was not governing her, at least for a few scattered hours. I was suspicious. This was anonymous spontaneous charity to people she normally wouldn't feel so charitable about. It was a wondrous transformation, though unfortunately, it was a temporary phenomenon that vanished with the Festival.

The El Monaco's new bank of fifteen real, working, bonafide pay phones was a scene unto itself. The uninterrupted lines of hopeful callers wove their way all over the grounds and out onto the highway. People were getting in these lines 400 feet away not even knowing what lay at the head of the queue. A 24-hour sitcom, the coin boxes were so full that no more coins could be added. No one from Bell Telephone could get there to empty the machines, so people were making calls for free. When it was all over, Bell found us. They said they lost hundreds of thousands of dollars in phone calls made from our phones. People called Pakistan, Delhi—remember, this was the 1960s and India was a very big thing then—Athens, London, Tel Aviv, Paris, and on and on. I personally enjoyed watching people make those calls. All those years of humiliation from Marie and her successors. When the Festival was over, I was still pleased, but Ma Bell wasn't. Ma Bell was mad. Tsk, tsk, I said to the Bell management supervisor who was sent to remove our bank of phone booths and collect money.

"I'll get your ass, Tiber. You should have protected them. We're suing you for $400,000. You don't fuck Ma Bell and get away with it!"

"Sue me! The whole county is suing me. Ask me if I care!"

Today, 27 apparitions, 18 phantoms, and 2 UFOs were sighted.

About the Earthlight Theater Troupe? They disappeared from our story because they disappeared from center stage at El Monaco to work for the Festival itself. The Earthlight actors left us to work for Mike weeks before the Festival began. The only news I had about Earthlight was from guests who were coming and going from the farm. They reported that the actors were doing puppetry, improvisation, instant theatre pieces, singing, playing their guitars and flutes. The company mascots—a great dane and a monkey—were part of the entertainment, too. Never saw them again. That's what happened with Woodstock. People came into your life and disappeared without a trace.

"Getting it Together"

Sometime during a vague several days before the Festival actually began, I hopped in our rapidly-expiring golf cart to take a security look at the bungalows out back in our swamp. I hadn't been down there in ages, and felt a look-see was overdue. There was so much commotion up front and on Route 17B that it was easy to forget there were 14 more acres of El Monaco swarming with people. What with driveways all over the compound, people checked in, and I never saw or heard from them again, except for when some came to the office asking for blankets, bed boards, tissue, and so on. But I had no idea who was staying where. It didn't matter, since we were totally without any supplies. Luckily, Momma had hidden a dozen cartons of bathroom tissue under one of the buildings some years before. They were found accidentally as we were digging trenches. They were World

War II surplus, left over from the hardware store basement in Ben-sonhurst, and moved when we relocated upstate. It is hard to describe the condition of 30-year-old tissue. But, to coin a phrase: *That's Show Business!*

I slowly drove along the blacktop path through the evil rain. The green slime and mysterious black holes gurgled on either side of the path. Not terribly inviting, but I was used to it. I wondered that guests didn't go ballistic when they first travelled this road less travelled. My brother-in-law, a big-shot insurance man, never once commented about the liability risk we assumed by renting the back woods. Who had insurance for swamps? Considering the nether-nether land of primeval ooze I had the chutzpa to call rolling lawns under whispering pines, it was better we had President Bill Clinton's intolerable plan in place, 24 years before he was in office, i.e.: Don't tell. Don't show. Don't ask!

As I passed a puzzling array of sleeping bags, pup tents, lean-to structures, hammocks suspended from trees covered with plastic sheets, and busses, vans, old taxis, a few hearses, all gaily decorated with flower-power designs, I felt frightened. Surely I would be stoned to death? But this was not a hostile crowd. This was an ever-so-grate-ful, down-to-earth, even down-to-muddy-earth crowd. All these people whom I had placed waved and called out my name. People were wrapped in plastic bags, so it was just one waving bubble after another. About a hundred cars were parked every which way near the bungalows. Most were fender deep in mud. Before Woodstock there had been something of a meager lawn, but not a trace of it remained. Actually, it looked like the pictures we were watching on TV of the trenches in Viet Nam. Except this was no killing field. Here everything was about love. While the Viet Nam barracks and fox-holes may have outclassed the El Monaco bungleholes, not to mention the "Doll House," here everything was decorated with peace signs, doves, hearts, love and all that. Even the cement cover over the cesspool was decorated with painted daisies.

I drove on carefully until I got to the barn theatre. It was filled with young kids who were having a big party. I heard music, laughing, and unidentifiable noises. I minded my own biz. Everything was nice and all was well, hickory, dickory, dock.

Only 1 UFO and 1.3 apparitions were reported. On our grounds.

As I surveyed the steaming ectoplasm that represented my estranged lifestyle, I was startled by a strange guest I didn't remember checking in.

She had a large umbrella. So, whoever she was, she was the prepared type. She was a hefty woman. Dressed in black sequins, fishnet stockings and spike heels. Her make-up was so thick you could have used it for wallpaper paste. Her faux eyelashes were like two pairs of vicious black teeth. Her faux hair, which was skewered with bejewelled oriental chopsticks, was dangerously bouffant; the type you shouldn't bump into or use to clean teflon because it is likely to mar the surface of whatever it touches. If I were into that type, I would have thought an angel from heaven had sent me the answer to the Teichberg Curse.

I know I didn't check her in, because there was no way I would have forgotten her. She did not "blend" with this crowd. I'm not sure she blended with any crowd that still lives on this planet. So, I figured Mama registered her, mistaking her for a "fency lady." Or maybe Pop, whose only concern was whether or not there would be any children in the party.

She stood in front of me brandishing her umbrella. A vision. While I stared, her spikes were sinking into the mud, so before she disappeared, I asked if I could help her or give her a lift to her room. She said, sounding like Marlene Dietrich with an extra hit of testosterone: "Permit me to introduce myself, I don't belif ve'fe met."

Standing under her black umbrella in the driving rain, spike heels deep in El Monaco slime, the Baroness informed me that she'd had her eyes on me for days.

"You don't look like the golf-cart type of man. Vot are you doing here?"

"I am the owner."

"Ah, a man of property. I knew you were more than a caddie and less than a cad. I am here to offer you my services. You look like a man who could appreciate me."

As she said this, she pulled from the handle of her black umbrella an impressive leather cat-o'-nine-tails.

I was not certain how to react. My first-hand expertise with S & M did not include, before Woodstock, a dominatrix.

"Maybe you have a brother in leather?"

"I can be most accommodating," she said parting her sequined skirt. *She was a guy.* Vilma was the first transvestite whose presence was apparent in the bucolic town of White Lake. While this was an opportunity of sorts, sex of any kind was not beshert between Vilma and me, though we would become friends. Twenty years after Woodstock she would even enroll in my "Absurd, Twisted Comedy" class at the New School.

Disappointed though she was, the Baroness nonetheless invited me in for tea. She didn't make any further plays for me, but she did talk and talk and talk and talk. Apparently, Vilma has as interesting a past as she does a present. She was a sergeant at arms for General Patton in World War II! I've actually seen the pictures myself, though she does look considerably different in uniform than in the elegant red suit, stockings, heels and blond wig she wore out there that rainy night. Nonetheless, she was unmistakably the man in the photographs and today she's a grandfather eight times over, plus a full-time transvestite and hooker. A hell of a guy and an inspiration to me.

Vilma had checked in as David Mosenchinski, and had some Russian dialogue with guess who? He did not eat cholunt. After tea with the Baroness, the rest of my day could only be anti-climactic.

I arrived just in time to observe a local White Lake bully painting a white swastika on the Disco window. A group of hippies descended upon him, fringes, hair and love beads flying and convinced the local lad to clean up his expression of free speech. Pop, who had quite a temper, rushed over wielding a baseball bat and supervised the scene. He wielded his influential bat to put things into legit perspective.

No UFO, no apparitions, no phantoms. Too much rain.

22

One Hundred Thousand
Points of Light

Monday, August 11, 1969...

Worried that something disastrous would still happen to prevent the festival from happening, I was a bit testy and on edge. A group of town officials, self-appointed guardians of the honor of White Lake, marched into the five-by-seven-foot El Monaco executive offices. The dimensions of petiteur (ad hoc opposite of grandeur), were intentional and not just because we were near bankruptcy for fourteen years. The office was designed to hold no more than one Teichberg and one guest at a time. This also implied that it did not have room for more than two Teichbergs at a time. This cut back on family fights in the office, or at least the two-on-one variety and, just as important, it kept the nosy Yentas from eavesdropping on the other guests as they registered. Eavesdropping was an important sport with our kind of clientele. From the simple act of eavesdropping on someone's registering, a good Yenta could determine who was rich, who came from where, who came with whom, and most importantly, which men were not married.

I think it's important for the reader to be able to visualize the class and style of my office, the site of this summit between the Teichbergs and the locals. The meeting began on the wrong foot, so to speak. The uninvited guests had great difficulty stepping over the crowd of bodies in front of our door. The sight of blanket-wrapped sleeping hippies, looking like piles of psychedelic stuffed cabbage arranged by an eccentric cook, likely put them off a bit. Like the cheap plywood door to this office, unused to so many comings and goings, the midnight visitors were unhinged. They were looking mean and agitated. I had no idea what could be bothering them. A good guess was the invasion of what seemed to be half a million of the people they hated most in the world. By the ruddy complexions of their faces, and considering that they had not just come in from an invigorating walk in the snow, I knew this was not going to be a pleasant chat.

"The community in White Lake has had enough. We do not want this Festival. It is out of control. We have declared a state of emergency. We have called Governor Rockefeller and asked him to declare us a state of emergency! You and your hippies and misfits have destroyed our lovely community. We will not tolerate any further damage. If you and your trash don't vacate this county immediately, we will block 17B with a human barrier on Friday morning! No one will get through to Yasgur's farm! This the only warning we're giving you. We represent the business community of White Lake, the merchants, homeowners, and even Yasgur's neighbors."

The end of the Festival? I was sick and getting nauseous.

"It's an election year, right? Didn't you get enough money? Want more? That it?"

"What money you talkin' about, careful what you say! You never saw no money pass hands."

"It's on the TV. There's a lot of money in this thing. This is getting big. You need more money? Or you just trying to get elected again?"

"It was one thing when you said twenty or thirty thousand people were coming here. This is not what you said. This is hundreds of thousands. Just look down 17B! You Jews are making big bucks here and pulled a fast one on us and you're not gonna get away with it! And if you think your Festival is going to happen, you're dreaming. We ain't letting no more hippies onto 17B."

"You're trespassing on private property. Get the hell out of here. Now!"

Pop brandished his broom and together we chased the townies out, as fast as could be expected when your front porch is lined with rolls of psychedelic stuffed cabbage.

Once again, my white knight, Mike Lang, an angel in ringlets, fringed suede and on a motorcycle, rode in to the rescue. I explained to Mike the rotten developments.

"Like no problem, man," he said, and picked up the phone. His ringlets danced like gold springs as he told our story, his head bobbing with every "Like no problem, we're on top of this barrier shit." Lang hung up the phone and said,

"Elli, how about you going on NBC radio in about an hour? It's a short walk. Room 102. Elli, I want you to tell the whole country to come up to the Festival now. Tell them not to wait. Tell them what's going down. Tell them about those rotten politicos, man. Tell them about the barricade. Tell them the Festival is alive and well and happening. Tell them it's the birth of a new nation, the Woodstock Nation. Use your own words, just make sure they know to come up now. Okay, Elli?"

Room 102, of the multi-colored pastel-doored original ten rooms that began the debacle of a resort, was not custom-designed for network radio and television coverage. With leftovers of three sisters' households, shabby and dreary, NBC did the best thing. They emptied out the garnishing, painted everything vertical and horizontal black, and installed their own generators. In place of Goldie's ancient dressing table were now banks of radio and television equipment. Microphones, wires, cables, monitors and lots of phones. Half a dozen technicians with headsets and microphones pushed buttons and adjusted knobs. They put a headset on me and sat me in front of a microphone.

The announcer indicated that they were live from Woodstock, and introduced me.

I was about to address millions of people. I was trembling in the panic dance of one who was gambling with his life's work and savings. The entire dream of the Festival, of survival—economic and emotional—was on the line.

I warned that the locals were planning to block the highway on Friday August 15, the Festival's opening day. Just three days away! I invited one and all to come up immediately. It was the beginning of a new nation of freedom seekers, music lovers, and anti-war-establishment brothers and sisters. It was the Woodstock Nation and the local bigots were trying to kill it by putting up a human barrier to block access on opening day. I then gave driving instructions from New York City. It was so strange. There I was in Room 102 talking into a microphone. I had no idea whether anyone was out there listening. It's not like you get any instant feedback on the radio, you're just talking to a metal mesh-covered object. The technical crew members gave me the okay sign and Mike smiled his transcendent smile. My improvised speech was "cool man," "right on, man," it was "like beautiful."

I spent that entire Monday and Mon-night not knowing if even one person had heard my plea. After all, I simply spoke into this metal thing that had a wire running from the toilet to a generator parked in front of 2A. Mike was pleased, but then, he maintained that blissful look with a constant. He was back at the site and shuttling via copter to the city in order to maintain control of the vast entanglement of obligations.

That night, the ongoing party in my Disco continued. People were hanging from the loose fiberglass ceiling. Substance abuses were, undoubtedly, taking place under our very roof. We were juggling the elements, both man-made and natural. The sweet smoke of marijuana wafted through the cool Catskill night air. And yet, there was something different. I don't know what, but it all felt different than the day before. I supposed the uncertainty of the effects of my radio plea naturally clouded everything. There was no point in arranging for a serious search for Bogart's Maltese Falcon. A goose chase was out of the question. Vilma tried to set up a 'pin the tail on the donkey' game, but there were no interested people.

Late that Monday night, the Disco was packed with people listening to a jam session given by a couple from Bombay. They were playing some mysterious string instruments which I assume were sitars. We had two crowds in the bar. The early crowd, for which Momma could now only stand guard as there was hardly anything to sell anymore. People were consuming whatever they brought with them. It was more of a village green or the corner malt shop than any bar or disco. If there was some new information, it seemed that Congress would announce it here. The assemblage was mostly a mix of Woodstockers, groupies, and anxious relatives seeking other relatives.

The late crowd drove Mom to prayer-mumbling. She thought this group would bring Moses back from the dead, dropping fatal plagues left and right. It was a nightly song and non-linear poetry fest. A good number of the impromptu singers and poets performed naked. They felt that stripped naked they were more real, more present, and more connected with art and their audience. Centered was the word of choice, then. They were also more centered by being naked. I was envious, but having lived forever with no self-esteem, carrying 30 excess pounds, and sexually unstable, it wasn't for me to be a top-less/bottomless barkeep or emcee even though our international audience was tempting.

This particular night when the sitar-playing couple performed, the crowd was quieter than usual. Maybe it was the sitar music, rippling, sinuous and so otherworldly. Maybe not. My nerves were ripply, sinuous, and very otherworldly too.

3:00 a.m. Tuesday morning...

The now-empty bar was eerily silent. Momma and Pop were sound asleep on mattresses in 9A, just beside the fake wall of the men's room. I too, was exhausted, though still vertical. I looked out the window at the peculiarly silent highway. It was about 3:00 a.m. and recently that meant little in terms of movement. This night, it was very quiet. I was convinced something blue and orange and pink and mauve and red and puce was about to happen. I was on edge. I locked up and then started my night patrol of the compound, but I was too tired. I went over to Vilma the Baroness' shack and asked him/her to dress up in a security guard uniform and patrol the grounds. Armed with a big camp flashlight and our one baseball bat, Field Sergeant Vilma was delighted with his/her new role.

Leaving El Monaco security in interesting and creative hands, I went back to the bar, slid open the men's false bathroom door where Mom and Pop were sleeping, and collapsed on the tatty mattress that was designated as mine. Within two-and-a-half seconds, I, too, lay there like a beached whale, dead to the world.

I must have slept at least 20 minutes. Sounds of horns and cars outside woke me. I had trouble standing up. I immediately thought that local goons were attacking, and so grabbed a hammer, and silently went to the bar window to get a discreet view of the grounds and highway. I nudged my pop who got his baseball bat and stood by my side. They were car horns. Car horns blaring away. Those were either

Eighty miles of cars on Route 17B,
Tuesday, August 12, 1969, 3:00 a.m.

Gabriel's trumpets or the rednecks' Armageddon arriving. It was only 3:20 a.m. I was still dressed, so were Mom and Dad. Who had time for costume changes any more? I grabbed my lead pipe, left over from my water pump mugging. Mom awoke now. Mom grabbed an empty bottle of kosher-for-Passover King David wine, and we raced through the bathroom wall into the Disco.

The Disco was silent. Dead silent. Some kids were sleeping outside. Nothing happening. Still, we heard the blare of horns, so I drew the curtains from the floor-to-ceiling window in the Disco. In the distance, Route 17B was now an immeasurable continuous snake of shining headlights. What we had was hope diamonds, one pair after another, blindingly bright. This was no Armageddon, this was the Second Coming.

This Second Coming was the beginning of an infinite river of vehicles of all sizes, shapes, colors and states of repair. Each car, bus, truck, was filled with every type of person you could and could not imagine. Old, young, in-between, black, white, Asian, Hindu, Native American, and even though nobody cared, the ten percent of gays and lesbians. The only people missing were Republicans in plaid pants and Forest Hills tennis-obsessives.

Cars were festooned with flowers and peace signs. Psychedelic colors were the order of the night. I was elated.

"I don't think these are the people who read our Swinging Singles ad in the *Voice*, what do you think, Pop? These don't look like your cook-it-yourself tourists, Pop. Lookit! They're here. It's for the Festival. Mom? Listen to the music. Guitars. The cars are coming from maybe even as far as Monticello..."

We hadn't turned on the radio yet to listen to the news. If we had, we'd have heard that the traffic jam, my personal Second Coming, extended all the way to the George Washington Bridge.

I did what I had always done in a White Lake crisis. I painted over the highway sign at the main entrance, a sign I had painted only two months earlier, that had announced: "Bustling Resort for Sale, Inquire Within." My new sign now heralded a very different attitude. It read:

WELCOME TO THE WOODSTOCK FESTIVAL.
WELCOME HOME!

Pop and I turned on all the Disco and bar lights. The Christmas lights did their twinkling, the neon beer signs did their flashing, and while Momma complained about next month's electricity bill, we threw open the doors. Route 17B's configuration of two lanes was now a five-lane one-way express route to Yasgur's. Within minutes of lights up, the bar and Disco were hopping. Meanwhile, the invasion of headlights continued, non-stop as it would until Friday morning when it would come to a complete standstill.

The next morning, we turned on the news on the one working television set. Helicopter shots of the jammed New York State Thruway, alternate highways, side roads, and a town of Bethel first, a shot of Route 17B that was now being called the "world's largest parking lot." This was the first time we had real perspective of what was going on.

I was not only in heaven, I was quite convinced heaven had come to me. Pop looked into my face beaming with pride at this heart-warming experience. I never saw my Pop in that way again. To see his dark flashing eyes, without pain, even if only for those precious moments, was a reward I never thought would be available to me.

23

The Rednecks Return

3 days and definitely positively counting!

Some mothers take an extraordinary amount of time to absorb the facts of life around them. Some will never accept that which they don't already subscribe to. Hellooooo Sonia! Wake up and smell the coffee, already.

"Ellinoo. Maybe we should borrow some money and build a new wing? Look at all the customers."

"Forget about it Mrs. Teichberg. When this is over, I'm gone. Away. With no phone number. Understand this once and for all, Mom. I hate it here, and don't ever want to see it again. The mortgage will be taken care of. You find a customer to sell at any price. I will not die in this god-forsaken hell-hole. I will never even want to stay in a motel in my entire life. Is that clear?"

She looked around at the strange assortment of types that did not fit into her scheme of things.

"I was also thinking. I don't want you to look close at any of the Jewish girls who are part of this Woodstock business. Not your kind of people. Wait 'till all the crazy ones go away. Maybe in such a big crowd, a nice Jewish girl is out there."

"I will stop talking to you lady, don't fool with my brains anymore! Okay, last time. Positively the last time. Get off my case. I am not ever going to marry any nice Jewish girl. These Woodstock people are exactly my people. Sell the motel or burn it down. This is my last time here. Pop? You tell her, but not now, later, when I'm not here!"

Mike Lang zoomed into the drive on a Harley.

"Let's see that fucking town board block the highway now! Is this the most beautiful sight you've ever seen in your whole life or what, Elli? Man, the traffic is almost at the New York-fucking-City line! Elli, let me know when you can get away, I'll send a bike to pick you up, babe. You just gotta see what we have going at the farm. It's beautiful, man, it's fucking beautiful."

Mike and I marvelled at the response the radio appeal garnered. I was surprised; Mike said he wasn't. I didn't comprehend how he could have been sure. As I look back, I realize that was his way of dealing with the seemingly interminable barrage of problems.

And he zoomed out onto the road and back to the farm site.

1863 alleged sexual encounters reported. 900 UFO sightings.

I assigned the ever-vigilant Vilma to "man and woman" an information desk. The former Chamber of Commerce booth was now resurrected as an official Festival Information Center. The new immigrants to Woodstock lined up instantly to get information and advice dispensed by this vision in black sequins, fishnet stockings and spikes. Vilma's see-through black lace face nets and black silk floral-hat-decor didn't jell with my parents' ideas of an information clerk, but once I told them she was not on salary and was paying extra just for the privilege of working for us without a salary, they decided she, he, whatever, was just fine. Having a cross-dresser on the front lawn was a treasure of perfection in this haven for rednecks! I prayed for another town meeting and having Vilma be the keynote speaker for our side. But my Mother's God didn't hear me. I guess removing the Teichberg Curse was all even a great divinity could handle at one time.

It was a glorious morning. Crowds kept coming, cars jammed the road. To add to the glory, young kids came to the motel asking to meet Elliot Tiber. Yes, people had listened to my radio broadcast. No, this was not just an unusually heavy turnout for a swinging singles weekend. Yes, Elliot Tiber was now famous and would be, not for fifteen Warholian minutes, but for an entire week. Unless someone else became more famous, then my position was fragile at best. Oy.

The same disarming clique of townie power brokers that visited us the day before came back again. Now this was 1969, pre-fitness walking, pre-walking as an olympic sport. So, they didn't know to use the walk as a cardiovascular exercise. They were steaming by the time they reached the El Monaco. Not one of them was able to use his car.

I don't mention the wives since it was an established understanding that women in Bethel didn't count for nothing.

Now, once again this world-class group of misfit bigots tumbled onto the El Monaco's slanted doorstep. And this time they brought a new weapon: The Instant Ordinance. They seemed mighty pleased with themselves.

"Elliot, we came to advise you of the new town ordinance. You guys are in violation of it. Public assembly of more than 50 persons is illegal. Music festivals are prohibited from being held in White Lake or Bethel. Here's a copy for you."

It seems that a meeting with a quorum had been held in the schoolhouse late the night before. A man then introduced himself as the new attorney for the concerned citizens of White Lake. His great distinguishing characteristic was that he shouted the loudest of the bunch. He shouted that my violation of the ordinance was punishable by a jail sentence.

I retorted with a few questions of my own:

"Would there be plenty of room in jail for all the officials who took very large kickbacks, too? Anyone care to take a boat ride?"

Now these land slugs were all quivering. Pop got out his roof-tar mop and shooed them out of the El Monaco entrance.

"Do you dopes see Vilma of the Vilma's Black Stockings Fetish Emporium, who the big boys sent here to take care of any bad news by the local trash... "

Vilma waved her cat-o'-nine-tails and handcuffs at the assemblage. Whatever message Vilma was sending, this crowd was getting. And they were confused and in disarray. If only I had been courageous enough to use it at odd hours as the backdrop for her thriving lawn information biz. She also was hustling her famous black stocking get-togethers under one of the bungalows in the swamp out back. She had such demand that her shack could not contain all comers.

We don't know if it was Vilma's long blowing-in-the-wind black leather scarfs or the black netting that seemed to dance around her as she gestured dramatically. She was in rare form as she took a variety of menacing poses directed at this local group. They departed without further comment.

24

Rain and Reality

2 days and counting. Almost home.
Wednesday, August 13, 1969.

Rain, rain and more rain. Food shortages. Water shortages. Skirmishes. Tenseness everywhere. The crowds kept coming. One of this crowd was Swami Cyrus V. Grubatsvana who was assisted by a very young, very blonde woman named Narayani Goldberg. Their enormous Ryder rental truck had difficulty maneuvering into the drive which was 200 percent filled with wanderers. The Swami, in his hooded robe, stood still like a buddha while Narayani Goldberg opened the rear door. She pressed the elevator gate at the rear, and out came several other hooded people. They lit tiny pen lights and stood in a circle. For a minute I thought they might be a offshoot of some KKK splinter organization deciding to have a meeting in front of my Coke machine. They wore robes, but no pointy hoods, so it seemed kosher. Each lit an incense stick and then they began chanting some language that broke the phoneme sound barrier.

I tried to observe without intruding, but this group, apparently very attuned to the presence of vibrations, all immediately turned to look at me.

"Welcome home, Elliot," intoned the swami. "We've been waiting for you."

"Who are you?" I asked, confused, certain I hadn't ever met this particular group.

"We are a group of old souls guided here just as you were guided, by the same light of the blue pearl, the great granter of dreams. You dreamed for years of a certain thing. You dreamed for years of other things. You dreamed for years of reaching those you left behind under the sea. I see tools, broken waffle irons and Pyrex measuring cups. I see spatulas, doormats, hammers and toilet seats. Does 'hardware from hell' mean anything to you? And as you were guided to a place I cannot name, so you have been guided to this circle of light now mandated to encompass and bless other nameless wonders. Who are you? Why have you called us?"

The swami didn't look Indian Indian. He looked more like an overdressed busboy in a Hell's Kitchen Ninth Avenue all-you-can-eat joint with pretensions. In mystic drag yet. How did he know my hardware store history? My name, okay. I was in the papers, but that fucking hardware store from hell in Bensonhurst? It was drizzling now. But the Swami's silk robes seemed dry and pristine. The dozen or so young disciples gathered around him also seemed curiously unaffected by the precipitation.

"Join us and you will feel the power of Swami Felonius. It was fate that brought you here and it is your moment to receive the greatest gift of the blue pearl—shaktipat."[1]

"Very nice. I think you have the wrong Elliot Tiber and I already have a blue pearl, my own shaktipat, thank you anyway. We have no rooms here at the inn, and if you'd move your truck out of the driveway, it would be also a nice thing since you are blocking the only emergency exit we have left here. Thank you for sharing and caring."

I wasn't trying to be rude nor nasty. I was just running on empty and, even though later on I was sure I was a dunce to pass up an opportunity for shaktipat, this was 1969 and I had no idea what shaktipat was. I didn't have the intellectual bouillabaisse[2] Yale grads had. My pathetic limited lifestyle at Brooklyn College did not allow for a discourse course in shaktipat, let alone a major?

There was no word from the war front and that disturbed me. I was sure the town council was up to something, but what, I didn't know. The phones were so overworked it was impossible to make calls. Now and then the motel office phone lines rang, but who had strength to go answer them? If I was standing at the registration desk, it was usually someone from Utah or Michigan who wanted to reserve rooms and get directions to White Lake and wanted to reserve Festival seats.

---

[1] State of ultimate enlightenment.
[2] A French fishy, spicy soup.

211

My hoarse throat wouldn't permit me to discuss anything with anyone on the phone any more, so I advised callers to stay at home or get another interest in life.

Sometime later during that hectic day, a "honcho from CBS" showed up. This limited identification is not just to protect the man's privacy, but is the only identification I ever got.

He was tripping on something. His eyes dilated as if the world they were seeing was wandering in and out of focus. He had wiry ash gray/brown hair, a trim beard, sparkling eyes, and a lean lanky body that was difficult not to notice in his khaki shorts and tie-dyed tank top. It might be I noticed some few small details because I was attracted to him. And where was it written that only the straight authors are entitled to talk about who and what turns them on?

Mister CBS did the cool, hot man's glide over to my immediate vicinity. His eyes were a good three to four inches from mine. I like someone who is secure and knows what he wants and how to get it. CBS took a joint out of his pocket and offered me a toke. I, who had already had more than enough tokes for the entire season, refused, on the grounds of maintaining a state of semi-alertness. We talked about regressive-aggressive-passive and eternal behavior. CBS did most of the talking. I couldn't listen too well as I was focused on the upward and downward moving patterns of his mouth. For reasons that escape me now 25 years later, this was fascinating. Actually, anyone who stood that close in my face so determined for whatever was fascinating to me. My self-esteem needed boosting just like the rest of the world's, so I let him serenade me with his quasi-intellectual yet poetic rambling about life in the middle. I don't remember the middle of what exactly, but he made sense.

He said he had seen me make my big radio broadcast, and thought we ought to discuss the ramifications of intense touching. Suddenly Mister CBS's hand was on my shoulder. Was this man making a play for me? In broad daylight? Within yards of my mother? Within yards of my father? I didn't know that my folks were so blind from pubic hair linen vapors that they wouldn't have known what they were seeing if they saw it. His making a play for me was fine.

I noted he was wearing a wedding band. Woodstock was the beginning of all kinds of personal freedom for all kinds of people. Now

212

I see that my never having made overt passes at men was a big mistake. There were so many over the years that might have turned into valid friendships and more. But being gay was, for me and my generation and those before us, treacherous. Oscar Wilde and Tennessee Williams and Truman Capote all paid high prices and suffered immense personal dangers because they were visible. Ergo, most of us had no choice but to remain invisible. It was always furtive, secret, in the dark, groping in movie theaters and never-revealed passions to strangers across crowded rooms. But in the middle of the world's largest and busiest parking lot? How would it look if the esteemed President of the C.O.C. of White Lake had his arm around a man's shoulder? For the hippies, it was groovy and cool. For the locals and family, it would be catastrophic and warrant calling in the state troopers. I gingerly put my arm on his shoulder—carefully enough so that if necessary it could have been the old buddy type of pat-on-the-shoulder type of gesture. But his squeeze of my arm made it clear that this was no accident. Then, he pulled a silver chain that was around his neck so that the charm, which was hidden under his tank top, was visible. It was a miniature set of handcuffs.

So, CBS and me went to Shack Number Two to dive into S & M games. Only after did I sense how much I needed that precious time in intimacy. My breathing for the rest of the day would be much easier. CBS faded into the throngs just as smoothly as he had appeared.

I was trying to set up an airlift network for badly-needed help via our unknown White Lake International Airport. An old friend of mine from Los Angeles had gotten through to me, and offered to help. He had made big bucks in real estate, and wanted to do a Woodstock out there as soon as I was finished with this one, and so he was now offering to fly into White Lake in his own plane with lots of supplies. A show of good will. Lenny was exceptionally bananas on the phone, and I said I'd welcome first aid materials, canned food, and bottled water and dry blankets. No problem. He got flying route information from wherever pilots get this stuff, and said to expect him within 14 hours.

I thanked him, he thanked me, and I assumed that would be the end of it. Lenny had been a boyfriend of my kid sister, Renee, a century before. Renee was out on a date with someone else or maybe it was someone else was on a date with her, same difference? He came over with a bottle of vodka and said one Teichberg was as good as the next, so we had an affair. The first for both of us. He went crazy, and moved to Hollywood to get away from the terrible sin we had just committed. I went to live in Greenwich Village to find others to commit more sins. So, crazy Lennie, on the coast at the right time, bought real estate at the right time, sold it at the right price, and was now a rich, rich man. Part of his shtick was to call me from time to time to cook up deals that sounded good. If one was speeding on snow and diet pills, these hot deals sounded terrific. After all, Lenny was a graduate chemist from Brooklyn College, so he knew how to mix powders. Lenny was very popular as long as he wasn't busy taking baths. He needed lots of baths.

Lenny saw me on TV and decided to come help. Nice. He needed an all-you-can-eat place. I told him to bring his own all-he-could-eat since we were out. Lenny liked baths. I told him to bring his own baths since he was so rich and we were out. He took ten to twelve baths a day. He never slept. He installed three commercial washing machines in his bedroom for a constant supply of fresh towels.

Lenny arrived by the smallest two-seater plane I had never imagined would exist. He landed atop the Presidential Wing. My pop was running for a shotgun he didn't own. Lenny opened the door, plopped out huge trash bags with food, enough for a 100-plate sit-down dinner.

We did the hug kiss hug stuff. And that was enough sentimental. Lenny had a box of legal papers for me to sign about the Hollywood Hills Woodstock he was going to do. But, first things first. Before anything, he was hungry. He then wolfed down whatever he'd brought. Raw as is. He then indicated his urgent need for a toilet. I pointed to the public one next to the Fred Astaire/Ginger Rogers Wing. He disappeared into the bathroom with his chemistry set.

There was a hell of a lot of things to do, and supervising Lennie wasn't one of them. I didn't. After a few hours, I glanced up at the roof, and the tiny plane was half hanging over the side, the remains of Lennie's packages dissolving into the muddy bog, and no sign of Lennie. I was accustomed to his m.o., and returned to the situation at hand. Two days after Woodstock was over, a truck pulled up, unhooked the mini-plane and towed it someplace. Not even an excuse me sir.

The hours melted one into another. Most of these days were blurry and fuzzy due to the rainfall and snowfall. There were incidents every hour that needed emergency handling, medics, and the extending of help from one to another. And that is how we were getting on.

The number of apparitions and UFO sightings were not being counted in any reliable manner.

Thursday, August 14, 1969.
One day and too tired to count...

I was so numb, I was beginning to forget that there was going to be a festival. We were so immersed in rain and mud and shortages that music and stages and performers seemed to be a remote business at best. Also, the only views of the site I got were on the TV set, when it worked or my eyes were focused enough to watch, and from kids and guests shuffling back and forth.

I was still focused enough to be on the lookout for trouble from the spirited community in Bethel, and so, when an emissary from the Teichberg Curse stepped onto the El Monaco grounds, I expected it, sort of.

He only looked like he'd stepped right out of Central Casting for a role in a gangster movie. He was miscast and more like the embodiment of Ooze from the Lagoon on Blueberry Lane. He was, in the middle of August and the intermittent monsoons for which Woodstock would become famous, wearing a three-piece shiny dark suit and dainty pointed shoes made from some dead reptile, which he vainly tried to preserve as he tiptoed his way through the ankle-deep mud to talk to me. He was from Monticello, the county seat. Your basic oily type. By this time, I was used to all kinds of threats and I hardly gave most of them much thought and when I did, I called Mike Lang who had a miraculous way of making them go away. I was so tired that I hardly had energy to care about another screaming-meanie local. But this guy gave me a jolt. It was his entire manner that unhinged me.

"Well, Tiber, you're gonna be in big trouble once this festival is over. My advice to you? Enjoy these last days for all they're worth. Look over your El Monaco real good because there are people—big people—who say you ain't gonna have no motel once these creeps and drug-crazed hippies of yours are the hell out of here. Tiber, I don't think too much of you or your kinda people. But, a guy's got to earn a dollar. There's legal stuff coming at you like a speeding train, but a few words to the right people—and I know the right people—and maybe we could save you some of your property. Whaddya say, Tiber?"

And he partially opened his jacket. I had never seen such a tiny metal thing that looked like a gun before. Once, I did get to feel a small metal gun placed against my chest by a vertically-challenged hit man who was acting on behalf of a Supreme Court judge, but that was in Manhattan, not in the fresh air of the mountains.

Before I could say "Mike Lang!" the Baroness Vilma Von Schlimpenblausch, just finishing a security round of the El Monaco compound, appeared. Here she was, an angel in a too-tight military uniform, her padded breasts straining the brass buttons of her jacket, her six o'clock-in-the-morning shadow of a beard showing through her thinning coat of make-up. Yes, to my rescue came an extraordinary decorated military man dressed as a woman dressed as a military man.

"Elliot? " the Baroness called out with a voice like a tuba. "Is this man bothering you?"

I mumbled key words including "extortion" and "blackmail" and "anti-semite" and the Baroness sprung into action.

She whipped out a small silver pistol which, for all I could tell, was a fancy cap gun. Whatever it was, Vilma never needed to fire it, because Mister Extortion put his hands up and did his best to tiptoe backward out of the parking lot.

Vilma explained about a series of articles she had written for *Boy's Life* and *Popular Mechanics*. These were how-to pieces on constructing sixteenth-century Spanish Inquisition torture instruments out of every-day items found in any suburban garage. As Vilma outlined her rainy-day what-to-do advice for restless teenagers across America, I felt such comfort in his madness, which no doubt saved my ass.

Speaking of saving ass and grass and hash and other good stuff, that is now in 1994 bad stuff again, I had my own private stash. All sorts of people with monumental needs were plugging into me, a natural outlet since I was the Woodstock liaison. I'd do someone a favor or provide help or information and, after a while, some of these grateful people gave me some coke or grass. Most of them couldn't understand that I wasn't into the variety of available stuff that dreams are made of. And neither could I. Good sense was prevailing and dominating my day-to-days, and that wasn't so terrifically satisfying. Why not? So they gave, I experimented, and since I was so cautious, it turned out to be relatively safe. And I had a good time. There was more than I would ever use. So my stockpile became considerable. Seeing my folks so tight about every second of the day, I decided that what Mamma and Pop needed most at this juncture was what the 1990s Grunge people call an "attitude adjustment." They needed a calming down, a mini-mental vacation. So, I decided to bake some hash into cookies.

I'd never baked anything before. This is not a political statement. This was 1969 when men still didn't cook, know what quiche was, or blow-dry their hair. But I was curious about cooking the hash. I'd heard of hash brownies, not cookies, but supplies of food were next to nothing, so I made do with some four-year-old left-over passover supplies, tossed in some chocolate chips and made matzo meal-hash-chocolate chip cookies.

The folks were sitting in the Disco when I walked in with this prodigious breakthrough in the culinary arts. The Disco, which was functioning more as a shelter from the rain and as the location of a working toilet and sink, was crowded but quiet. Since food was already scarce in White Lake, my entrance with a tray of cookies made quite a stir.

Mom didn't seem upset about my baking on the Shabbos.[1] They were too tired to notice that it was the Shabbos. I put up a fresh pot of coffee—also illegal on the Sabbath—and they eagerly drank and ate and passed the goodies around to anyone who was interested.

And so, I got my innocent kosher parents stoned on matzo meal-chocolate-chip cookies laced with an illicit weed. I didn't think they'd actually be able to get stoned. The two of them were so serious, so scared, so worried all the time, so fucked-over by their mismanagement of every phase of life, that there didn't seem any room for

[1]Hebrew for the Sabbath.

laughter. They never had sex. I didn't think it was possible for them to kick back, chill out or do anything vaguely approaching relaxation even with the benefit of the evil weed. I thought they were immune to anything that could loosen them up or that wasn't business. The only side of either of them I ever knew had to do with selling pots and pans, then rooms and beer. I was convinced that they were apart from the human race, lacking the feelings and responses the rest of mankind had.

Clearly my evaluation was off the mark, because within ten minutes they were giggling. Within fifteen minutes they were laughing. Within sixteen minutes they were howling. While they were roaring with laughter, they tried to explain that they had no idea what was so funny. As anyone who has done hash or grass knows, the dialogue became a gurgle of twisted phrases and incoherent words. Meanwhile, they wolfed down more and more and even more cookies.

"These are the best cookies I have ever tasted in my life!" Momma declared, giggles erupting as she tried to speak and chew and swallow simultaneously.

My Yenta's Pancake House on Route 17B.
Traffic at a standstill, no more gas, no more pancakes.

Pop just kept laughing and giggling. I had never seen his body move in such a totally relaxed way. I was over-stoned, so it was not difficult for me to be objective in this eye-opening experiment. Three hours later, with my recently gained expertise on drugs and their effects, I knew to quickly drag a mattress out from behind the bar so that they could collapse into the sweet marijuana sleep that was going to sneak up on them any moment. Sure enough, these two worn-out and stoned immigrants suddenly slumped in their chairs and I rolled them onto their waiting bed. The cookies bought three hours of R & R for my parents and three hours of R & R from them for me. Such a deal!

I was numb by four in the morning. I had to take full advantage of the maybe two hours before dawn that I could sleep. Everything was quiet, and the sea of bodies laying in every direction, on the grounds and out onto the highway, seemed to be resting up for the big day coming. Just a few more hours!

Friday morning, August 15, 1969. Day One!

Most of my energy during these 48-hour-days was spent handling motel logistics. There was no longer any contact with Lang and the Woodstock entourage. It was as if they were in some other time warp. Which is exactly where they were. I got touches and bits and pieces of news about my Woodstock "family" from TV and radio. Mostly, news came from the non-stop parade of kids who were traipsing to and from Yasgur's.

There were lulls to be sure, but mostly the sparks, not unlike those California wild-fires, flew erratically from mouth to mouth. Talk about rumbles with Hell's Angels, hundreds—on one occasion rumors had it there were thousands—of accidental deaths due to someone gone bonkers with a hand grenade! New York City cops were hired to help out with damage and crowd control. Either they were excessive in their violent behavior or badly trained or there were conflicting purposes, but it all misfired. Then political stuff was injected, and poof, they were gone. Many cops stayed on to help as volunteers.

It was difficult to know who were the good guys and who were the hooligans. The big conclusion that came about suggested that these kids were not from the moon, after all; they were neighbors, sons, daughters, uncles, aunts, moms, dads, cousins; we all got the picture. White Lake was suddenly a legitimate media dateline. The C.O.C. didn't take advantage of that either. The list of how the local business and social community fucked themselves over would require volumes.

Even though I was technically on the sidelines, I was in my own nirvana. I have always loved upheavals. I love storms, lightning, tornados, earthquakes, hurricanes—especially when I'm watching from a safe vantage point. I even relish rain—especially when it does one of those big downpours for ten minutes and you get drenched and somehow feel so cleansed. A good snow storm? A blizzard? That's my kind of weather. I bundle up and traipse through the silent white fluff. My physical and mental numbness was enervating as well as energizing. As I sat there in the midst of all this upheaval and chaos, when there were free moments to reflect, I relished the joy of this invasion which overturned life as I had known it. A side pleasure was that the tourist and swinging singles plague were shunted into instant ancient history. Relics of the stone age. No the ice age, this was the 'stoned' age to be sure.

Adding to the peripheral mayhem were the chopping sounds of Army helicopters flying in supplies and medical personnel. It was a peace and love festival with the sound effects of a grade B war movie. Those whirling olive birds hovering and whizzing over the tourist information booth on my swamp bog were a very strange combination, totally alien to the quiet sky that was the norm. I couldn't get over the irony that I was definitely, most definitely not going to get to the Festival site. Wishfully, each hour I'd reconsider and try to work out some escape plan so I could get to the farm, but that was hopeless. There was no way my folks could be alone, as they were losing their health rapidly and their remaining strength almost minus 200 percent. And I was so alone, not part of any personal network or support system, there was no one to help or share responsibilities that might have provided a slight respite. But, nobody asked me to do all this, so I'm not complaining at all. Absolutely not. This was a moment in time that was meant to be, and I relished it. Then, and still, now.

Looking around the bedlam of panic and the sheer overweight of numbers, no question, I understood I wouldn't get to go!

But at least I heard the Festival. The speakers at Yasgur's farm floated the music onto the winds, across the valley, over Route 17B, and then, into my open arms. And face and heart and ears. Maybe it was the mountains, the lakes or some special configuration unknown to motel operators that caused such incredible amplification, nobody knew for sure. Some people told me they were hearing the music as far away as Monticello—a good fourteen miles. It was a semi-sweet revenge on the townies. They fought us, they fought dirty, and the hills and lakes fought back with a natural amplification system that would bring the Festival to everyone in the county. I like to think that some of the good vibes, if by no other method then by osmosis, sunk into their brain-dead brains.

As it turned out, over the past quarter of a century, if one reads interviews with some of those left over and some of their like-minded replacements, it is clear that osmosis alone wasn't enough to penetrate bigoted uneducated wasted minds. The way the local press reported events, they must have been happening in some other county or some other continent, which is how it seemed to many of us.

25

The Town Board Blockade
Brigade Fights Back

Augst 15, 1969.
Friday, Day One of the Concert:

A few more hours and counting till the Festival's opening. It's morning, and I'm still uncertain there will be an actual Festival. In my mind I imagine it all disappearing into the purple haze keeping us all aloft like some flotilla. A thousand and one incidents and unknowns could have scrambled it all to hell, and I envisioned the National Guard making mass arrests and sending the rest back to the four corners of the globe. And I'd have to refund everybody everything. This was a "Shlechteh Chaloymeh."[1]

As incredible as it was, a dozen members of the Town Board of White Lake, with wives in tow—not unlike the image of Arab wives walking behind in the shadow of their powerful hubbies—did try for the human barrier, the big blockade brigade. They held little soggy paper plates with ball point-penned messages reading:

Festival Canceled By Order of Town Board of White Lake.
Vacate White Lake immediately!

One of my big regrets, along with trashing a pile of Woodstock posters and all the unsold tickets, (which sell for thousands of dollars now), was not taking photos of this polyester and plaid protest line across 17B, interwoven with the oncoming throngs of hippies who were totally oblivious to it. Such a classic example of dopes or, in more

---

[1]Yiddish for 'rotten bad terrible dreams.'

adult terms: Mismanagement by Corrupt Government at the local level. It was not an effective protest. The rains, the mobs, the opposing agendas of townies and Festival-goers made this attempt at a blockade a non-attempt. Woodstock was already a human barrier and White Lake could support just so much barrier.

And their signs? There were so many signs; people looking for lost friends, people inviting you for the next enlightenment opportunity conducted by one of the dozens of impromptu swamis in town, or a mystical psychedelic sampler under the fourth oak tree to the right of the Disco, and the plethora of "Ride Wanted to Calif," or Philly or Tokyo, that the dull town signs didn't have any chance at being noticed. Had they had a Harvard consultant on their picket line, they would no doubt have been advised not to expect their wet paper plates, with their improbable dictates, to compete with the flood of more colorful and apt signage. When the blockade and sign brigade realized their lack of impact, they welcomed Leon Lapenis' offer of his bungalow colony's sound stage and microphones. Leon "the tractor" Lapenis grabbed the mike:

"Leave White Lake immediately! By order of me! All non-residents leave immediately. Unless you want to rent a nice bungalow for next season, in which case, the Lapenis office is now open and taking cash-only deposits. The rest of you trash, get out of the county before we run you out of here!"

Attempting to broadcast a message against music blaring from the countless portable radios and the exhaustive display of musical instruments from all around this and other worlds, was a little like pissing into the wind. In this case, it became "hissing" into the wind when the wiring shorted out, causing a small electric fire. And so, the Town Human Barrier Festival Protest went up in smoke, smoke so insignificant that it couldn't hold a candle to the burning incense of the countless spiritually-awakened hippies who had taken over White Lake.

Innocent and ignorant of the latest, newest and most up-to-date White Lake legislative activity, the hippie and not-so-hip pilgrims continued to arrive. By this time, all possible physical space leading up the winding country roads to the farm was transfigured into a serpentine parking lot. All road shoulder-space was impassable. Left with no choices, people left their empty cars wherever they happened to be. Effectively, Route 17B and Route 55 were closed. Effectively, Route 17B Quickway was now closed. Effectively, traffic stopped moving for 50 miles or more. And they hiked, biked and, in fortunate cases, rented horses from farmers and galloped to White Lake.

"Do you think that maybe our regular customers can't get through? Maybe some of these people are looking for our swinging singles-package vacations?"

It was a distinct possibility that my mother, expressing herself in this insane manner, was almost ready for the funny farm. How she could even find the mental time to think back to pre-Festival craziness was beyond any lunacy I could have conjured up. Watching her dance her Yiddishe Mamma stuff amongst these thousands upon thousands of kids, was akin to a voyage in outer space. She was handling money and feeding hungry kids simultaneously. Her two biggest passions. What her mind was processing, I didn't know then. Only some 20 years later, when she was living in a nursing facility, and the subject was discussed, did I get the full impact of what she thought of the entire happening.

"I hope you don't mention my name to anyone in your book. Don't tell people where I am. What would I say if reporters asked me what went on? I would better shut up and not tell them anything, since I don't want to ruin your book. I hated them, all those dirty shmutz,[1] feh, dirty sex everyplace, drunks, drugs, kids who should have been home with their mothers. It makes me sick to remember. Rotten. Disgusting! I hated that music too.

"And all those awful people, naked and sleeping with strangers. I was ashamed. I was ashamed you were there. I don't know why you are reminding people who you were and where you are now. They will blame you because you were the one who made it happen. They weren't our kind of people. I was proud of you when you were teaching art. And I'm thankful you came to help us now and then. But I am ashamed of you and Woodstock."

She instantly wrecked me again. I thought I was experienced enough and wise enough, 20 years totally away from her, that some

---

[1]Yiddish for dirt.

stupid jerky remarks like these couldn't affect me anymore. Wrong. Her limited corrupt navel vision, still strong in spite of Parkinson's, kidney failure, eyesight failure, memory loss, and deterioration of every moving part of her body, still went on and on. Like the Energizer Battery bunnies in those television commercials, on and on and on. And it was enough to make one homosexual? No way. According to the latest studies, environmental exposure to raw elements (such as impossible Jewish Mamas), are not to be considered the cause of sexual deviation. The X chromosome, (given by the mother naturally), determines sexual direction. Who could hate a mamma so overwhelmingly devoted to her son that even near heaven's gate, she is able to still push her corrupt self-serving agenda up the mountain? Eeeyuch!

By Friday, the few remaining exhausted El Monaco resources, never functional to start with, were devoted exclusively to crowd control. I looked behind the bar parking lot where I could see Yenta's without risking the ire of the hoods who were its temporary landlords. It was all locked up and surrounded by twenty-foot high piles of garbage, soda cans, clothes, blankets, car parts, and assorted remnants of bric-a-brac. The stinking mess was encircled by piles upon piles of kids in various states of disarray. Unfortunately, none of these festival goers were experiencing anything remotely resembling a music festival. It was impossible to determine if they were already returning from the farm, or if drugs and booze had simply made them plop onto the nearest pile of refuse. Whichever, not a terrific sight.

Since Yenta's appeared to be out of business, I cautiously stepped over the debris, to assess the damages. I was enormously relieved to find the tenants had mysteriously disappeared. Their two big black limos with opaque windows were no longer there. I could see the imprint of these behemoths in the mud. I have no idea how they managed to move those hearses past the mounds of refuse and piles of sleeping people, but I was ecstatic. I went inside hoping to find food supplies, but there was nothing but refuse and mounds of wet and muddy rotting who-knows-what in all the rooms. I did find several small unfamiliar paper boxes. They were empty ammo containers, something I'd never seen. Perhaps they were just being recycled and used to store jelly beans. The good news, however, was that I could use the space, as wrecked as it was. At least it was indoors and, if those

They are all sitting on my mamma's motel blankets.
Go know, at the site, August 1969

crazy rains were going to continue, people would be grateful for a room with a roof.

Jesus was spotted walking on White Lake. 18 UFO'S hovered over. I got a crew of volunteers to sweep the floors and haul out the wet rotting who-knows-whats.

"Hello. My name is Lilly of the Valley. Can I am be of help here? I am a licensed dietician and have returned to Earth from the future to restructure the misguided past.

"I see you are slightly overwhelmed here and since my duties with the Sunshine Salvation Sluts are not required, and I notice you are in the midst of something clearly demanding, and I do have an advanced degree in thermo... thermo-something, what can I do?"

She had to be six feet-five, not a usual height in White Lake for a graduate thermo-whatever. Her long brown braided hair reached her ankles. In spite of the wet and muddy, previously sunshine-type outfit she wore, her face radiated squeeky clean and wholesome.

"We're cleaning out the Pancake House and are going to try to set up some makeshift emergency shelter here for whoever needs a break from the rains. I've gotta get back to my post next door at the motel. Could you handle this here?"

She nodded, straightened up her blouse and pants, and began organizing a few of the kids in her path. I sensed she would be able to do what had to be done, based on nothing substantial, of course, except her willingness, and retreated to the motel. I peeked out at her a couple of times and saw her, effectively comforting the most desperate kids, those freaking out on bad drugs and those who had first aid needs. The logic was that a dirty Yenta's was better than a clean bog.

White Lake, in short, looked like a war zone. The helicopters were continually chopping overhead. Victims of bad acid were air lifted to hospitals for emergency care. And the schoolhouses in the county— even the White Lake site of the Town Board and Chamber of Commerce meetings—were converted to emergency medical care centers. After it all, I read that school gyms, libraries, shops, religious places opened up emergency shelters and first aid centers for a 60 mile radius. Every inch of space and every available supply were being overtaxed, but effectively being inducted into the emergency. Professionals and amateurs of every description were volunteering their desperately-needed services. If nothing else, and at a great price, the Festival mayhem brought together people helping people, which was a total unknown in the county before. As I mentioned earlier, if it wasn't hotel- or room renting-related, it wasn't on anyone's agenda.

By Friday afternoon, many of the locals started to soften up. Once they realized these Festival freaks, in overwhelming numbers, were kids with overgrown heads of hair, and much like their own family members, albeit with different tastes in clothing and color combinations, they proffered their help. A bit of intelligence slept in.

Sadly, some people were "gouged" for medical services, otherwise known as possibly inappropriate fee scheduling. Examples of a small handful of doctors charging extra-large fees for their emergency first aid services were evident in many villages and towns. Certain physicians had their daughters, wives, and friends dress up in nurse's whites, and administer injections. Of course, illegally. I personally knew of two such doctors. I didn't hear of any dangerous results and I suppose the doctors took precautions but, in order to make money on this emergency situation, resorting to faux nurses administrating medications which they were not qualified to do, was beyond.

Reports of long lines, like those in supermarkets, in front of any medical doctor's home or office, and of ladies in uniforms dispensing pills and injections, perpetuated images of a cashier at Sotheby's ringing up auction sales, while the fever for her services grew.

There was also gas gouging, price inflation at food and supply stores of every kind, and taking advantage of the situation by local business persons who were foolishly unprepared for this influx of customers. I had tried for weeks to warn everyone to stock up, but in vain. While Lapenis was selling water for five dollars per glass, some of his tenants were more thoughtful. Even the worst of the normally lowest of the low-lives provided hose showers, sandwiches, and dry clothes. Never mind the taste levels. Dry and clean was terrific. Since no new supplies were getting into White Lake, there was a physical limit to what generosity was possible.

26

Vass Iss Dass Under the Sealtest?!

Later: Exactly when is impossible to say. Still not counting...

It was late afternoon on Friday. The concert had still not officially begun. All day hysterical concert-troubled rumors wandered in and out of the El Monaco. Frantic stories of musicians not showing up, the opening act arrested, car explosions, skirmishes between locals and outsiders, knifings, and excited National Guardsmen throwing everyone out, travelled like wildfire.

There was so much improv music by wandering guitarists, improv drummers and instruments enough to form dozens of orchestras that, in the immediate motel area, it was uncertain if the festival had begun four miles away, or if we were being bombarded with echoes. But when it did begin, it was cataclysmic. The mountains moved and were moved when Richie Havens opened with his improvised, now-famous song, "Freedom." This part is all music history. The cheering and shouting of millions of young voices began echoing for miles! It makes me want to cry, just thinking of it and thinking what this very first call for freedom meant to me at that time. Freedom to be gay or straight or bi. Freedom not to be invisible because if people knew what you were they'd hurt you. Freedom from my indentured servitude to my parents. Freedom to be an artist, of whatever kind. Ninety percent of those in and around the compound didn't seem straight enough to focus, so they were not entirely sure if the music was the Festival or portable players or nearby kids' improv performing. The one-big-party atmosphere, coupled with the continuous onslaught of everyone high on grass and hash, clouded serious judgement. But no matter, not to me anyway; I knew the difference.

It was Friday night, and I knew Woodstock had been born. The weight of the gnawing constant fear I'd been carrying on my back for weeks—that it might all be closed down and poof, gone—was now history. The pain was not one of economics. Had there been no Woodstock, we'd have had to walk. My folks would have gone to Israel somehow. I'd have returned to New York City and found yet another job. But the fear of returning to the status quo, the living death of White Lake, the motel, and my parents was, finally, lifted up and shot out of existence. It was clear that the man on the moon would soon enough be able to see this new nation. And the moon man had better hurry since, as we all know, as soon as something this good and wonderful happens, it don't last.

Suddenly, so much good for so many people, and for free yet, somebody would surely come along and try to bottle it and keep it available for only a few who could afford it. With that in mind, as exhausted as my brains and feet were, I made sure to relish every aspect of the here and now. Someone was presenting this moment, this gift, and I knew how to say, "Thank you."

My folks and I took turns grabbing half-hour naps whenever there was a bit of a lull. The back of my car, parked on the mud next to the Underground Cinema, was the most advantageous spot to be able to continue the swivel head method of watch out for...?

We never woke each other unless there was an urgent situation needing instant handling. So when I heard the tapping on the windshield, I jumped up quickly. It was Mom.

"Elli, wake up. Wake up, I have to talk with you."

"Ma? What's the matter? Are you okay?"

"I'm okay, it's you who worries me. I found dis in the freezer, It's not normal. It's not normal to put dog poop in plastic bags and in the freezer. We keep food there. Kosher food. What's the matter with you? Talk to me. You can trust me."

She was waving a plastic baggie packed solid with frozen dark stuff and frenetic.

"Mom, there were other bags like that. Hundreds of other bags like that. Did you touch them?"

Those little plastic bags of "dog poop" were actually bags of hashish left with me for safekeeping by certain people. These people were friends of certain other people, whom I never met. If I did meet them, I didn't know. But in the state of chaos, there was lots I didn't

230

know. Ultimately, people were sure doing me favors, and when someone needed a favor, I tried.

How could I reasonably refuse to lend a bit of ice cream box space? And here was this madwoman, beyond redemption, waving one bag out of thousands, each of which could have been worth thousands. I couldn't imagine how much hard cash I'd have to find someplace to pay for the freezer full of shit. This was a 'shlechteh chaloymeh' of major proportions. I was terrified. I saw my head on the block and the cleaver coming down.

"Mom. Did you touch the other bags?"

"I trew it out. And now I have to trow out the freezer. Who could use a freezer that has had such traife?"

I knew I was safe when she said she threw it out. My mother never throws anything out. Not even a toothless comb—you never know when you could need it. Every object that passed through her life was used to death and then stored somewhere. She was so terrified of poverty that, for all her faith in God, she was determined to make certain she would never starve as she had in Russia.

She had admonished me countless times when I was a kid. She would hold up a huge eight-pound ball of string and teach:

"Don't throw out string. One day when you'll need string, everybody else will have to buy string, you? You'll have string."

And sure enough, when I searched long enough and deep enough in the recesses of El Monaco's basement, I found the hundreds of bags of hashish, stowed away under some buried aluminum pots from World War II years that were now used to store cholunt leftovers. The smell alone kept away even sewer rats, so it was a safe place.

What on earth could she have been thinking of doing with bags of dog shit? Put it in her cholunt? Use it for meatloaf extender? I was relieved and my hysterical shaking subsided. They watched as I gathered up the bags, stuffed them into huge canvas sacks, dragged them out to my car and locked them in my trunk, safely, until the good witch of the east came to pick up.

Before they phoned a madhouse to take me away for a lobotomy, and I had explained that this was not dog shit frozen in individual portions, but hashish, and worth hundreds of thousands of dollars, they calmed down. I thought that would be that, but they went that one last step with a follow-up question:

"What is hashish?"

"Hashish is medicine from India and Japan and the Himalayan mountains that priests, goyishe priests, use to help their believers. You saw plenty of goyishe priests in long robes and smoking funny sweet-smelling stuff in funny pipes. They are here, they are everywhere. One of their rabbis asked to put his supply here because he was afraid somebody would smoke it all on their own, party until death, and there wouldn't be any left."

I sent one of my minions to find one of the runners at the farm with a simple message: *The Sealtest Ice Cream is melting.* Within an hour, a young long-haired man on a motorcycle with a sidecar with State Police markings on it drove up to collect the goods. He was not the same guy who had brought it, but he knew what to say and how to say it, so he was legit. I was glad to see the stuff off the compound since there was so much paranoia about drug arrests that I didn't need to be involved in something I was not involved in. In fact, I still wouldn't swear it was hashish. I never opened one bag, nor was offered a toke. People came and went and told me all sorts of things, which I mostly discounted. For all I knew, it was doggie poop. But I didn't know the poop-scoop maven, Fran Lee, in those days, or I would have called her for a professional say.

27

A Twenty-Minute Love Story

More victims of blue acid, whatever that was, floated into my lap. You should know my bar door was actually five feet out on the highway. Even if you were not headed for my step, you tripped over it. I set up blankets by the pool under the standing umbrellas. Didn't take long for the operating grapevine to get the information out: Under the Hebrew National Hotdog pool umbrellas, you can get help in coming down. And the line of unfortunate kids now coming from the top exit from Route 55 was snaking its way in circles around the frozen custard ice cream stand which, in fact, unknown to the owners, was having its parking area used as temporary headquarters for some big drug cartel from Bogota. Oy, the funny stuff behind the frozen malts.

My brains were now completely numb from the cold rain. I felt a peculiar sense of isolation. As I watched the moving waking zombies, I feasted on leftover cans of vile Rokeach kosher unlabelled cans we found behind the hot water boiler. Hunters had left these cans several winters before, and Mamma never threw anything out. It is also possible these cans grew there. Anyway, this was the only nourishment we had left for the duration.

28

Miz Scarlett, I Don't Know Nothing About Birthing Babies!

Saturday, August 16, 1969...

On this, the second day of the Festival, I had no time or strength left to even think about much of anything. What Festival? I knew I was missing my chance at Crosby, Stills, Nash and Young, The Who, Joe Cocker and Santana, but they didn't know they'd be missing me, so it evened out. Sort of? I've missed out on much more before, and even more since.

Not to let you think it was boring back at the compound. A very pregnant woman, in a hot-Schott leather jacket and hot jeans, screeched into the drive in front of the bar doorway. She almost ran over my outstretched feet as I was in the wrong place at the right time.

She plopped the bike at my feet and started screaming. She was standing in what appeared to be her own personal puddle of water. What do I know about baby birthing? Zilch. I looked at the puddle she travelled and it looked different from the rain puddles all over the drive. Not that I was thinking, but it hit me that was the broken water so many characters in hospital TV series screech about during focus-on-emergency-baby-birthing. So it was clear this was no victim of Mamma's cholunt. But beyond that and whatever I'd seen in the movies, I had no idea what to do in a medical emergency. I flunked Biology because I wouldn't slit open my frog for dissection class. I couldn't do heroin or anything that involved a needle because I'm afraid to puncture my skin. I look big and burly, but show me where it's written big 'n burly is able to deliver babies, live, without an appointment?

It all looked a bit like a Russian Revolution battle scene from *Doctor Zhivago*, except Julie Christie was nowhere to be seen. The rain was pouring non-stop and the muddy ground was covered with bodies of the tired, the tripping, the ill, the confused, and now, one pregnant woman. There was no room to manoeuver without trampling someone else—people were laid out like pieces of a weirdly mis-crafted mosaic. I was the most together-looking person in this circus. There was no other option than to play doctor.

I looked down at this young girl. She was maybe twenty. Her long brown hair lay on the ground, framing her face. Her large eyes got larger by the second. She was screaming in pain. Her howls cut through my terror and I began functioning automatically. I looked under her skirt, figuring maybe that was the general area to be focused on. I tore off her underwear, and, remembering from some TV show that you're supposed to scream "Push," screamed "PUSH!" What did I know? This lady with no name was lying on the ground and I was vainly screaming "Push" and looking for something to happen. And then something did. A dark hairy head started to emerge from between her legs. I was so excited, I had no idea what to do other than continue shouting "Push" and grab hold of the head and pull.

While I was pulling the baby out, Papa rushed over to see what the commotion was. "Get help!" I ordered, and Papa, apparently having leapt directly into adrenalin-mode, ran off to fix the lawn mower. Mamma peeked out from behind her Louis IV-Sloane Fifth Avenue Damask drape in the rolling office, and decided to do windows. She immediately covered the window with opaque window wax.

The cries and moans signaled me something new had happened. All the mud, the noise, the dirt, the rain, the collection of fools and nitwits in attendance at this birthing notwithstanding, a tiny Woodstock baby girl was born in my arms. And it was crying, and this long bloody umbilical cord was dangling and I was attached to this woman even though my attachments to women over the years were peripheral. Thinking about it much later, I assume my relationship with the mamma and little girl could qualify for more than peripheral.

I wasn't sure what to do about the umbilical cord. Even a full-impact adrenalin shot couldn't propel me to cut human tissue, so I motioned to someone standing above for help. It was Vilma. She took off her sheer see-through black silk cape and Paris designer scarf, and wrapped the child. Someone shouted something about 911, and an army copter would be there in minutes, and to hang on. I plopped, carefully, onto the front steps of the Disco, the cord connected to the mother, and we waited. Light years and seconds later, the crowd pulled back and a copter landed on the roadway with an emergency medical team. I looked at the bedraggled mother and child and naively asked,

"How could you, in your advanced condition, have come to this Festival?"

"I didn't know I was pregnant. I don't know how this happened."

The state trooper on his horse asked, "Are you the father?"

Mamma rushed out from the office and made it very clear:

"No! No! Not him! That's my son. He wouldn't have a baby in the mud. That girl doesn't look Jewish, how could it be him?"

Twenty years later, when *Life* magazine did an anniversary issue about Woodstock, they published this incident along with my phone number and a request to the grown-up Woodstock Baby to call me. Along with wanting to meet her and see how the mother was doing, I thought if we were going to film this story, she could play her mother. I got calls from foreign countries whose languages I didn't understand, so it may well be that the baby or the mom called, but I'll never know. Office hours in London, being six hours ahead of us, enabled may secretaries on supper break, or at the end of their work day, to make 'free' long-distance phone inquiries, with various claims about the Woodstock Baby.

Three hundred crank phone calls later, from coast to coast, and 1,000 more calls from around the world, I have concluded that it is not necessarily a good idea to place one's home phone number in *Life* magazine. I still get one or two calls a month from would-be grown-up Woodstock Babies. Must be those old copies of the magazine lying around in dentists' offices, I surmised. Many calls were from curious youngsters of high school history classes who were writing papers on the Festival and wanted some first-hand information. Others were from freaked-out stoned-out nuts, aged hippies, wannabe hippies, perverts, and lots of anxious strange types. Many were young ladies who were being held prisoner in their country of choice, and nobody would believe they were born in Woodstock, ergo, if I'd send them their Woodstock birth papers and an airline ticket, they'd come see me.

The only call out of all of those that even seemed remotely possible was from a shy woman from New Mexico who said she was in fact the mother, but she was ashamed that she gave birth to her daughter under such circumstances, and didn't ever want the child, now 20, to know. I tried to get the woman to give me her name and how I could reach her. She refused. I gave her my address and asked her to write me in confidence, but she never did.

Robert Stack's *Unsolved Mysteries* phoned, and said they might be able to help with a nation-wide search. But, after a while, they informed me this wasn't a mystery enough for them. Okay for you, Stack. Cancel my subscription.

29

Let Freedom Ring!

Still Saturday Morning. If I could count, I'd use the strength instead to make a nice hot cup of coffee, and make a clean dry warm bed, and go to sleep.

In order to give aid and comfort during the remaining Festival hours, the highly respected and responsible local rag, *Times Herald Record,* in cahoots with the Teichberg Curse, declared the Aquarian exposition of Woodstock a Sodom-Disneyland combination. They screamed "Fire" by exaggerating some three deaths that had occurred, unfortunate accidents that were just that. Those were three people out of at least a million and, considering the immense potential with all the bad drugs going on and dangerous conditions, it was a slim statistic.

One death was a seventeen-year-old boy in his sleeping bag in the mud who was run over by a tractor. The other two were drug-related. Full details of which, to this day, I've never known.

The rumor mill spread the word that hepatitis and other infectious diseases were running rampant. I've no doubt in my mind that many of these damaging vicious claims could be traced to misfit townies looking to wreak havoc and perhaps prepare the way for legal battles later on. Several people came into the compound to claim that Yasgur's was serving gourmet champagne dinners to the Woodstock staff and elite performers, while a riot of hungry Festival attendees was about to break.

I had given my Navy speaker mikes freely to those wishing to make loudspeaker announcements in the immediate vicinity of the compound and lake. Big mistake. While they were being used to locate missing people and alert medics of needs that required immediate attention, they were also being used by crazed people whose agendas still remain a mystery to me. Perhaps fracas was what they had on their

The posters were free.
I lost thousands of them in the rains.

minds as they abused my efforts at helping. Some of the craziness they were announcing included warnings of roaming psycho-killers, rapists in the woods, stabbings, poison foods, poison in the water supplies, and sexual sales in order to raise monies for drugs. Once that became obvious, I just shut down the system for the duration.

30

Sunday Morning Shoot-Out

Saturday night, Clearance Clearwater Revival played until dawn. I only heard vague sounds wafting in and out of my Caddie. I was so cold and numb, it wasn't possible to differentiate between one performer and another. Kids were still playing guitars, trumpets, accordions, mouth organs and other instruments I am not able to describe. That, along with noisemakers, loudspeakers, roars of motor bikes, copters, made it impossible to filter out one sound from another.

When I woke up from my nap, I vaguely remembered that this was the last day of the Festival. As groggy as I was, I began hoping that when the Festival was over, it wouldn't be over, ever. It must have been akin to delirium, but I fantasized that this amazing crazy quilt of people would stay. I had already forgotten what life was like at the El Monaco pre-Woodstock.

I heard exciting new rumors. I hung on every word of the stories that a whole bunch of people intended to become squatters in Bethel. When the music was over they would not leave, but form a nucleus for that new nation the press was talking about. That I would even consider being part of such a hopeless nutzy impossible effort shows how dilapidated my rational thinking process had become in those few hectic crazy weeks.

31

Exodus

There was a strange feeling in the air, so thick you could slice it and serve it atop the state troopers' car hoods. Everyone felt it. The concert had this last day of performances, yet by early morning it seemed the vacuum cleaners were turned on too early. The state troopers had obviously had strategy meetings the night before. They were organized as they arrived and moved cars to the side of the road. With tow trucks and cans of gas, they were clearing a width equivalent to one-and-one-half lanes, in one direction; out. What an impossible task. Most of the cars were out of gas, and there was, of course, no gas to give them. Nevertheless, they were making a heady path. One of the troopers told me they would have one-way traffic to all points out of White Lake in a matter of two hours! Emergency traffic plans called for all roads to become one-way exit routes.

Meanwhile, this final day of the Festival was getting underway. Jimmy Hendrix was scheduled for the finale, and I thought maybe I would be able to regroup my face and make a chance to get to Max's farm. With my folks all but panting for rest, I had to take their health and wear and tear into utmost consideration. I'd have to stay put. The closest I would get to Max and his farm was a brief phone call. Max called some time on Sunday just to see how I was doing. I described just a mini-bit of the meshaggaas at my end, and he described the thousand-fold craziness at his end.

"What I wouldn't give for a nice ice cold buttermilk or a wonderful bottle of chocolate milk or some yoghurt!"

"Forget all that. There is nothing at all left here on the farm. My barns and storage are totally empty. There is not a drop of cheese or milk left for a hundred miles! We'll get together later this week. There are things we should talk about. Nothing I can say now, my phone is not private anymore."

And that was the very last time I ever spoke to Max. When I was living in Paris some time later, I read in the *International Herald Tribune* that Max had died.

Those final hours took on a moon-surface atmosphere. We were moving in slow motion. It was later in the afternoon and Mom and Dad were operating on empty. The night before I had plugged in the trusty golf cart to get its batteries working, if possible. Like the little train that could, the cart energized itself for one more day. Its grand-finale role was as a mini-ambulance, taking many drugged-out kids to our shelters. Now, Pop needed it to get around the compound to shut down. All we didn't have was the Medal Chevalier from Paris. As people abandoned their bungalows, Pop loaded whatever supplies he could muster up, boards, nails, chains, locks, tools, and drove around in the over-abused yellow golf cart we now called 'life saver.' Without those golf wheels, none of us would have had any feet left. Pop drove around boarding up the windows and doors. There wasn't much left to protect, since everything was caving in, soggy, empty, torn, worn and muddy, but it seemed the prudent thing to do.

Mom was harvesting what was left of her linens—torn, worn, soggy and muddy. I ran around, worn, soggy and muddy, sorting out whatever I could. I looked over my shoulder and jealously eyed the last of our guests who were together enough to walk the four miles toward the farm.

At about 4:30 Sunday afternoon, the rains resumed. We are not talking about minor precipitation. We are not talking about a minor monsoon. We are talking about an explosion, a gale force hurricane. I ran into my Caddie for safe cover. It seemed a lot more secure than the wilted El Monaco office. Looking out the foggy splattered windshield, I witnessed a scene that could have come out of the *Wizard of Oz*. People, blankets, tents, plastic sheeting, love beads, peace paraphernalia, drug pipes, all went flying in every direction. My signs—"Motel for Sale," "Underground Cinema," "Coming Soon: 87-Story Condominium," and even the famous "Presidential Wing"—floated, spun and twisted in the sky. It was like watching my life pass before my eyes, except that it wasn't my past, it was my present. And the most precious present I'd ever had in my life. As much as I loved dramatic weather, this time it was excessive, even for me. I realized that this downpour could ruin the end of this heavenly Festival. I would have cursed God, but I knew that this was no Godly event. If there is no God, there is no curse from God. Since there are Teichbergs, it was the Teichberg Curse.

But, at approximately 4:32 that afternoon, just as I was taking total genetic credit for the destruction of the final moments of the Woodstock Festival, not to mention the rude interruption of Joe Cocker's act, the downpour ended. The signs flew back to their posts, the blankets, tents, plastic sheeting, and love beads landed in the mud. A victorious cheer filled the air as the rain-soaked hippies, like so many munchkins in Oz, emerged from under doorways, cars, trees and bushes and cheered the sunshine.

I emerged from the safety and protection of my Caddie.

Jimmy Hendrix sang and sang and sang. Only years later would I read in some of the several books about Woodstock who, what, where, and why. Those twilight hours were very unreal to me. The strange, filtered-gray orange color that filled the air, the dampness, and the eerie sound of cars being started up and heading all in one direction. Away from White Lake. As cars passed by my vantage point in the Disco, where I was lying like a corpse atop the jukebox by the window, I looked for familiar faces and perhaps, some of my recent new friends. I could see nothing but the red lights of the tailgates.

By early evening, the exodus became serious. More and more cars were flowing in one direction. The one-and-one-half lane was now three lanes in one direction.

It was strangely silent, as though someone had turned the sound down on the television, but the picture kept moving. A silent blur dissolving into the damp summer night.

I found an old can of Oxo broth some hunter from the winter kills had left atop a closet that obviously nobody had cleaned since a year or more. I heated it up, and was nursing the hot beverage, watching wistfully out of the Disco window. The folks were long since dead asleep.

By one in the morning, wiped-out and alone in the deserted motel, I gave my last sentimental glance. I turned off all the motel lights. I peeked into Room 9A where I found Mama and Pop passed out cold on a mattress on the floor.

I adjusted the last sign I'd made so that it leaned upright in the window:

**Closed for the duration. No vacancy.
Everything is out of order.**

There was only one dry place in the compound where I could get a private quiet night's sleep. I walked to Shack Number Two, where I climbed into my leather sling, surrounded by my leather and metal toys, and fell dead asleep.

32

Rude Awakenings

What a deadly silence. A letdown. It was over and nobody was saying anything. The entire community looked like it had survived a war, and the troops had gone. It had. They had.

Monday morning the county-wide cleanup began. Pop was hosing away mud from the steps and path and driveway. Two thousand volunteers from a New Mexico commune stayed on to pick up every last piece of garbage and refuse. The vicious attacks about the Festival leaving the county in total filth were clearly not going to be true. These volunteers stayed two to three weeks, walking hunched over with huge plastic trash bags, picking up every last blanket, sneaker, towel, shirt, bottle and can. Other volunteers—many of them performers such as my Earthlight troupe—also stayed on to give of themselves to leave the entire county as clean as possible. The garbage could be blamed on a million people. The rains and mud couldn't.

Mom was surrounded by huge piles of muddy stained linens. She called a linen service to come pick it all up. A major step for her to consider paying for a cleaning service? Maybe there was a God; for her, not for me.

Wet muddy blankets lay like corpses on a battlefield. My thoughts were not of sending them out to be cleaned. Burn the entire mess, and not to start fresh. Burn down the fucking motel, and sell the ashes as a souvenir. It would be an ecological gesture, since the land would look much better without any of El Monaco's questionable improvements. The rumble of trucks moving in to collect the debris was the sound of the moment.

Some locals passed by in mud-splattered vehicles and gave me the finger. They shouted at me and jeered incoherent warnings, but I was too tired to care. Whatever was going to happen would happen

The Bar and Disco entrance from Route 17B.
Where is a broom here?

anyway, and I'd call Mike Lang and he'd smile and everything would be fine. Or so I thought then.

"Pop, we can't do this. We will drop dead here in our tracks. We need to go to sleep. It can all wait 'till tomorrow. Let's close off the driveway, shut down."

Dad put chains across all three driveways, and the three of us collapsed in three different motel rooms and slept for the next thirty-something hours.

Several weeks passed, everything was quiet. Our place was in some kind of order, and I was packing my car, headed who knows where? It was done, and like in Zen studies, I was going to turn the page.

33

Aftermath Math—
A Morally-Challenging Moment

Somewhere along the line I realized how much that summer had totally changed me. My fifteen-inch tall hair, bell-bottom jeans and tie-dyed shirt? My black pants and black shirts, and obsession for noir, had changed into psychedelic madness. Everything was different. But not just my clothing and my hair—and my long sideburns. Something about me had changed. I hadn't really come out of the closet to anyone outside the secretive gay world in Manhattan yet. Hell, it would be twenty-four years before I told my mother I am gay. When I finally did she was 92, in a nursing home, and her response was that she was late for bingo. Even so, at this moment after the Festival, I was more "me" than I'd ever been. Woodstock changed me. It was more than a dream-come-true out of control. It was as if the whole world had come into my backyard to demand and celebrate freedom, just when I needed it most, just when I thought I'd be enslaved forever to a crappy Catskill Mountain motel.

Part of this revelation and change may also have been due to economics. For the first time in twenty years, the Teichberg/Tiber clan was not in debt. Not only was the clan not in debt, it had substantial fees tucked away in the bank and two big sacks of cash.

We did spend a lot of post-Festival time counting money. We had to. First, there was a lot of it. Second, our record keeping wasn't too good. We desperately tried to match totals with the exact number of tickets Mike Lang had given us and relate it somehow to the number of unsold tickets we had left. At some point, I gave up and threw the leftover tickets in the garbage—tickets which, if we had them today, would be selling for $2,500 a pair!

A few weeks passed and neither Mike nor anyone else from the Festival contacted me, so I put in a call to Mike. I told him I had some cash for Woodstock—$28,000 or $35,000 of ticket-sales proceeds, depending on one's bookkeeping. Later that day he arrived at the motel, grateful. I had no idea at the time that he'd been through the meat grinder. Financially, the Festival was a disaster for him and John and Joel. Warner Brothers would make big bucks with the movie later on. But this was now.

Who knew? I threw out thousands of Woodstock posters! I only kept one, which we used as a prop in my film "High Street." That is all I have left, the original poster Mike Lang gave me when they were printed. Now they fetch $2,000 each. Who knew? I had three thousand unsold Woodstock tickets! Now they go for $2,500 a set. Who knew that the several drawings in my Shack Number Two, under the floor mats, that Rothko and Reinhardt had given me when I was studying with them, would one day be valuable? Paintings going for six and seven figures? I did! But my mother didn't. She threw the art work in the garbage when she cleaned out Shack Number Two in order to rent it during one hunting season for fifteen dollars a night.

Mike didn't look exhausted, but it was obvious he was. We had a warm reunion. He gave us a receipt for the money, and matter-of-factly, thanked us. Only 20 years later did I read that he was being accused of all sorts of money-handling errors. That he was suddenly able to bring in $35,000, a legitimate return of ticket sales, was clearly a big boost in his favor. As usual, he didn't comment more than he needed to. It wasn't any of our business the troubles he was having. And we certainly were not able to offer him any help.

I asked him about the threats of a slew of law suits for a long list of reasons including Mafia collaboration, drug dealing, and sex-ring management.

"No problem, man. We'll take care of everything."

With that, Mike Lang got back in his helicopter and disappeared. I wouldn't see him and his smile again until 1989, at the twentieth Woodstock Reunion.

34

Westward, Oh No!

My old New York City lifestyle and its values were in sharp relief against the pastiche of humanity that had peopled this bizarre fantasy come true. My old life now seemed trivial, hollow, and was one that I couldn't return to.

Installing rain forests complete with live birds in rich womens' foyers—one of my sub-specialties—seemed like a terrible way to spend my life. What could I have been thinking of? Yes, it meant good money in my pocket. What did it matter if one more Park Avenue grande dame or West End Avenue Yenta had a drop-dead living room in taupe or mauve? The ultimate dining room? A bathroom that included a damask reproduction of the Shah of Iran's second cousin's marble toilet seat cover? And a dressing room inspired by the Parthenon? Who cared what was in the window of Sloane's or Lord & Taylor? Did it matter if the world had one more Louis-the-anything loveseat or one more scandal about Scalamandre's derivative floral chintz? It was clear to me that my former professions took up valuable time that could otherwise be spent in pursuit of... I had no notion of what. I had no idea what I was put on this earth to do, but surely, it couldn't be to decorate foyers with flair.

I was confused, bewildered and alone. I was suffering from what some mistakenly call a mid-life crisis, but which I have noticed occurs continually during the life-time of a reflective person who engages in anything remotely resembling self-examination. I was also suffering from post-partem Woodstock depression. And since this was 1969, there were no twelve-step groups to join or even identify this secondary malaise.

And so, that was the frame of mind I was in as I stuffed the trunk of my Caddie with the contents of Shack Number Two. The rest of everything White Lake I burned next to the pool showers.

That was the frame of mind I was in when our attorney was on the phone. Urgent.

"You better get in your car and get out of New York State. And now! Go someplace far! Don't tell anyone where you will be until this Woodstock stuff fades out of memory. They're going to send someone from the D.A.'s office out there to arrest you. They have compiled some kind of incriminating evidence about the two million dollars Woodstock gave you under the table. Why the hell didn't you tell me about the two million? They are also claiming you sold your permit to Woodstock in collusion with the Mafia. I'm your lawyer, you're supposed to talk to me. I'm on your side. What the fuck else have you been up to? We have to talk about this two mill and the Mafia."

I was stunned. I wouldn't be teaching absurdist humor for another 15 years, so this was a bit of a shock. If I had two million anything why would I still be in While Lake answering the phone?

And so I, the promoter extraordinaire, dreamer whose dream came true, closed the Caddie's trunk, said goodbyes and drove out driveway number one of the El Monaco Motel.

I wasn't exactly concerned with Mom and Pop and the sharks and barracudas. They survived the Nazis and the Cossacks, they'd survive the Bethel Beasts of the Bogs.

They never signed anything. They had nothing on paper to do with the Festival. All they had was whatever legit money we took in from renting the motel rooms, spaces, whatever. From an aesthetic point of view the El Monaco should have been illegal, but we didn't do anything technically and practically illegal. And everything was cash.

My pop didn't seem disturbed as he assured me,

"We'll be okay. You'll be okay. If anyone asks, I got one answer— Vat Festival? Who's Elliot Tiber? I'm Jack Teichberg. I never saw no Festival. Gei gezuntah hei,[1] son. I'm proud of you."

---

[1] Yiddish for 'Go in good health.'

35

Vandals, Mafia and the Long Trek Home

January 1970...

I was in Los Angeles, staying with Lennie of the chemistry sets and towels. I was trying to put together some kind of life that had fun built into it. In the middle of a vast array of creative projects involving a film, a festival, and Marie Dressler's old house, Mamma called to tell me the El Monaco had been broken into and vandalized.

I should have hung up on her and changed my number. Instead, I got on the red-eye to New York. Go try booking American Airlines from L.A. direct to White Lake? Oh, please.

I climbed over the snow pilings left by the county plows and waded, snow-bootless and hip deep through the drifts to get to the motel office. I had no keys, but they were unnecessary. The office door was ripped off its hinges and the entrance was snow-drifted in. The room-key rack was empty. There was graffiti covering the walls. It was chilling.

Swastikas.
Fuck off faggot. Keep the kikes out of White Lake. Sonia is a Old Jewess Whore. Christ-Killers.

Stuff like that. I went out to see the rooms. It was worse there. Anything of value—which wasn't much, granted—was gone. Cracked toilet bowls. Feces smeared on the walls and floors. Pillows and mattresses slashed open.

It was clear, seeing as my footprints were the only ones around, that the place was trashed before the snows. Questioning neighbors brought only invective about Woodstock. Even the State Police said

251

they had not noticed anything. It was a natural mistake, when they saw the open doors, to think we were merely getting the place cleaned out.

"Did it ever occur to you, Tiber, that it was your dirty hippies? I heard talk that plenty of them didn't go back to hell, or wherever they came from, and were hanging on and living in the woods and breaking into homes and hotels in the neighborhood. It's your own fault, Tiber. You tried to ruin this county with your fucking Festival, but we know how to deal with hippies. Bunch of fucking draft dodgers. I'll tell you one thing—any hippies we find, find out real fast that they shouldn't come back here. You understand?"

With that, the trooper handed me a form to sign. I called my attorney who said the good news was there were no more warrants for my arrest. Everyone was suing Woodstock and Warner Brothers. But personally, he was dying to know about the Mafia connection.

What about the two million dollars from the Mafia? You heard it here first! Someone in a trench coat, holding an Uzi machine gun, came to my room with a dead horse's head at 3:00 a.m., and gave me one hundred million dollars so that I would betray my county, Sullivan County, and divulge all its nuclear warhead secrets so it could blast Miami Beach's tourist industry to Iraq. Get real.

The next morning, I got to JFK and got the hell out of New York.

36

"Because I Love Her."

A couple of months in tinseltown, and I was digging in for the long haul. Trying to get into films via my Art Direction, and trying to forget everything White Lake, things were moving right along. Mom called. Pop was gravely ill. Could I come back?

There was a Nazi nurse on duty at the Monticello Hospital. We fought over my coming after visiting hours. We fought about my bringing Pop ginger ale, as it wasn't on his charts. We fought over the absentee doctor out playing golf. She was about to ring for security, so I said,

"Don't touch that bell, I'm warning you. I'm no ordinary man. I'm a violent faggot who does un-Republican unspeakable acts in bed with men! I'm the one who let Woodstock come to White Lake. I'm the hippie-loving faggot who gave them their permit!"

Bingo! The veins in her neck bulged purple and she dropped her hand from the alarm and stepped aside.

I visited. I just sat next to his bed, my hand under the oxygen tent so I could hold his. We were never much for talking, so the silence was familiar. But knowing that it wasn't possible to talk made it painful. I just watched him sleep and watched him wake and open his tiny eyelids and stare into space. When his eyes were open, I'd talk to him. Mostly about the happy times we had during Woodstock. Those were, after all, the only happy moments we shared.

At the end of one visit, I was about to get up and leave when Pa grasped my hand so hard it hurt. I held my ear right next to the plastic tent to catch every whisper.

"My little boy, my son. I love you. I know about you. I know what you do. I know about your life. Your friends. I just want you should know it's okay by me. I hope you find somebody and you can be

253

happy. I have just one thing to ask of you. When I go, please do something for me. I want to be buried facing Woodstock. There's a little Jewish cemetery just near Max's farm. That's where I want to rest."

I promised. And then I asked him the one question that had dogged me for years.

"Pop. If you can hear me, please tell me one thing. Why did you stay with Mamma all these years? Why did you work so hard? Why didn't you just run away? You were so tired. Why didn't you ever tell her to stop?"

"I love her," he barely managed to whisper

I made a right turn into the first El Monaco driveway. Mother was sitting on a folding chair with our neighbor Sol Mondlin in front of the office, under a Yenta's red-and-white umbrella that was still exhausted from the Woodstock rains. Sol and his wife Thelma, both lovely warm people, ran a run-down rooming house a short way up the hill. Their place was often a haven for me. Many, many times over, I'd run to Sol and Thelma's kitchen for sage advice, a glass of tea and sympathy. Sol took one look at me and asked what was wrong. I said I needed to talk to my mother alone and ushered her to windowless, behind-the-men's-toilet's-graffiti-wall Room 9A, which ever since Woodstock she'd been using as her bedroom.

We sat on her unmade bed, the only piece of furniture in the tiny room. She asked why I came up so early. It wasn't Friday yet. "Poppa's dead," I said. The words were barely out of my mouth before she started shrieking. She turned in frantic circles in the tiny patch of floor space, shrieking. It was a scream I'd never heard in my life—it sounded like all the animals from pre-history till 1970 who'd ever been slaughtered were all screaming at the same time and the sound was coming out of her mouth.

It was as if I were invisible. I watched, terrified, as she then started ranting and raving, and shouting words I could interpret but never understand:

"Yankl! How could you do this to me? How could you leave me here alone at the beginning of the season? How will I manage? How will I rent the rooms and make the beds and mow the lawns by myself? How could you leave me alone in the motel for Decoration Day? You never gave me one good day in mine life! Not one moment of happiness! Never! You never gave me even one good day in mine whole life!"

I stood staring at this display, amazed and disgusted, my entire body trembling. Suddenly, Mama saw my image in the mirror on the wall and stopped her wild frenzy in an instant. She switched immediately to a different dance, the one I would see the next morning at the funeral. She rocked back and forth and went into "bereaved Jewish wife and grandmother from Russia" mode. Hebrew prayers spewed forth from her mouth and she wailed to her mother in Heaven. She wailed to her father in Heaven. She wailed to God and the angels in Heaven in a mixture of Hebrew, Yiddish and Russian.

This display was interrupted by a clarion call. No, it was not Gideon's trumpet, it was the sound of a car horn that summoned Mama from her mourning dance. She opened the door to 9A a crack and peeked. "Oy, a customer," she mumbled, wiping her face with the skirt of her dress. With a cursory look in the mirror, she opened the yellow door and ran to welcome the new motel customers.

I followed her in disbelief. She took the couple who'd arrived into the office and launched right into her rent-a-room Yenta routine. Sol went to her and said he'd take care of the customers, not to worry. Of course, from all the screaming, he knew Pop had died. But no, Mother wouldn't trust him with her business. No sirree. As for me, she wouldn't even look at me. I couldn't stand it for long, and while she searched an ancient Yasgur's milk box for a room key, I announced to this unsuspecting couple: "Sorry, the El Monaco is closed on account of my father just dying. My father, this woman's husband! Please leave!"

Mother went wild. She shoved me aside and tried to make out to the couple that I was some kind of nut. Her effort was useless, since they were rushing out the door after hearing my announcement. But this didn't stop Mamma. She ran after them and, when they gunned the motor, she ran to the driveway to block their exit.

I ran back into the motel and threw myself on the bed. Sol ran out to drag Mom from the driveway and let the couple drive away. Then he brought her back to her room. She quieted down. She dropped to the bed and buried her head in the pillows. Sol and I left her there on the bed and returned to the office where we put up the "No Vacancy" sign.

In a few days, we were in the Jewish cemetery near Yasgur's farm. Family around, the whole thing was revolting to me. I stood a brief distance in the woods, smoking a joint and crying.

My mother was making wailing noises about the 'only' son has to be at the grave site and say Kaddish.[1] I refused to acknowledge her pleas. A few attempts by the ridiculous rabbi and more ridiculous aunts and uncles informing me about my filial duties, and the charade continued.

Mother threw herself into the grave atop the coffin and shrieked: "Jake, mine friend! Jake mine friend! How could you leave me?"

No more apparitions. Just grieving funeral relatives in the pool.

---

[1] A Hebrew prayer for the dead.

37

Sing Out

June 4, 1970...

This was the last piece of unfinished business. I was going to stay and dump the dump. Get rid of the fucking El Monaco at any cost. Ship Mom off to Israel to be close to her religious shit, and I'd be free to return to Los Angeles, and the new life I had begun.

I had no plans to develop anything for that summer. I put a bit of energy in painting "For Sale" signs and other absurd comic signs to conjure up some excitement and interest to amuse me while I had to wait there. I didn't intend to let Mom apply her heavy craziness and obsessions to me any longer. The Woodstock monies were all but used up. We were okay financially, but I'd still have to get a job, unless we could sell the compound and I could recoup some of my past salaries and investments. That likelihood was remote and hardly on the list of possibilities. Times stunk. There was no business. The locals wouldn't permit any capitalizing on the past glory of 1969. Any of my signage indicating what had been, was quickly knocked down. Any memory or effort at Woodstock anything met with horrendous attacks from both residents and authorities.

I gave up on my "Rent my rooms" mantra. My new mantra was now: "Sell, sell, and if you can't sell, give it away!"

And so I began the final El Monaco marketing plan. I listed the motel with every agent that ever listed its name someplace. I sent letters, I phoned, I pushed, I annoyed. I gave press interviews about the firm plans to hold a second Woodstock Festival, though this time it would be a completely El Monaco production. I said I'd optioned a 500-acre site in White Lake, and the El Monaco would again serve as the Festival headquarters. The papers, desperate for news, printed this garbage, and I was happy to now have news clippings I could photocopy and use as sales literature. That this was total bunk took the press a few minutes to figure out. The Chamber of Commerce, of which I used to be President, was now null and void and defunct beyond dysfunctional. That winter the town had passed an ordinance that required a permit for gatherings of more than 50 people who were not members of the Republican Party or the Klu Klux Klan. This was obviously an anti-semitic ordinance designed to prevent Bar Mitzvahs, but a clear side-effect was that it would effectively prevent another hippie invasion, as well. My additional sins included that I had not applied for a public assembly permit nor had I bought or optioned any parcel of land.

That June, before the July Fourth weekend, I was banned from advertising the motel pending inspections for alleged code violations. All month, local White Lake inspectors crawled under and over every rock on the El Monaco acreage. They demanded health and occupancy permits, they tested the water in all four wells. They sent fire marshals to inspect for fire and safety hazards. Their inspections turned up no major violations and I was free to advertise again.

Woodstock Festival Headquarters Resort, El Monaco Motel, For Sale. Unlimited Potential. Future Location of next Woodstock Festival.

The threatening phone calls began immediately. Goons came by at night shouting and kicking lawn furniture around. When I called the police for help, they gave a clear indication of what position I was in locally:

"You made your bed. We don't want your dirty hippies here. Don't expect us to help you out."

But, aside from some stolen folding chairs and some anti-semitic graffiti, nothing much really happened.

Nothing much really happened from a business point of view either. Once or twice a week some young people who had never made it to the Festival came by to see where Woodstock happened.

In a last-ditch attempt at capitalizing on the Woodstock event, I tried to create a Woodstock Museum in the former Underground Cinema bungalow. However, the County Clerk quashed those plans saying that because the building wasn't fireproof, the town could not issue a permit. I argued that 99.25 percent of Sullivan County was not fireproof. What did it matter? Zilch. And so the summer went by as if we were on a moonscape. Eerily quiet. There was virtually no business. We hired no help, and there was little to do except send sales pleas to agents everywhere. And there was no response.

After Labor Day weekend I emptied the pool and closed up all the bungalows. With each nail I hammered as I sealed the doors, I fantasized about a big bonfire getting out of control and burning down the whole motel. Then I realized the grounds—the bog—were too wet and the bungalows too far apart for that to work.

The crunch of gravel—the sound of a car driving into the driveway—stirred me from this stupor. I was surprised. It was Tuesday after Labor Day. No one came for Labor Day, why should anyone come after Labor Day? I ran outside and saw a big, black stretch limo drive in and pull into a parking space. Then came a second limo that looked just like the first. Then a third, a fourth, a fifth, until we had nine fucking limos in the El Monaco parking lot. Mother got frantic and started rushing around looking for room keys. I ignored her as I had learned to do that summer. I just watched in amazement as nine identical-looking chauffeurs opened nine identical doors and out piled nine identical-looking families with hordes of children. Not nasty children, not the kind that Pop didn't want staying at his motel and peeing on his mattresses. Nice, well brought-up quiet kids.

The men, in dark suits, approached me.

"We're not interested in renting rooms," one of the men said. "We're interested in buying."

My heart took off with the speed the El Monaco Trot was supposed to have had.

"It looks like a nice place here."

"Oh, yes, it's a beautiful place."

"A nice place to raise children?"

"Oh yes, a wonderful place to raise children. We have the White Lake School just a mile down the road and terrific fresh air and countless super-duper desirable attributes of life perfect for the large fembily—uh, I mean family looking to settle down."

I then took the nine brothers on a tour of the El Monaco compound. They inspected one room in the main "wing," one in the

Presidential Wing, and one bungalow. As far as I could tell, they were pleased with what they saw.

"We have four spring-fed wells," I began, but the spokesperson brother cut him off:

"It looks good to us. We have nine families and we need this kind of space. Basically, we'd convert some of the bungalows into year-round homes and we're looking to make an Italian restaurant out of your bar. We have four Italian restaurants in the Bronx, but it's no place for raising children. So, let's talk business."

The oldest brother and I went into the bar to "talk business." The rest of this mega-family waited politely and quietly outside in the scenic El Monaco parking lot. The older brother asked the price for the motel.

I gave him our best price right up front. Just enough to make up for the lost salary checks I had poured into the motel, and to give Mama enough money to live on without worrying. The story I gave was that since my Pop died, it was just too much work for Mom and me alone. El Monaco needed a big family, and coincidentally, they were just such a perfectly-numbered family. Mother then dragged in a few shopping bags with muddy, illegible receipts from the Woodstock summer. I was now forced to come up with some kind of explanation. I began again with the fact of the Festival and the hundreds of thousands who came, but he interrupted me. "Woodstock? What Festival? We aren't interested in festivals. We just want to open a good Italian restaurant, with good food at reasonable prices in a place that would be good for our children to grow up." Apparently this guy didn't move in circles I understood.

The brother then said that our price seemed fair and that if it was acceptable to me, he'd give me 50 percent in cash now and the balance the following weekend. They had to be able to move in the following weekend because he wanted the children to enroll in school at the beginning of the semester. That would give me one week to pack it up and get out. It was perfect.

It was too perfect. I was bewildered. The older brother took a huge stack of cash out of the pocket of his suit jacket and counted out half the asking price of the motel.

"Cash? Now? No lawyers?" I asked trying to keep my jaw somewhere in the vicinity of my face.

"Well," said the buyer. "I suppose your lawyer should make up some sale papers. But I don't need lawyers to make a deal. I trust you and your mother. Your mother—she reminds me of my mother. She's a fine lady and I offer her all my respect as if she were my own mother."

"What do you mean, cash?" the attorney asked.

"Cash."

"Where did they get it?"

"I don't know."

The brother said the money came from income from their four restaurants in the Bronx, and sure, I should feel free to have it examined. They knew it was good money. No offense taken. They had no problem driving me and Mama and the money to Monticello to have the money checked and the legal papers drawn up.

When we went into the parking lot, it felt like Woodstock all over again. Neighbors were lined up along our driveway, staring at the nine limos. No doubt they assumed we were up to our dirty hippy tricks again. Little did they know that we had a very large dream in common: That I'd get the hell out of White Lake. And little did they know that, the Teichberg Curse willing, their and my dream was about to happen.

Now if the money was not counterfeit, my lawyer would draw up papers, we'd sign, money would change hands, and it would be over. The 14-year nightmare-turned-wet dream, would be over. Let nothing go wrong. What could go wrong?

Mom was having some kind of second thoughts.

"Sonnileh, maybe this is not the thing to do. What kind of life will you have without the El Monaco? People know you're a Teichberg here. You have respect. You have property. If we sell, we're selling your future. Maybe we should stay here. Together we'll make a life. You have fresh air here. What do you have in the city? Your Greenwich Village bum friends? No life. No respect. I don't want to sell. Here you'll find a nice Jewish wife and have children. I won't sell."

It was all I could do not to explode, but I had to keep quiet, because I didn't want to scare off our lone customer, this God-send.

"Mom, I'm warning you. For ten years, nobody ever wanted to buy this stinking rat-trap of a motel. It killed Poppa and it's going to kill me. Listen up. If I stay here, I will die. You sign those fucking papers. And you sign them now. This is our first and only customer and I'm not letting you fuck up this opportunity I've been begging for ten years."

"Vat do you mean no customers? There were plenty customers, Plenty. And they offered. Plenty. I just wouldn't betray you and your future bride, so I said no."

At this news, I nearly collapsed. I stood, shaking, beads of sweat running marathons down my neck as Mamma nonchalantly rattled off a list of offers she'd received over the years when people responded to my many ads offering the resort for sale.

"People answered those ads? And you never told me? You didn't think I needed to know? You didn't think I needed to get out of White Lake? Sign the papers, Mom. Sign them now or your hands will never make cholunt again! Sign the fucking papers, Mama, or I'll kill you right here, with my own two hands, right now in this office right across the street from the County Court House and County Jail."

With that, I dragged mother, who was still clutching the Italian restaurant bag of money, back to the room with the lawyer and the older brother.

"Everything's fine," I said. "Mother was getting sentimental. She built the place with Pop. It's a little hard to sell your life's work and dream."

The limo drive back to the motel was in total silence. I and Sonia would have one week to pack up our personal belongings. As far as I was concerned, everything could be tossed in for the sale of the century!

38

Going, Going, Gone!

What a wonderful week it was! I called a tag sale specialist and auctioneer to get rid of our "personal effects." Mama was impossible at first, because she thought she needed every personal effect in the place. Then, when she understood that in exchange for the personal effects she got money, she turned into a personal-effect maniac and started dragging out everything that wasn't nailed down.

A small notice appeared in the local rags that the former headquarters of the Woodstock Festival was selling documented memorabilia of the Festival at a historic sale to be held that Friday. The auctioneer had cautioned against the sales pitch, warning that the mention of Woodstock would alienate the county residents. She was wrong. Friday morning, the people of Sullivan County, who claimed they hated Woodstock, had filled up the lawn in front of the barn.

They bid for every crummy box of rusty tools and broken dishes. They bought every crumbling piece of Bensonhurst furniture—stuff that wasn't even good the day it was bought in 1926. Mother was convinced she was onto something wonderful. It was all I could do to keep her from selling the furniture from the motel rooms—things that were sold as part of the motel deal.

I was happy bordering on delirious watching every last piece of dreadful crap go! Rusty lawn mowers, old pots and pans, pubic hair-stained sheets, leftover shmutz, old jars, rotting everything, and items too numerous or well-covered to identify.

I only felt twinges of past recall at seeing the trusty, now broken-down golf cart and Pop's roofing supplies go for coins.

They took in about $5,000 that day—a fortune in 1970. Saturday, the Sabbath, Mother rested while I finished cleaning up to prepare for the new owners. The next morning, Mother, all smiles and happy with

Me, after Woodstock, in a meditation program circa 1970

the winnings from the auction, announced special news and a decision that was sure to please her son Eliyahu Teichberg:

"Sonneleh, we're going to open an auction house. Vee can buy the Kenmore Motel across the lake. It has a kosher kitchen. This is a business for miracles. It will be your future. A bride won't be hard to find with..."

"Mother. No. It's over," I said. "It's over. Finito. Ganuk." I made a nice roaring fire and watched the paperwork and paraphernalia of sixteen very weird years go up in smoke.

Later that morning the nine black limos arrived. Many sons and daughters, aunts and uncles swarmed over the place. The older brother asked for help with the keys—which key worked what.

"The keys have no numbers. During the Festival, the nuns of charity were helping with the ill kids, and they messed them up," I said with a straight face. I had no choice.

"Not a problem. My brother there, is a locksmith. The others are carpenters, cement workers, electricians. And our wives and children will clean the rooms. Do you think we might enter politics in this nice little town?"

And it was finally over. Mom went to Israel to talk to God. I went to Greenwich Village to party in the S & M fuckbars.

1994: UFO sightings in White Lake: zero. Apparitions: zero.

Epilogue:
Woodstock, Twenty-Fifth
Anniversary, 1994

In 1989, for the twentieth anniversary of the Woodstock Festival, one of the television networks drove me and some others up to the Festival site. It was the first time in twenty years that I'd been back in White Lake. I broke down into uncontrollable sobbing when I stood next to the stone grave marker a local artist placed on the hilltop, the site of the Festival. All the fields were green again, just as if no event had ever taken place. Lots of talk had gone on, however, that Max's cows produced 10 times the normal amount of milk years after. Even several prizes were awarded for the quantity and quality of the milk. Research was conducted into the effects of the cows eating all the marijuana that had sprouted after the festival. Zillions of seeds were germinated, no doubt, in all that mud.

The WPIX-TV Producer offered to drive me to my Papa's grave at the tiny cemetery. I wasn't up to doing it. He isn't there anyhow. Travelling through White Lake was entering a time warp, and very little had changed. The El Monaco was a thriving italian restaurant, mostly cemented over. The Floridian colors were still there. The bleak emptiness was pervasive. Not a nice place to spend one's summertime, for sure. I still was passionate in my hatred for the area. We stopped for pizza. It was okay. I went into my old bar, Disco, and office. It was no longer there. It was a sprawling restaurant, bar, and gigantic men's and lady's rooms. Oy.

A mammoth reunion party was held in New York City. Beam me up Mike!

My lover, Andre Ernotte and me at work on our first French TV show, "Sketch Up," in 1972 in Bruxelles, Belgium. I did not dare even mention Woodstock then.

And I met Mike Lang and Lee Blumer and Stan Goldstein, Joel, John, and the others at a splendid reunion party at the hot Ritz Disco on Fourteenth Street in New York. Everyone but me got older-looking. Grey hair, pot bellies, etc. And nobody smoked anything. Not even cigarettes. Most were into health foods and were, like myself, vegetarians. And it was sweet.

Now, in 1994, the twenty-fifth anniversary of Woodstock, I am still receiving phone calls from high school and college students world-wide. They who are writing term papers about the Festival for their history classes. They who just want to talk to someone who was there. Those who are curious to know how it felt. And so many who thanked me for giving their personal feelings a route for expression. Those old *Life* magazines with the Woodstock Baby story, are still in dentists' waiting rooms and, of course, reference libraries. History. It doesn't seem possible that Woodstock took place a quarter of a century ago. A generation ago. It's now, officially, "history." For me it isn't history and it isn't past. It's still alive in my head as if it were yesterday.

What was it about? It was about music and freedom. Music was the medium; freedom was the message. For me, the Festival was about free choice. About reminding people about the importance of simple human values. The values that make life worth living. Values that had been obscured by the rush of the industrial and technological revolutions. 1969 was the cusp of all the freedom movements of the last part of this millennium. And Woodstock lives on as the call for self-realization on every level for everyone. And everyone is not just the people who made the historic trek to White Lake during three rainy days in August twenty-five years ago. Everyone is also those who came after them.

I miss Woodstock. I still play the album. I miss Hendrix. I miss Joplin. I replay the movie every August. I talk to Mamma every August and foolishly ask her what she remembers. She only remembers it was filth and dirty sex and dirty hippies and she advises me not to tell anyone I knew anything about it.

Woodstock transformed my life. It rescued me from the motel from hell which rescued me from the hardware store from hell. It taught me some important lessons: Sometimes pipe dreams, even ridiculous improbable pipe dreams, send out smoke signals. You have to dream hard enough. And as the song goes from *South Pacific:* "If you don't got a dream, how you gonna have a dream come true?"

Woodstock taught me how to dream. And that's what it is about. Creating dreams and creating your life. Thank you, Woodstock. And thank you my Woodstock Nation. And thank you Mike Lang and may you never stop smiling.

P.S. I have sighted UFO'S, apparitions, and phantoms on my own.

Special Offers
While Supplies Last

"Knock on Woodstock," The Book
The uproarious, uncensored story of the Woodstock Festival, the gay man who made it happen, and how he earned his ticket to freedom. 1994, 288 pages, over 20 photographs.
Quality Softcover, $14.95 plus $3.50 shipping and handling.
Hardcover, $22.95 plus $3.50 shipping and handling.
Special. A limited edition hardcover copy of *Knock on Woodstock*, numbered and autographed by author Elliot Tiber, $63.95 including shipping and handling.

"Ticket to Freedom: Woodstock," The Video
This feature-length video is based on the book, *Knock on Woodstock*. It features actor/author Elliot Tiber, Richie Havens, who has written three new songs especially for this movie, and famous actor Michael Moriarty, among others. VHS format, $29.95 plus $3.50 shipping and handling.

FRAMED PLAQUES
These unique collector's items have been produced exclusively for Festival Conservancy, Inc. Each plaque is accompanied by a certificate of authenticity.

The Woodstock Festival Plaque
A panoramic color photograph of the enormous crowd at the 1969 Woodstock Festival, along with an unused, authentic ticket to the Woodstock Music and Art Fair, beautifully matted and framed. Autographed by Elliot Tiber. $119.95, including shipping and handling.

Richie Havens Plaque

An exclusive photograph of Richie Havens by renowned photographer Martha Swope, along with an unused, authentic ticket to the 1969 Woodstock Music and Art Fair, beautifully matted and framed. Autographed by Richie Havens. $119.95, including shipping and handling.

The Woodstock Festival and Richie Havens Plaque

A panoramic color photograph of the enormous crowd at the 1969 Woodstock Festival, plus an exclusive photograph of Richie Havens by renowned photographer Martha Swope, plus an unused, authentic ticket to the 1969 Woodstock Music and Art Fair, beautifully matted and framed. Autographed by Elliot Tiber and Richie Havens. $159.95, including shipping and handling.

Special Collector's Limited Edition Package

A numbered, limited edition hardcover copy of *Knock on Woodstock* autographed by author Elliot Tiber, *plus* an autographed photograph of Richie Havens by renowned photographer Martha Swope, *plus* a panoramic color photograph of the enormous crowd at the 1969 Woodstock Festival, along with an unused, authentic ticket to the 1969 Woodstock Music and Art Fair, beautifully matted and framed. $189.95, including shipping and handling.

For ordering information, please see the Order Form on the next page.

Order Form

Yes, I want to take advantage of your special offers. Please send me the following items:

Qty	Item	Each	Total
	Knock on Woodstock Softcover	$ 14.95	
	Knock on Woodstock Hardcover	22.95	
	Knock on Woodstock Limited Edition	63.95	
	Ticket to Freedom: Woodstock Video	29.95	
	Woodstock Festival Plaque	119.95	
	Richie Havens Plaque	119.95	
	Woodstock & Richie Havens Plaque	159.95	
	Special Collector's Package	189.95	
	Shipping and handling (where applicable)		
	Subtotal		
	Sales Tax (Michigan residents only)		
	Total		

Payment must accompany order. For shipment to addresses in Michigan, please add 6% sales tax. Allow 2-4 weeks for delivery. Please make check or money order payable to "Bookcrafters Distribution Service" and mail the completed order form (or a copy) to:

Bookcrafters Distribution Center
615 E. Industrial Drive
Chelsea, MI 48118

For fastest service, order using your Visa, MasterCard, Discover or American Express card by calling **1-800-879-4214**, Monday through Friday from 8:00 a.m. to 11:00 p.m.

Our Guarantee: Return any item in saleable condition within 30 days for a prompt refund. Prices subject to change and availability. Thank you for your order!